THE BIG BOOK OF BREAD

THE BIG BOOK OF BREAD

Recipes and Stories from around the Globe

JAMES MORTON

Contents

INTRODUCTION

Bread.

Flour, water, salt, maybe some other bits.
Baked, boiled, fried or griddled
into buns, loaves, pancakes, muffins, bannocks and endless more
for the sustenance of the rich and the poor, for millennia.

An industrial, manufactured staple, and an artisan's calling.
Domestic nourishment and the national pride of countries and cultures;
A fascination that intertwines the geography, genetics and society of a place.

Bread.

The Big Book of Bread

First, break bread.

Bread straddles borders. It blurs the boundaries between cultures and nationalities. As you make your way through this book, you'll see we all make bread, everywhere. We share common and related ingredients, mutual processes, common biology: as in every aspect of humanity. I hope that by baking breads from around the world, by sharing this experience, we can understand a bit more about each of us.

The process of putting together this slab of a book has been gruelling at times: a labour of love, yes, but one filled with self-doubt. I originally started to write this as a World Atlas. Following in the footsteps of Jancis Robinson on wine and James Hoffmann on coffee, I wanted to tour the world in recipes, with each bread representing a respective country or region. But as I started work, I felt uncomfortable. I saw I couldn't be yet another in a list of white men from a colonialist country to explain cultures in which I've never lived, no matter how much effort and time went into the research and testing and travel.

So we changed tack. I sent out a call for contributors and had hundreds of suggestions from every corner of the globe, many of which have made it into this book. I've diligently researched every recipe, tested and re-tested, expanded into about 90,000 words or so, then over an intense three-week period, they've been beautifully photographed for your pleasure.
This book will never be perfect in everyone's eyes – I'll face flack for misrepresenting even my own local recipes, I'm sure. I'd just ask you to consider me a neighbour, and it's OK if I don't make something exactly the same way you do; and it may be that both of our methods have merit. I hope that you'll find me open and reflective and willing to correct and improve if required. I'm up for some harsh cultural scrutiny, so if you find something you don't like, write to us, and we'll remedy it and credit you in future editions (see page 320).

Still, I have done my utmost to showcase the most interesting or enlightening aspects of a bread and the culture surrounding it, and to pick breads not that represent a particular place, but that I felt had the most distinct processes or story behind them. Through understanding the way each of us cooks and eats, I think we can reach a greater shared understanding and empathy – one that goes beyond language or border or culture or religion. If this book will prove anything, it is that we have more linking us than dividing us.

About Me

I'm merely a compiler with an awesome opportunity. I write stuff, and with a certain conversational style that I hope you enjoy; I have done it before and people have liked it, and so I've been asked to do it again. This time, with considerable scale.

It can be tricky at times, as each word is spoken in my head as it is written: it feels like I'm explaining processes to a blank screen, over and over, with no idea whether anyone can understand it or not. So I'm grateful to the whole team involved in this book for putting up with me bouncing things off them.

My background is as a doctor, a general practitioner, and now with an emerging interest in the health of the planet as well as the health of the people I look after. I've had this parallel career as a food writer and one-time media personality since appearing on a TV show called *The Great British Bake Off* back in 2012.

Despite everything I've done since (this is my eighth book, and fourth on bread), I still see myself as an amateur baker and cook. These recipes are not tested in commercial bakeries or using specialist equipment: they have been made in my own humble kitchen and the homes of my friends. They are all achievable at home.

How to Use This Book

My favourite thing is when people tell me they've read the book cover to cover. In a way, it's designed for you to do this. Every recipe is a story, often with detailed technical or historical context, and so even they can be read back to back. I'm considering an audiobook.

You don't need ever to have made bread before to make world-class bread. In fact, it helps if you haven't, as it's easier to start fresh rather than challenge misconceptions. Start with ingredients and equipment, make sure you've got the basics, then check out my process chapter on How to Make Bread (pages 30–63). This contains everything you'll ever need to know.

Many of the recipes will reference stages explained during this chapter – unfortunately, there are some processes to learn, but you can always turn back here for a refresh.

If you are an experienced bread baker, things might look a bit different to what you're used to. I don't hold sourdough on a pedestal, for example: it's just an old-fashioned, slower (and delicious) way of making your bread rise. Most recipes contain both sourdough and yeasted versions. I've adapted sourdough versions for many yeasted breads around the world, and vice versa.

I don't bother with technical info for most recipes, such as hydration and baker's percentages, because they are essentially meaningless once you take into account the differences between ingredients. Instead, you'll see the adaptability of bread: that you could take any one of these hundred different doughs, and shape them in a hundred different ways, add a hundred different personalizing ingredients and suddenly you've got 1,000,000 different combinations.

While commercial bakeries strive for consistency, the wonderful thing about baking bread at home is that each loaf you make is unique: there has never been another like it in the history of humanity, and tomorrow you can make another just as unique.

Glossary of Bread Terms

Autolyse: An initial rest that occurs before kneading to allow easier bringing together of the dough and rapid gluten development. This rest is not always included in the process.

Baker's percentage: I don't use this here, but it's useful to know for recipes online and elsewhere. This refers to all ingredients as a percentage of the total flour weight. So a recipe of 100g strong white flour, 2g salt, 2g yeast and 65g water, would be 100% strong white, 2% salt, 2% yeast and 65% water. They make sense in a mad way, as they allow easy scaling of recipes into industrial quantities. See also *hydration*.

Baking steel: A thick piece of cast iron or steel that's placed on the oven shelf and preheated, adding rapid heat through the bottom of the loaf, much like a baking stone, below.

Baking stone: A flat piece of stone, either natural (such as granite) or synthetic (ceramic, cordierite), that's placed in the oven and preheated before baking. The stone regulates the heat of the oven and provides heat from the bottom for an even crust and good rise.

Banneton: Another word for a proving basket, especially of the wound cane variety.

Batard: An oval-shaped loaf. Be careful with spelling and autocorrect!

Bench rest: An extra stage after dividing the dough and pre-shaping but before creating its final shape. The dough sits on the bench to relax, usually for 15–30 minutes.

Biga: Italian for pre-ferment.

Bird's eye bubbles: Tiny bubbles that form on and within the crusts of breads, especially sourdoughs that have been proved for a long time.

Boule: A French name for a round loaf, equivalent to an English cob. Whenever I refer to shaping round, I will use this term.

Bran: The brown bit of wholemeal flour; the fibrous outer coating of grains. See page 20 for a full explanation of wheat.

Bulk fermentation: Another name for the first rest or first prove, especially used if splitting the dough into multiple loaves.

Caramelization: Sugar plus water plus heat equals caramel. More heat, darker caramel. Basically, varying degrees of burnt, from mild and tasty to severe and not.

Carbon dioxide (CO_2): What yeast makes and what makes bread rise. Contributor to climate change. Makes beer fizzy. You know, that one.

Couche: Heavy linen cloth, floured and folded, and used to support the second prove of various breads as an alternative to a proving basket.

Crumb: The middle of the bread, especially if examined in cut form; any bit of a loaf that's not the crust.

Development: How well formed the gluten in a dough is, usually created by kneading, or by stretching and folding at intervals.

Distribute: To mix together dry ingredients so they are evenly blended.

Ear: When your score opens up during the bake and leaves a darker, raised edge along its length, this is an ear. Generally a good thing.

Egg wash: A brushing of whisked egg (or yolk) prior to baking to give a deep brown shine. Usually a pinch of salt is added, helping break down the protein of the egg and allowing easier brushing.

Endosperm: The part of a whole grain that contains starch, to feed the growing seed. This is the part of grain that makes up white flour.

Enriched dough: Adding butter, oil, sugar or eggs to your dough to create softness and sweetness.

Extensibility: How stretchy your dough is. The opposite is tenacity.

Fast-action yeast: See *instant yeast*.

Feeding: Adding flour and water to your sourdough starter to keep it alive or to prepare it for the next bake.

Fermentation: In bread, any process involving your yeast breaking down starches and sugars into carbon dioxide and alcohol. Used interchangeably with prove or rest.

Gluten: A complex of proteins (glutenin and gliadin) that stick together to form a mesh that can contain carbon dioxide (CO_2) to create lightness (page 23). Wonderful stuff. Also the devil of the wellness industry, ridiculously.

Hooch: The acidic, alcoholic layer of liquid on top of a sourdough starter if you neglect it.

Hydration: How wet your dough is, often expressed as a baker's percentage. For example, a dough of 100g flour and 65g water, is 65% hydration. A dough of 50% hydration or less is firm and even difficult to form. A dough of 55–60% hydration is dry; 70–75% hydration will be sticky and soft, usually a good balance for yeasted doughs. A dough of 80–90% hydration is usually challenging and requires careful dough development and shaping.

Instant yeast: Tiny dried pebbles of yeast that are easily incorporated and often contain enzymes to help kickstart a fermentation. Also called 'fast-action yeast' or 'dried, long-life yeast'. Don't confuse it with active dried yeast that needs hydrating before using and is generally not used in this book.

Knead: Bakers often interchange with 'mix', but kneading is a prolonged, vigorous mixing stage to develop the gluten in the flour (page 35).

Knock back: To force the developed carbon dioxide out of your dough after the first prove, redistributing heat and yeast, for a very even, small-bubbled crumb.

Lame: A handled razor blade, or razor blade holder, used to score bread.

Lamination: A method of developing gluten or incorporating chunky ingredients (page 60).

Leavened: Bread that has been risen. This usually refers to yeast-risen bread and some consider those risen with chemical agents to be unleavened for religious or cultural reasons.

Levain: The French term for starter. Some Americans use this word to describe a sourdough pre-ferment, or a young, fresh starter.

Loaf: A name for any baked bread.

Maillard reaction: A browning reaction in the presence of heat, involving the bonding of protein and sugar, that creates savoury flavoured compounds.

Mixing: The first step after weighing, involving the combining of your ingredients. Some people refer to kneading as mixing.

Oven spring: The rise of your loaf during the initial stages of the bake.

Pain: French for bread. Also an emotion experienced when your sourdough doesn't work out.

Peak rise: The point at which a sourdough starter is at maximum volume, before it starts to deflate.

Peel: A flat, usually handled surface used to slide dough or bread around (page 18).

Pre-ferment: A mixture of yeast, flour and water, left to ferment, then added to a new dough to create a more complex flavour. You can even ferment bread using a piece of yesterday's dough, kept back as a pre-ferment. I have generally avoided using them in this book, as a similar complexity can be obtained by adding sourdough starter as an additional ingredient. Types include biga, poolish or sponge.

Pre-shape: A gentle initial shape following the first prove, especially if splitting a dough into multiple smaller loaves. This develops greater dough strength, as long as it is done gently to preserve the developed structure so far. Followed by a bench rest.

Prove: Another name for the resting stages.

Proving (or proofing) basket: A basket, often made of cane or lined with linen, that supports a loaf during the second and final prove.

Rest: Another word for the proving or fermentation stages, when the bread rises.

Retarding: To chill your dough to 'retard', or slow down, the activity of the yeast. It can be in the first or second proves, but most commonly the second.

Scoring: Slashing or cutting the bread before baking to control its rise.

Shaping: To hand-craft the dough into its final shape. Surprisingly important, but becomes less so if you've got a dough of great strength.

Sifting: To pass an ingredient through a wire mesh sieve. Used to remove bran to create whiter flours.

Sourdough starter: The natural raising agent used in sourdough and the bane of your life henceforth (page 27).

Starch: Carbohydrates found in wheat, specifically the endosperm.

Strength: The ability of the dough to hold its shape, especially over time and after long proves.

Stretch and fold: A method of building strength in the dough through manipulating it.

Tangzhong method: A small amount of flour and water is heated and added to the dough for stability and a soft crumb (page 278).

Tunnels: Large bubbles that permeate the entire length of a loaf, causing cavernous areas of the crumb. Usually down to poor dough strength.

Yeast: A fungus that makes bread rise. It is available fresh, dried (which needs to be reconstituted) or instant active dried, which is what I use.

BUTTERMILK

Equipment (Some You Need, Some You Don't)

The first fallacy of bread-making is that it's difficult, and the second is that you need lots of specialist equipment. You don't. An oven, I'll concede, is handy, alongside a tray or tin, and a bowl. That's it. You can make, and I have made, world-class sourdoughs in a near-bare kitchen. The only piece of specialist equipment I do recommend is a dough scraper, but even then, you can use an old credit card, at a push.

This first list of equipment – the essentials – is what you can get away with. You can make nearly every recipe in this book using this simple collection of things you may well already have. You may also have bits and pieces from the second list – they can make your life a little easier, or allow you to do certain things that are otherwise impractical. Mostly they're indulgence and consumerist self-identification as a serious baker – and that's no bad thing.

The Near-Essential

Oven

You can make bread using any oven. Modern, expensive ovens may have fancy bread and steam functionalities, but I don't really know anything about them. Turn your oven on and use it. If it's a fan oven, I recommend the standard fan setting.

If there's no fan, I recommend baking on the middle shelf at the higher temperatures given, and you might need to turn your bread halfway through for an even bake. Fanless ovens work best with a baking stone, baking steel or a heavy cast iron pot rather than a thin tray or tin alone: the heat inertia of these heavy baking surfaces really helps give you a strong bottom-heat and even bake. But as long as your oven gets hot, you can make great bread.

A Tray or Tin

Whether glass, ceramic, stone, metal or silicone, you can use it.

I recommend baking most of the little breads in this book on a baking tray. Line your tray with a sheet of baking parchment (non-stick greaseproof) for ease. But if all you've got is a roasting dish (with sides), that's fine too: you can even cover it with a little hat of kitchen foil for the first 10 minutes, allowing you to capture the steam released during baking.

Most larger breads can be made in a loaf tin. The simplest metal tins are best, as you want thin sides to allow the heat to penetrate easily. Some tins, called pullman-style tins, have lids that slide on and off. These are ideal if you want a square shaped, toaster-friendly loaf.

A Cast Iron Pot

A cast iron pot or Dutch oven is the single biggest change you can make to improve your larger loaves and sourdoughs: the heft gives a stone-baked quality, and baking with the lid on traps steam to give a beautifully caramelized crust with magnificent oven spring. If you remember nothing else from this book, '20 minutes lid on, 20 minutes lid off' will satisfy me.

Cast iron pots work best preheated, which can be done on the hob over about 3 minutes if you're in a rush. Once they're hot, you can pop your bread in. I use baking parchment for this, not because I'm worried the bread will stick (it won't) but because I can make a little cradle of paper, score my dough, then safely lower it into the pot without burning my fingers. The lid goes on, and if there's a bit of frayed paper poking out, so be it.

The very best sort are those that can be turned upside down, so you bake on the lid: or you can use one of the many specific cast iron home bread ovens designed for the purpose. These are very expensive and have no other purpose, whereas a casserole pot can be used for... casserole.

Dough Scraper

If you're new to bread, this is the only piece of specialist equipment I strongly recommend buying straight away. Don't start with a rigid metal scraper, but instead pick up a flexible, thin, dirt cheap plastic scraper. It should cost £2 or less. Get two, if you're prone to losing things.

These can be used to help with mixing, with kneading, with stretching and folding, with transferring every last bit of dough from bowls to surface and vice versa, with cleaning your hands, with scraping surfaces and even when washing up. They are brilliant, invaluable tools, and when I am making bread without my usual set of tools, these are what I miss.

Having said that, there are many different sorts available and having a few to hand is an indulgence I can get on board with. Metal scrapers are great for chopping and dividing doughs, and they are particularly good for scraping surfaces of dried-on dough, but be warned they can be prone to scratching soft surfaces like wood. To me, that only adds to the patina.

Bowl

Any bowl will do, so long as it's big enough to fit the amount of dough you're making. Ceramic, glass, plastic, steel: it doesn't matter. Wood, despite often being sold as suitable for bread, isn't the best, as it's most difficult to clean.

Electronic Scales

If you don't already have a decent set of electronic scales, you really have no excuse. Go out and get a cheap set. They will make your life so much easier. Stick your bowl on top, zero, weigh, zero, weigh, zero, weigh, done.

And this may be radical to some, but please, please measure in grams. All the recipes in this book have been deliberately given in grams to avoid the use of a nonsensical, non-metric system of pounds and ounces. Grams are accurate and decimal, and they allow easy scaling and translation of recipes. Do not use cups, for the variation of volumetric measurement is vast.

Something Sharp

Before bread is baked, it's scored (most of the time) to control how it rises in the oven – oven spring. Anything sharp can do the job – so long as it's properly sharp. If you don't have anything really sharp, a serrated knife, such as a tomato knife or even a bread knife, can do a decent job.

The sharper your tool, the faster you'll be able to score, with little chance of the blade catching on the dough and sticking or dragging. Typically, commercial bakeries use a lame (pronounced 'lamm' – it's French), which is basically a holder for a razor blade: the same sort of razor blade you can get in your pharmacy for using in a double-edged safety razor.

I used.to use a bare razor blade for scoring, pinched between my thumb and forefinger, but I no longer recommend that after I left it lying out in its paper wrapping, and my mother innocently lifted it up thinking it was a piece of scrap paper. The resulting bloodbath led me to now use something altogether safer and more sustainable: a vintage folding straight razor. If it ever gets blunt, a quick drag across a sharpening stone or strop on my leather belt and it's brand new.

Proving Basket – or Make Your Own

A proving basket supports the sides of your shaped dough, to help it keep its shape and avoid it splaying everywhere. They tend to be made of wood fibre, cloth-lined wicker or spiralled cane. Doughs are proved in them smooth-side down (seam-side up), meaning that when they are turned out of the basket, any pattern is imprinted on the top of your bread.

Many doughs are difficult to make without them – especially wetter, longer-proved sourdoughs, as they would stick and spread if left to prove on a tray. They are, then, another piece of specialist equipment you're going to want to buy. But you don't need to, initially. All you need is a bowl, alongside a dish towel or fairly heavy piece of cloth. Spread the cloth with flour to saturate the weave of the material, then stick it flour-side up in a bowl or basket and sprinkle with some more flour. There, a makeshift proving basket.

The Less Essential

Electric Mixer

This book is designed for anyone to make bread, regardless of whether they own a piece of luxury kitchen equipment. Having said that, many of you do own a KitchenAid or Kenwood, and both do a great job. Maybe you have one of the new generation of mixers: I've heard great things about the Wilfa and the Ankarsrum. Indulgently, I use a Varimixer Teddy at home and it gives me joy every time it smashes through as much dough as you can throw at it.

A mixer isn't a panacea. It simply takes effort away and gives you back time to do other things as the dough mixes. And all home mixers tend to be spiral mixers, and as such they have a tendency to mix in a cęrtain way that can develop gluten well, but they don't necessarily impart much strength. It can really help to add a stretch and fold or two (page 46) after mixing.

The other advantage is for making doughs that involve adding butter or eggs after the dough has been mixed; this becomes super-easy, and you can save time by cracking your next egg or softening your butter as your dough mixes.

Baking Steel or Stone

In my first book, I recommended everyone have a baking stone in their oven; and to be fair, from a purist's perspective, if you go to the effort of preheating your oven for 40 minutes before every bake, then a baking stone will be an improver to nearly every oven.

Now I'm a pragmatist and an environmentalist. Doubling your baking time with preheating, sending huge amounts of energy into heating up a stone, is hardly a good thing for the environment. Then, realistically, not everyone is organized enough to remember to preheat their oven so far in advance, and if you're baking first thing before work, this means you've got to get up even earlier.

Using cast iron pots is far more energy efficient and gives you all the advantages of a stone. Otherwise, you can use a baking steel rather than a baking stone: this is a hefty bit of cast iron or stainless steel that heats in your oven, but takes far less preheating. Then, it releases its energy into the dough much faster, optimizing oven spring.

REAL
BREAD
BakeryBits
For The Artisan

Couche

A couche is a stiff sheet of linen cloth. It's a useful thing to have for baguettes, where you fold it between each proving dough, and it's stiff enough to hold its shape. Its weave is coarse enough to hold plenty of flour and it's thick enough to draw moisture out of your dough, helping to stop it stick.

And indeed, if you've got a couche, you can simply make those folds bigger, and prove much larger loaves between those folds, as long as you've got something at either end to stop the whole thing unravelling.

It's not essential as you can do the job, just not so well, with any large sheet of material or a large dish towel; if going down this route, make sure to prove on a tray for some support, and use plenty of flour to try to prevent any sticking.

Peel

A peel is a thin piece of metal, usually aluminium, on the end of a stick, that's used to transfer bread to and from your oven.

A peel, of sorts, is a nearly essential thing if you're using a baking stone or steel: you need to turn your bread out from your proving basket onto something so it can be scored. That's the peel, usually dusted with plenty of semolina to stop it sticking: the semolina acts like little ball bearings so the dough can roll from one surface to the next without sticking. Then you can slide the dough onto the stone.

If you don't have one, a thin metal baking tray can do 99% of the job: the thin edge can get under the dough to remove it from the oven, and they usually have a lip you can grab to lift the dough from one place to another. The handle only really becomes necessary if you were trying to get breads deep into a baker's oven, or if you're using a pizza oven, as opposite.

Please avoid peels that are made of wood and bamboo, as even if they're tapered, the edges are not sharp enough to get under breads or pizza without causing some dough destruction.

Pizza Oven

Quite a few recipes in this book – and of note, my entire pizza section (page 109) – give the option of using a pizza oven. These ovens are able to get far, far hotter than a domestic oven (450°C (840°F), ideally), allowing the rapid expansion of bubbles in doughs for a super-light and pillowy bread. This is ideal for the Neapolitan-style pizza, or to get the authentic effect of a tandoor for flatbreads, for example.

Apart from the technical appeal, you've got the social pull of being able to host pizza parties, and for everyone to get stuck in to making their own personalized pizza after pizza. A word of caution: get comfortable making pizzas first before buying a pizza oven. A pizza oven doesn't make great pizzas: you do. And if you're not comfortable making pizza, you'll spend the entire pizza party trying to salvage stuck, soggy doughs while hungry onlookers consider ordering a takeaway. We've all been there.

Having said that, once you get the hang of it (and put together your own Standard Operating Procedure as per my guide, page 109) the modern iteration of pizza ovens is truly brilliant. The best are by Ooni (sorry Gozney lovers) and I have used the Karu 12 at home for years: it runs on kindling and charcoal and is highly efficient. For this book, I upgraded to the Karu 16 for the glass door, larger cooking area and the fact it can take logs, which means I need to stoke it only once or twice during a session. Don't be tempted by one of those cheap knock-off versions on eBay and AliExpress.

Ingredients & Variations

I'm going to take you through what we need to make bread, and what I might ask of you to make certain breads. These are different things. Please feel free to overrule me.

As long as you can get flour, yeast and salt, you can make the vast majority of recipes in this book. If you can grab some rye and go to the effort of making a sourdough, and your local shop has adequate ingredients to make a simple cake, you can make nearly every recipe, with a couple of modifications and substitutions. The recipe will still work. That is the beauty of bread.

Flour

Flour is made by grinding up seeds. If a seed is grown commercially, there will be a flour made from it. And if there's not and you have a couple of stones to grind together, you can make one. Most commonly, flour is made from wheat, or from similar grassy cereals that contain gluten. This might be rye, barley or a number of ancient wheat-like grains. Grind down these seeds and you've got wholemeal flour, as it contains the whole of the meal. If the grain happens to be a form of wheat, much of the English-speaking world refers to it as wholewheat flour.

Before we get to **white flour**, it's wise to check out the structure of each seed. For simplicity, we'll look at wheat, but most of the grains we'll be using are structured in a similar way.

On the outside, that's the **bran**: the hard, brown stuff that's rich in fibre and turns many a toddler away. It's texturally divisive, but filled with both fibre and flavour, and an essential part of many of the recipes in this book. It can largely be removed through manual sieving, as when grinding it tends to snap into large flakes.

Then you've got the **germ**: this is a very rigid part of the wheat, and creates the building blocks out of which a new plant will form. It's the plant equivalent of the yolk you'd find in eggs, and adds flavour and structure to breads, but is also removed as part of processing in the creation of white flour.

Finally, and most uninvitingly named, you've got the **endosperm**. This is the bit of the grain that we want for most recipes in this book. It contains the fuel for the young seedling to sprout: starches, protein and various nutrients. When you think of white flour, you're thinking of filtered endosperm, that's often bleached using alkaline to make it extra white.

White flour exists for two main reasons: the first is that it is shelf stable: bran holds on to moisture and thus wholemeal flour tends to spoil quicker. The second is that it's delicious. Nowadays, there's a classless comfort in the enjoyment of white bread: enjoyment shared by all. It wouldn't always have been: look at pre-revolutionary France, for example, and you find a society where the poor had bread predominantly made up of bran. Refined white bread was an aspirational product. Today, it might be the ancient grained, bran-heavy sourdough that's a marker of wealth or status, but I know of no-one who doesn't succumb to the white, enriched crumb of a plain white loaf.

MULINO MARINO
MUGNAI DA TRE GENERAZIONI
CONSERVARE L'ETICHETTA / KEEP LABEL
PRODUCT
PERIYAR
www.periyar.com
PAN
Whole Wheat
500g
MULINOMARINO.it
GROSSA MAIS
POLENTA
COARSE POLENTA FLOUR
FARINA INTEGRALE BIOLOGICA
MARINO
SFARINATO DI GRANO DURO
BIOLOGICO
MISTO ITALIANO
PASTA, PANI DEL SUD, FOCACCIA TIPO BARESE
STONE GROUND DURUM WHEAT FLOUR
PASTA SOUTHERN ITALIAN
BREAD AND FOCACCIA
MULINOMARINO.it
BỘT NĂNG
FARINE DE TAPIOCA
TAPIOCA FLOUR

It's worth noting that white flour isn't an absolute term, and there are many shades of white. The technical term for this is '**extraction**' – as in, how much of the original grain is extracted – and is expressed as a percentage. Wholemeal flour has an extraction of 100%, for example, whereas a white, white flour might be 65–70%, meaning that 30–35% is lost as bran and germ. Many smaller producers making stoneground flours both choose not to bleach their flours, giving them a grey colour, and to manually sieve the flours to maintain a little bran and germ. This gives a beautifully moist texture, though you often have to use a little extra water and they can be a bit trickier to work with. If you can get these unbleached flours, use them. They're better for you and for the planet.

What's 'on' Flour

Flour is more than the grain. Those grains aren't alone: they are teeming, as we all are, with micro-organisms. These bacteria and yeast have landed on your growing wheat as the ears swayed in the wind, or actual little creatures have brushed the grasses as they've landed or flown past.

Then, as the grain is milled into flour, they can be distributed widely, and so there's almost no part of the flour without different species of bacteria and yeast, waiting for their chance. Store flour in suitably dry conditions, though, and they shouldn't be allowed it, as they do need moisture to multiply. We give them their chance when we create a

sourdough starter: this is when we hydrate them by mixing the flour with water, allow them access to their fuel and they begin to grow. What flour you have, grown in whatever conditions, then what water you've used and in what kitchen you've built it up: that will create a sourdough starter that is unique to you.

Some flours are richer in interesting bacteria and yeast than others – as such, if you're looking to culture a sourdough starter (page 27), I'd suggest **stoneground flour**. Unlike in roller-milling, where the friction means great steel rollers that crush the grain get very hot indeed, stone grinding flour is slower and cooler. More of the bacteria and yeast survive and you have a greater chance of success.

Gluten

Bread flour is **strong flour**. This means that it is rich in gluten. And gluten is wonderful. Lots of people don't like gluten and most are misguided through misinformation – I can say this confidently as a medical professional. Still, about 1% or slightly more of the population, or about 80 million people worldwide, can't have gluten due to coeliac disease. There are a few gluten-free recipes in this book that will help you if you're catering for the 1%, but if you're after a collection of gluten-free breads for you or someone close to you, there are loads of guides available and this probably isn't the book for you. That's because I love gluten.

Gluten is made up of two proteins called gliadin and glutenin, which tangle together to form a big sticky lump when you mix your flour with water. But through the kneading process, or any process of stretching the dough, you build up layer upon layer of elastic film that, when filled with the carbon dioxide created through fermentation, gives you bubbles. And those bubbles make bread light.

Almost all of what we do to dough is to manipulate gluten for a lighter, tastier bread with a beautiful smooth crust. It's an obsessive passion – hence I've written all these books on it. And it's why making half-decent gluten-free bread is difficult.

Not all strong flours are of equal strength. Those grown in Canadian or American super-farms under ideal, non-organic conditions may be 15% protein or more, with much of this being gluten: these can be useful in very high hydration (wet) doughs, or during long sourdough fermentations. They're forgiving, but they tend to lack flavour.

Your local, organically produced grains using older grain varieties will have immensely better flavour, and often texture. But they can be a bit tricky, can't take quite as much water, and during very long fermentations, the bacteria in sourdough can break down what structure they have. This isn't a bad thing, but you can't expect the same level of web-like crumb.

Cake flour (or plain flour) has less gluten in it – this might be due to intentional variety or poorer growing conditions. This can also be good – this creates a more crumbly or tearable texture perfect for cakes and biscuits. You might even see me specify plain flour in quite a few bread recipes; this means I'm aiming for that more cake-like texture, or for a puffy lightness during a fast bake.

Types of Flour

Wheat flour is first split into 'white' and 'wholemeal' ('wholewheat'). Avoid any flour labelled as 'brown' – this usually means it's a reconstitution of previously separated bran and white flour. White flour is then split into 'strong' (bread), plain (all-purpose), extra low gluten (cake).

Wholemeal flour is generally trickier to work with than white flour. Those big brown bits of bran tend to get in the way of forming your intricate gluten network, so you end up with a dough that's less stretchy, which results in a heavier bread. One way around this is to simply use less wholemeal flour compared to white, but if you're still keen on using large amounts, you can sieve out the bran and keep this aside. You knead and ferment and develop your 'white' sieved dough normally, and then fold the bran back in at a later stage. This allows you to maximize the fibre and earthy, wholemeal flavour of a loaf.

Most big commercial flours tend to use '**commodity**' wheat, of a few homogenous varieties, grown in a fairly industrial way. If you have access to it, seek out wheat flour that's been grown in a sustainable way, with soil health at the core. This is often achieved by growing a mishmash of ancient varieties together: they're much tastier, have an amazingly moist texture and can be used to make almost any recipe in this book. Check out YQ population flours, or excellent producers such as Wildfarmed or Hodmedod's.

Spelt is an ancient form of wheat that's suitably distinct enough to have its own identity. It has a lower gluten content but a fairly high protein content, and a yellowish tone. It also has a distinct nutty flavour and is great to dose into breads in smaller quantities, usually 10–20% of the total flour weight. **Einkorn** and **emmer** (including varieties like **khorasan** or **kamut**) are other diverse and ancient wheat varieties that make great additions to predominantly white loaves, or denser but very flavourful loaves if used on their own.

Durum wheat is a descendent of emmer, and the majority of it is used to make dried pasta. In flour, it's most commonly referred to as **semolina** (though confusingly, there's a separate British product made from waste wheatgerm that's also called semolina). Durum semolina is grainy because durum has a very hard endosperm, and for bread-making benefits from a second milling to make ***semolina rimacinata***. Look out for this if you're planning to make bread with it.

Rye is one of my favourite grains – very hardy, it grows even in very cold and wet environments and yields a small, deeply flavourful grain. It's very low in gluten but makes a beautiful dense bread complemented with seeds and whole grains, or adds flavour and texture to largely white breads when dosed in smaller quantities.

Barley – a grain most often used malted (left to germinate and re-dried) for beer and whisky – can also be made into flour, but is rarely used as it is low in gluten, and other flours tend to give a more pronounced flavour.

Gluten-free Flours

Buckwheat isn't wheat at all, but rather the seeds of a rhubarb-like plant, and works well for a variety of pancakes, noodles and a few breads. **Teff** is a subvariety of **millet**, and has tiny, hard seeds from a widely distributed collection of grasses. **Rice flour** is ground white rice, mainly used for noodles, and **tapioca (cassava) flour** and **potato flour** are both made from the dried starch of their respective root vegetable.

Maize flours are varied: you've got standard white **cornflour (cornstarch)**, which is the refined and very fine starch from corn, and tends to be used as a thickener rather than a bread flour. Whole corn kernels that have been dried and ground up become **polenta**, or **cornmeal**, which can be fine or coarse textured. If you're wanting to make breads such as tortillas out of this, the corn needs treatment by nixtamalization, or boiling with alkaline (usually lime) before being dried and ground – creating ***masa harina***.

Substitutions: You can substitute most strong white flours from different countries, but may need to adjust the water content if the dough seems too wet. I recommend substituting unbleached, organic flours for most of my white flours, if you have access to them. Most wholemeal and ancient flours can be substituted for each other, and you can substitute a portion of the white flour (as a rule, let's say 10%) in most of my recipes without dire consequences.

Water

I'll say what I've said before: **water comes from your tap**. It doesn't matter whether it's soft or hard, clean or unclean – nearly any water can make great bread. Don't be buying special water to make bread, or going to great lengths to modify it or filter it. Even the most inhospitable, soft chlorinated water can ferment a good sourdough. Even the most contaminated water will be sterile by the time the bread is cooked.

The key with water is to use plenty of it. I've done many bread demos where I've asked my audience to remember one thing from the whole hour: '**wetter is better**'. Depending on whose bread philosophies you've followed before, you might find many of the doughs I present as pretty wet and sticky. They have lots of water, or other liquid portion, in them. This can make them challenging to work with if you're not used to it, but once you relax and accept that sticking to your hands and the surface is actually a good thing, and allows you to stretch the dough further for better gluten development, you'll find some of the drier doughs in this book a little weird.

Hydration is simply a measure of how wet your dough is – how much water you've used. It tends to be expressed as a percentage of the total flour in a recipe. For example, a dough using 1kg of flour and 700g of water would be 70% hydration; 600g of water would be 60% hydration, and so forth.

Most doughs are between 60% and 80% hydration: the difference between these levels is utterly stark. 60% is a dry dough that won't stick and gives a close-textured traditional loaf. 80% is into the realms of ciabatta, where you'll get a web of very sticky dough that's difficult to contain if you're used to drier doughs, or new to bread baking. The minimum you'll find is 50% and the maximum around 100%, or equal parts flour and water. This is only possible with some types of flour, and usually requires significant development of the gluten prior to the incorporation of all the water, or else you just end up with something akin to a batter.

Adding wholemeal flours means adding bran which absorbs water. The higher the proportion of wholemeal flour, the wetter your dough should be, and recipes are adjusted here accordingly. Similarly, white stoneground flours tend to have some flecks of fine bran within them, and require a bit extra water.

Temperature

The temperature of the water is important, too: this helps decide the temperature of your dough, and thus how fast or slow your fermentation is going to be. While it's difficult to alter the temperature of your flour, or the bowl you're mixing in, your water temperature is easily adjusted.

For most recipes in this book, we're aiming for tepid: this is a warm room temperature, and if you plonk your fingers down into a jug of tepid water, it almost feels like nothing at all: neither warm nor cold. If you get it perfect, close your eyes and your fingers won't sense they're being dipped in water.

If you're using sourdough, which needs a bit of oomph to get going, you'll tend to want to aim a little higher than this: a warm temperature close to body temperature. This should be like a slightly mean bathwater, or between 25–30°C (77–86°F) or so. You could measure it with a thermometer once or twice so you get a sense of what it feels like, but I can't be bothered with any sort of faff.

Substitutions: You should rarely need to substitute water. But if you want extra softness, you can substitute liquid for liquid, so milk, eggs and purées should all lower your water content on a 1:1 ratio.

Salt

Salt is sodium chloride. It makes bread taste nice. Don't use fancy salt – use **table salt**, because it's finely ground and dissolves quickly. All sodium chloride, once dissolved, does the same job. Don't pay for expensive crystals and origins if you don't have to.

This book marks quite a shift in how I recommend you use salt: I've always before recommended salt at about 2% of your total flour weight. This is 10g in a 500g loaf. Now, I recommend adding a teaspoon to a teaspoon and a half, or 6–9g. The main reason for this is mostly that electronic scales are not reliable enough to measure salt accurately down to the gram, and if you go over what I specify and add 11g of salt to a large loaf with 500g flour, you'll find it far too salty. For most people, 10g is the threshold between deliciousness and saltiness.

The other reason is that the teaspoon is actually quite a good measure – a level, 'measuring' teaspoon, or exactly 5ml, is a very consistent way of measuring 6g of table salt. And we all tend to have a set of measuring spoons lying around, whereas many do not have a set of electronic scales.

Make bread without salt and you'll find it tastes rotten: the only way they seem to get away with it in Tuscany (*pane Toscano*) is by covering the bread in loads of salty meat and cheese. You'll also notice quite a few changes in unsalted dough, which will rise much faster, as salt inhibits yeast, and it will be much more fragile, as salt stabilizes the bonds between the proteins in gluten. Sometimes, as a result, salt is added after fermentation has started, so the dough can get properly stretchy and sourdough can get going before it is hit with its inhibitory action.

Substitutions: You can, of course, substitute table salt with fancy salt, but I suggest dissolving it in the liquid portion of your dough so it is evenly distributed and fully incorporated. Substitute 1:1 by weight, but not by volume. Volumes for crystal salt haven't been given, so you'll need to use the scales.

Yeast

In short, the yeast makes bread rise.

Yeasts are microbiological marvels. Your dough is alive because your yeast is alive. Yeast are living fungi, and specifically, the sort we use in bread is a fungus – *Saccharomyces cerevisiae*. This turns the starches in the flour into alcohol and gas – carbon dioxide (CO_2). They breathe out the same stuff we breathe out.

You can buy yeast in many forms. Most widely available is **instant yeast** (fast-action yeast) – these are fine granules that you can simply incorporate into your flour, without any extra steps. I recommend you use instant yeast because it is easy, cheap and widely available. The other dried option is **active dried yeast** – which is the same stuff but in bigger granules and with a far longer shelf life. This tends to require rehydration and re-activating prior to use, which is a faff, and I don't like faff.

Whichever dried yeast you use, the cells contained within those granules do gradually die over time. The number one cause of a yeasted loaf not rising is dead yeast – that's yeast granules that are too old, or that have accidentally been left in the sun or on an oven and got very hot indeed. Even if it's still before its sell-by date, yeast that's a year old will have a fraction of the potency of 'fresh' dried yeast. You can slow this deterioration down markedly by keeping it in the fridge, and I recommend you do.

If you've got access to it, **fresh yeast** is a great option, and often your local bakery will give you some for free – just ask. It comes in big crumbly, squeaky blocks, must be kept in the fridge, and you've got a couple of weeks to use it before it gets hopelessly slow. If you're using fresh yeast, I'd recommend ***tripling my specified quantity of yeast for each recipe***. You can add it in exactly the same way as instant yeast, by just rubbing it in at the beginning.

Yeast work faster in warmer temperatures, up to about 40°C (104°F) or so. Above this, they become really stressed and die. Until this point, as yeast get warmer, they work faster, they try harder and harder to make more yeast, and this can lead to some undesirable flavours. Therefore, doughs proved too warm may achieve lightness quicker, but tend to taste and smell like the bad old bakeries of yesteryear.

Prove too fast, and your fermentation will be over before the yeasts can complete their other jobs: before they can make CO_2, they need to first break down that starch into sugars. They do so in abundance, meaning that the longer you leave a loaf to ferment, the sweeter it will be. That means a shiny, crackling crust and a tastier crumb. Then give your dough some time, and you give the bacteria within your dough a chance to contribute a more complex and interesting flavour.

Substitutions: You can switch equally between instant and active dried yeasts, but you'll need to rehydrate the latter in your liquid portion first. Triple the specified quantity of yeast for fresh yeast, and rub it in to your dry ingredients.

Sourdough Starter

A sourdough starter also makes bread rise, just more slowly than yeast.

Once upon a time, we didn't know much about microbiology – indeed, until the 17th century, the idea that it was billions upon billions of tiny living organisms that were rising our bread would have been fanciful.

Commercial yeast is therefore a relatively modern discovery – indeed, the first isolation of yeast for bakeries came from the brewing industry in the 18th and 19th centuries, where bakers would take the dregs from beer fermentations and use it to make their bread. This was a significant step up from before, when bakers had to make do with sourdough.

Yes, the sourdough starter, that aspirational gloop we're all dying to conquer, was once scorned as a pain-in-the-ass. Bakeries were desperate to get away from a slow process that 'polluted' the taste with a distinct sour tang, especially in sweet, white doughs.

Now we know better – most of the recipes in this book have sourdough starter listed in the ingredients, but it's not necessarily to make the bread rise. Instead, it's precisely for the flavour that was once scorned. It adds a slight tang. It adds complexity. It also helps the dough relax and stretch out, creates more sugars, and the higher acid and alcohol content of the final bread is brilliant for longevity.

You can find my full guide on how to make a starter on page 50. Alternatively, like for fresh yeast, just ask your local bakery, and if they make sourdough starter, they'll give you some.

Substitutions: If your sourdough is unhappy or non-existent, it can be substituted for a teaspoon or two of instant yeast. See the recipes for details.

Sugars

Sugar is not necessary when making simple breads. Your yeast or sourdough creates an abundance of sweetness during their fermentation – adding sugar is both unnecessary and can even slow the yeast down. Yeast prefer to stick to one sort of sugar, and the switch between maltose (the sugar made from breaking down starch) and the sucrose you've added is likely to cause some yeast displeasure.

Having said that, sucrose gives a different sort of sweetness, and in many of my sweeter breads, we are adding small amounts of sugar to give a lift. Go further, into cake levels of sweetness, and this can draw water out of the yeast cells and slow them down to a snail's pace: this is why many of my sweeter breads incorporate sugars in other ways, whether icings, syrups, fillings or dustings. Plain caster (superfine) sugar is my usual weapon of choice, but sweetness can come in many forms. Plenty of breads have some honey content, and it's doubly important you don't go too generous with this, as the enzymes and sugars in honey have additional effects that can break down the structure of your dough. Treacle (molasses) gives a nice caramelly flavour to breads, as well as a deep colour, and I use it in several rye breads.

Substitutions: Most sugars can be substituted for each other, in equal quantities. Granulated sugar can be used, but you might find it more difficult to incorporate. The darker the sugar you use, the greater the treacly flavour. You can substitute honey for sugar and vice versa, but consider the different flavours and what you're after.

Fats

You'll start to see a theme here: oils and butters are not necessary in bread. They can be useful in certain situations, though. For buttery richness, by all means. For creating the super-light, flaky structure of a laminated dough, go for it. For a little extra lift and a softness in an uber-white bread, they can be wonderful.

But they do have a big effect on the dough's structure, so if you add too much you'll find yourself in a pickle. Fat acts as a lubricant, and so can stop your tangly mess of gluten from sticking together and forming the beautiful matrix you need for a light bread. A little bit, rubbed in at the start, is totally fine, but if you've got a particularly buttery, rich dough, then I'll specify the butter is softened and incorporated after any kneading takes place, so that your structure is already developed.

Substitutions: Vegan block can be used instead of butter, as can baking margarines, ghee, lard or any solid fat. Most oils can be substituted for each other. Consider which flavours will work before substituting.

Eggs

Eggs give a cakiness to bread – the yolk contains a significant fat content, which softens the dough, but the white contains lots of protein, which can aid in the overall structure for a lighter effect. They have to be used appropriately, though: if baked into a well-fired bread, the protein in the eggs can become firm and give a dryness that's much like an over-baked cake. The key is using them in softer breads or in larger loaves where you're after that specific egg flavour, and alongside plenty of butter for softness.

An egg-wash is applied to many of my recipes here – this is basically a whisked whole egg that is brushed over the raw dough prior to baking, enhancing crust and shine. Adding a pinch of salt will give flavour, and the salt helps break down the protein in the egg for easier brushing. You can even apply an egg wash at the start of the final prove, then another egg wash just before it goes in to layer it up, and for the most decadent or deep-dark crusts, brush only using the yolk.

Substitutions: Eggs can, for the most part, be substituted with aquafaba (chickpea/garbanzo water) or vegan egg substitute, 50g for each egg, though these will not give the richness required for most bread doughs and I'd recommend separately incorporating some fat into the dough.

Milk, Yogurt and Buttermilk

Milk is an emulsion of some fats, protein and sugars, mostly. So, you can imagine that it acts much in the same way as adding a little bit of oil, and a little bit of sugar: it gives a subtle sweetness, with the fat contributing some softness. It's often used instead of water in sweet breads and gives a characteristic white softness to shokupan and milk loaves. You absolutely can substitute for the various vegan options.

Buttermilk is the milky liquid that's left after you churn cream to make butter, that then usually undergoes a lactic, yogurt-like souring process. It gives a lovely softness and a slight tang to doughs, and unsurprisingly can be substituted with natural yogurt.

Substitutions: Any vegan milk can be used instead of specified whole cow's milk; my favourite is oat. You can also use milk from other animals, and switch between whole and skimmed milks without huge consequence.

Bits

Bread is freedom. You absolutely have my permission to add whatever bits and pieces you want to enhance, customize and personalize your doughs. Just bear in mind that it might have some detrimental effect on your dough, though. Larger pieces, such as chunks of hard cheese, nuts, large seeds or dried fruit, are the easiest to incorporate, as they don't tend to get in the way of your gluten matrix, but are rather held in place by it. I like incorporating them after kneading for ease and to stop them getting in the way.

Smaller ingredients such as herbs, small seeds, brans and grain are the biggest issue, as they do rather impact the structure of your loaf. As when making breads using a high proportion of wholemeal flours, it can be useful to add brans and fine bits later on in the process, after gluten development has taken place. The lamination method (page 61) is ideal for this.

Ground spices are also tricky as, depending on the spice, they can have a profound effect on your yeast. Indeed, many have been prized in traditional medicine for antiseptic properties and those properties extend to yeast and sourdough. Cinnamon and nutmeg are notable examples and my recipes including these in the dough tend to have a generous yeast quantity to ensure a reliable rise.

Add soft fruits and vegetables as a purée, substituting a proportion of your water. Better yet, consider that they might work better as an accompaniment or topping. It's difficult to get chunks of soft fruit through bread without them becoming mush, with the exception of hard chunks of unripe fruit or uncooked veg that then soften in the oven.

Substitutions: Most nuts can be substituted for each other, as can most dried fruit.

HOW TO MAKE BREAD:

A MASTER CLASS

If there's any chapter I'd recommend reading, it's this one. While all the recipes have a method, it's impossible for every one to go down into the detail: into the why and what for. Then there are the variations: the innumerable differences between every kitchen in every country, every flour or water or yeast. You might have to adapt if things go wrong, and it helps if you can understand what happened and fix it for next time.

This is a lot of information and there's quite a bit of reading to do. But, I mean, you bought a book. What did you expect? TikTok?

This is how you make bread, or rather, how I make bread – and most of the time it works out pretty well.

How to Make Bread Without Any Yeast or Sourdough

U

BP

Bread without any commercial or wild yeast (such as sourdough), falls into two categories: true unleavened breads, which have no raising agent at all, and breads that use chemical raising agents.

The advantage of these breads is that they tend to be simple and quick. They don't require the memorization of loads of steps, they (mostly) don't require kneading, resting, shaping or the worry about an inherently erratic biological process. Then they are delicious served warm, they tear easily and you can achieve a cake-like 'fluffiness' that's not possible with yeasted doughs.

The downside is that they tend to be heavier, they stale quickly and they lack the depth of flavour of a fermented bread. The lack of fermentation means that they tend to be very starchy, and so often there's the addition of sugar, such as in scones, for a hint of sweetness. Chemical raising agents can leave a soapy taste, especially if you add too much bicarbonate of soda (baking soda).

Some unleavened breads like a bit of kneading and resting to develop a soft stretchiness that allows them to be stretched out very thinly. This means they can be easily layered with fat to create flakiness, or cooked very quickly, but this will be covered in each recipe.

Chemical raising agents, on the other hand, work very quickly: they have to be mixed in just before baking. If you were to mix them into a kneaded dough, or one you've overworked, then all that lovely gluten remains very taut, and then is immediately put under pressure by the release of gas. This causes your bread to remain steadfast and tense, and your bubbles don't expand. The result is a dense, tight and chewy structure.

So, when making these breads, a gentle hand is often warmly welcomed. If you are careful with the dough, you'll see great tears and splits open up and they will achieve their light and fluffy potential.

4 Steps to Making Dough Without Yeast

1. Weigh and mix the dry ingredients – less than 5 minutes
2. Add the wet ingredients and mix – less than 5 minutes
3. Shape and divide the dough – less than 5 minutes
4. Bake or cook – 30 minutes

***Total time**: less than 60 minutes*
***Time spent in kitchen**: less than 30 minutes*

1. Weigh and mix the dry ingredients

Use electronic scales and put your ingredients straight into the bowl you're going to mix in. You might see some bakers do something fancy where they make a well in a pile of flour on a work surface, before adding liquid into the middle and gradually incorporating it. There is literally no reason to do this – except if you don't own a bowl.

Once you've weighed all your dry ingredients, distribute them. Because the next stage of mixing may be quite gentle, it's important that your salt or sugar or bicarbonate of soda (baking soda) is well distributed through the flour.

If I've specified butter, it's easy to rub it in at this stage, using your fingertips to crush your lumps of butter into the flour until they look a bit like breadcrumbs.

2. Add the wet ingredients and mix

Weigh your wet ingredients on top of your dry. Don't use volumetric measurements, such as millilitres, because measuring jugs for home use tend to be very inaccurate. There's no need to mix your wet ingredients beforehand – just dump them on top, then start to mix.

If your loaf has bicarbonate of soda (baking soda) or baking powder as a chemical raising agent, it's important to mix the dough together but to avoid overmixing and gluten development. Overwork, and you'll have a tough dough with minimal rise. Some doughs can still be lumpy when you stop, and this is fine. The odd lump of visible butter is fine, too.

If your dough is a very thin flatbread, your recipe might suggest kneading and then resting. This can allow you to stretch it out very thinly.

3. Shape and divide the dough

Unkneaded doughs tend to stick to everything, so use plenty of flour to allow you to handle them. If your fingers get caked, make sure to clean them off, flour them, flour your dough and continue. A dough scraper is your friend.

The shape, or whether the bread needs to be rolled out, will depend on the recipe. Be gentle, don't overwork or handle the dough more than you need to. If the dough sticks to something, scrape it off using a scraper and dust everything with flour.

4. Bake or cook

Larger breads will need to be baked in the oven, but the smaller and flatter the bread, the faster and hotter the heat can be applied, so these can be cooked on the hob, or even over an open flame.

Apply too much heat or for too long, and you will drive off all the moisture from the dough, leaving you with a (possibly delicious) cracker. Apply too little and your dough will be limp and stale quickly and lack the flavourful, caramelized and savoury notes from those browning reactions.

If your dough is chemically leavened, the structure will be very, very fragile until the dough has not only cooked, but cooled: think about a cake that sinks after it comes out the oven. So be careful with them during cooking, only open the oven and take them out if need be, and if cooking on the hob, flip gently and don't push down on the top with your spatula. Most of them will continue to cook as they cool, and an impatient baker might be disappointed to find that when they rip open a hot bannock straight from the griddle, it's still raw in the middle.

How to Make Bread Using Yeast

This is how I recommend making bread to most people. Many are put off by the brief kneading step, but it's fun, and if you have an electric mixer, effortless. A kneaded dough, compared to a no-knead method, tends to produce a slightly lighter, more even-crumbed bread, that's generally more stable and easier to handle.

10 Steps to Making Bread Using Yeast

1. Weigh – less than 5 minutes
2. Mix – less than 2 minutes
3. Autolyse (rest) – 15–30 minutes
4. Knead – 10–15 minutes
5. Rest (first prove or bulk fermentation) – 60–90 minutes at room temperature or 8–12 hours in a fridge set to cold
6. Shape – less than 5 minutes
7. Rest (second prove) – 45–60 minutes at room temperature or 6–12 hours in a fridge set to cold
8. Score – less than a minute
9. Bake – 30–50 minutes
10. Cool – 30–60 minutes

Total time*: 3–24 hours*
Time spent in kitchen*: less than 30 minutes*

1. Weigh

Weigh your ingredients – flour, salt, yeast, water and the rest – one by one, into a large bowl on some electronic scales. Use grams, never volumes, except for very small quantities. There is no special order to weighing and, if using dried yeast, no need to separate any ingredients. If you're using fresh yeast, rub or crumble this into the flour before adding your salt.

If a recipe lists butter, it will specify whether to rub it into the flour now or add it later. Almost all yeasted recipes have the option of adding some sourdough starter, which you can find out about a bit later in this chapter (page 50) – this isn't to make the bread rise but to add flavour.

Add your liquid, weighing it on the scales rather than using silly and inaccurate measuring jugs. Your water should be tepid: this means that you stick your fingers in and can't decide whether it's warm or cool. Indeed, every ingredient should be at room temperature or just above, for optimum yeast health. A bit colder and you'll maybe have a nicer flavour and a slower fermentation. Play around a bit – you might need to adjust timings and temperatures for your own home or by the seasons.

2. Mix

You could dive straight in with your hands, but a just-mixed dough makes quite the mess. Use a wooden spoon, or start out using a butter knife, then you can finish off with one hand if you like (keep one hand clean in case the doorbell goes). Stop once all the dry flour is mixed in but the mixture is still lumpy.

If you have an electric mixer, by all means, use it for this stage, but I'd switch the weighing order a bit: weigh your liquid ingredients first. If you don't, you can sometimes get a shell of firm floury mixture stuck to the inside of your bowl. It can easily be scraped off later, but it's annoying to have to.

3. Autolyse (rest)

Let the dough rest. Here, the yeast is slowly kicking into gear, while the tangles of gluten in the flour relax slightly, stick together and become more stretchy. This allows you to bring the dough together with minimal effort, and it makes the kneading stage far easier. You can cover your bowl, or leave it uncovered and just knead through the thin, dry skin that forms. Don't worry about it. Don't worry about anything.

Autolyse (pronounced auto-lease) is a French misappropriation of a scientific term meaning microbial destruction, but is widely used to describe this first, short rest before kneading.

4. Knead

When your dough is first mixed, if you were to zoom right in, you'd find a dense and not-very-stretchy tangle of proteins: sticky, tense and bounc to each other in many places This is gluten. In this tangled mess, gluten isn't able to form the lovely flat layers that can hold carbon dioxide and give the bread lightness.

There are two ways to change this. The first is with time, where the gluten relaxes and untangles and splays out. Then, through occasional stretching and folding (page 47), you can accelerate this process and give the dough some strength.

The second way to achieve these lovely flat layers is with effort – kneading – taking those tangled, tense complexes and shearing them apart with your hands. You apply these forces and in a relatively short period of time you've smashed these protein tangles into the layers that can hold gas, while creating trillions of new bonds by forcing them together.

Of course, these methods are not mutually exclusive, and in making sourdough, for example, I do tend to recommend a bit of both. In sourdough, you've got billions of bacteria working against you, breaking down the protein you've been building up, and it's similar in very wet doughs, where even after kneading, your dough sags and flops. Combining both approaches can be game changing.

I've described two methods of kneading below, for wet and dry doughs respectively. I've recommended these two methods for 10 years or more, but there are infinite ways of doing this, so do give others a try if you find one elsewhere that works well for you. Use the slap and fold for wet doughs – the stickier the better. Use the stretch and roll for dry doughs, that you can easily lift off the surface to turn after each roll. If it just sticks when you try to do this switch to the slap.

By all means, use your electric mixer if you've got one. Weigh your liquid first, then weigh in the dry ingredients on top, then mix on a low speed (setting 1 out of 5, for example) for 5 minutes. Use your dough scraper to scrape the sides down if everything isn't incorporated. Then, use a low-medium speed (setting 2 out of 5) for another 5 minutes, before finishing with a stretch and fold (page 47) for some strength.

Slap and fold – the French fold

1. Scrape your dough out onto an unfloured surface
2. Slide your fingers underneath the dough
3. Lift it up – don't worry if bits break off
4. Turn the dough over and slap it down
5. Grab the end nearest you and stretch it towards you
6. Fold it over
7. Repeat, turning the dough every few slaps and using your scraper to scoop up any stuck dough
8. Transfer your stretchy developed dough back to your bowl and cover

Stretch and roll – the 'English knead'

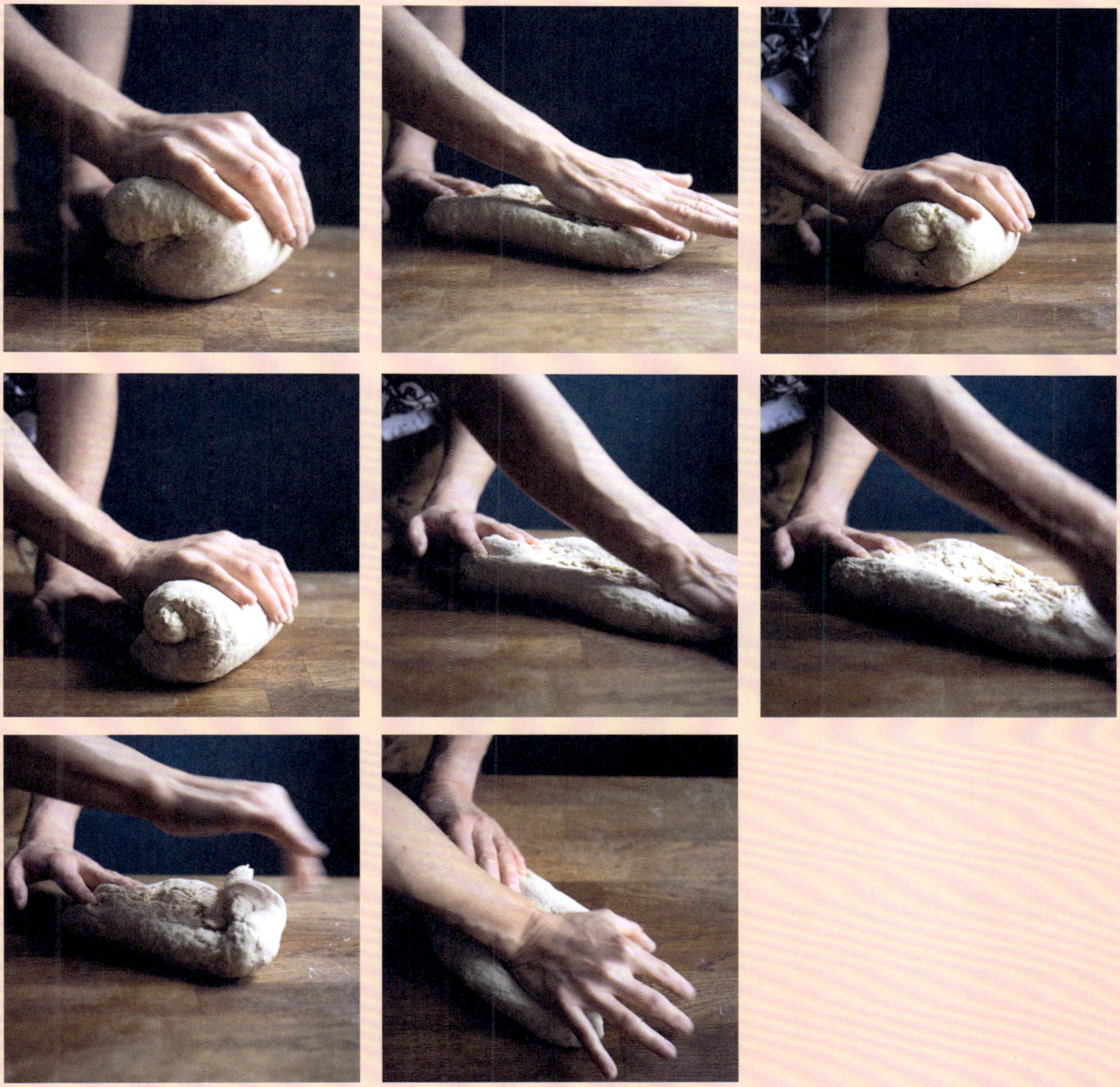

1. Turn your dough onto an unfloured surface
2. Stretch the dough away from you using the heel of your hand
3. Quickly use the same hand to roll the dough back towards you
4. Turn a quarter turn and repeat

5. Rest (first prove or bulk fermentation)

This is where you leave your dough to rise – for the yeast to break down starch into sugar, then sugar into alcohol and carbon dioxide (CO_2), filling between your layers of gluten to inflate them into bubbles. An excess of sugar creates sweetness.

As your dough rises, two opposing things are happening: your gluten is relaxing and becoming stretchy; but the yeast is pumping out the gas, putting some tension into those strands, giving your dough strength and shape. That's why, if your dough is flat and saggy or feels overly wet, it might be due to often-blamed factors like poor-quality flour or not enough development of the dough, but most of the time the yeast is old or unhappy. If this happens, stick your dough somewhere a bit warmer and add a stretch and fold (page 47) about halfway through the first prove.

How do you know when this stage is done? The truth is, there is no one-size-fits-all test to knowing this, and we all still get it wrong. The point you're aiming for is when your dough has grown to its full potential but remains stable: it can be comfortably cut and moved and shaped.

Too far (overproved), and it will deflate and lose its structure. On the other hand, if your dough feels heavy and firm and difficult to shape, this means it needs a bit more time (underproved) or that your yeast is old or too cold. As mentioned above, it might be small but feel stringy, wet, sticky and stretchy. This often means your yeast is unhealthy.

As long as you have happy yeast, feel free to prolong your first prove and just stick your dough in the fridge for 6–12 hours to overnight or while you're at work. If you are doing this, make sure your fridge is set to cold (ideally close to 2°C/36°F) or reduce the amount of yeast by half.

6. Shape

Here, we shape our bread into the shape we want it to be. Sounds simple? For a new baker this is the most difficult step to learn and does require practice.

Shaping is far more important than the aesthetic. It controls the final form of the bread, inside and out. If you want a nice texture and light crumb without huge holes or tunnels, you need to understand shaping. If you want a crust that's crisp and flaky rather than dense and hard, then it's shaping your dough that will help.

Having said that, if you've put in some effort and had a great fermentation, the shaping required to create a strong dough is often minimal, and actually by being very gentle, you can create a beautifully light crumb and crust.

Start each of the following methods by scraping your dough very carefully out of your bowl onto a floured surface, to preserve its structure. Shaping modern, open-crumbed breads requires a light touch. If ever a recipe calls for you to 'knock back' the dough, I will tell you: this extra step gives you a particularly small-bubbled but very even textured loaf, and also helps distribute the salt, yeast and heat better within your dough. It's a classic step of old-fashioned English-style bakeries.

Shaping a boule (round loaf)

1. Scrape your dough onto a lightly floured surface
2. With floured fingers, grab opposite sides of the dough and gently stretch them out
3. Fold them over each other
4. Turn the dough 90 degrees and stretch out two new 'ears'
5. Fold these over, giving you a squarer piece of dough
6. Repeat with the 'corners' you've just made
7. Flip the dough over, smooth-side up
8. Tuck and twist your hands under to cuddle it into a round shape

Dividing and shaping rolls

1. Create a cup shape with one hand
2. Place your hand over a divided lump of dough
3. Make small circles with your hand over the work surface, 15–20cm (6–8in) in diameter
4. You should feel your dough catching underneath. If it sticks, add some flour next time; if it slides, add less flour or add a spray of water

Shaping a batard or for a loaf tin

1. With floured fingers, grab one side with both hands and stretch a little
2. Fold it over the middle, crossing the midpoint by about half
3. Grab the other side
4. Fold it over
5. Grab the top of the dough, stretch it gently away from you and fold it over towards you
6. Grab the top corners of the dough and fold these into the middle, rolling it up
7. Keep rolling the dough towards you, like a swiss roll

Shaping a baguette or long baton – the easy way

1. Start by shaping for a batard (page 41)
2. Roll the middle of the dough between your palms and your surface
3. Keep rolling to stretch the dough out to the end. Roll the tips between the heel of your hand and the surface to create a point
4. Place the baguettes between folds of floured stiff fabric (a couche)

7. Rest (second prove)

This is where we let those bubbles fill again, but we don't want them to fill so far that they become fragile. If you give your loaf a shake and it deflates, this is a sign that your second prove was too long (don't worry – it's worth baking anyway, it will mostly puff back up). Too short, and you'll tend to have a more uneven texture with a mix of large and very small bubbles. Usually, the dough should increase in size by about one and a half times during this step. It should feel like you want to be careful with it, but still robust enough to take some knocks.

For larger breads, this prove tends to be done in a proving basket, smooth-side down. A basket is used to support the sides of the dough and so that the dough can be flipped before baking. This means it has both a nice floury pattern on top and (more importantly) it flips the structure, so that the weighed-down dough at the bottom is now on top, and is unimpeded in its rise, creating a more even texture.

Or you can use a tin – but make sure it's the right size for the loaf. Too small a tin and you'll find that your dough presses up against the sides and creates a dense line of flat bubbles, then spills over the top. Baking with moderate bottom-heat (so on a baking stone, baking steel or having a fancy oven) can help give you a boost and prevent potential bubble distribution issues.

Some doughs – such as some flatbreads and some pizzas – don't have a second prove. This is usually because the heat transfer of the bake is enough to puff them up, without needing this extra step. Others – such as some ciabatta recipes – don't have it because the aim was to fill the dough up as much as possible during the first prove, then handle it super-carefully to preserve an open and uneven structure. The stretchiness of these wet doughs allows them to expand even further in the oven.

8. Score

Before you start scoring, you want the smooth side of your bread facing up. If you're using a tin, this means you don't have to do anything, as the smooth side is already on top.

If you are using a proving basket, you should gently turn your dough out and onto your tray or pot, ready for scoring. There's no need to use baking parchment to stop sticking – a sprinkling of semolina will do – but if you're having to lower your loaf into a high-sided pot, I would tip your dough onto a sheet of baking parchment for scoring, so you can lower it gently inside.

Scoring is a skill I get a lot of questions about. Start off your scoring journey simply: use something sharp and make slashes in your bread wherever you want. Take a photograph before and after and learn how the tension you've created during fermentation and shaping is released by scoring. That is what scoring does – it allows your loaf to rise in the oven (oven spring) to its full potential. Fail to score and your crust will form but then crack in random places, giving you a misshapen and, if unlucky, an oddly small and dense loaf.

What matters most – more than depth, or what you use, or the angle of the blade – is the direction in which you score. You want to score to release as much tension as you can – so for example, if shaping any oblong dough, like a baguette, baton or batard, it's important to score it down its length. All the folding and rolling in shaping has created tension in the horizontal direction, which is aching to be released. Cut to release this tension, and you give it the best chance to thrive.

By all means, learn some decorative scoring, which involves making little nicks just beneath the surface. For this to work visually, it helps to add extra flour on top. Your little nicks do still need to be paired with some deeper cuts to control the overall direction of your rise.

9. Bake

Baking changes your dough into bread. The intense heat causes CO_2 in the gluten bubbles to expand, helping your dough rise for the last time: this is called oven spring. Then the bread cooks, the proteins and starches are set in place, and most of the water and alcohol are driven from the bread. The bits on the outside edges caramelize to form a crust. If you want to watch this process, I recommend sticking a Pyrex bowl over your loaf like a cloche for the first 20 minutes.

Your recipe will have specified to preheat your oven to a certain temperature – usually hot, definitely at least 180°C (350°F) fan (200°C/400°F/gas 6). Too low, and your bread won't get the energy to rise so well, and the crust will end up as dense and thick, if you ever get it to the right colour.

For most loaves, I don't recommend baking on something, but in something, so as to trap the steam produced as they bake. This delays the crust forming, helping it reach maximum rise, and helps caramelize the sugars on the crust for a crisp, flaky and sweet loaf. A cast iron pot or Dutch oven is perfect, but any lidded vessel will do, so long as it can safely take the heat.

You can now buy a dizzying array of bread-baking cloches and domes, either including a base or to put onto baking stones or trays that do the same job. Many are very expensive but they rarely do a better job than the metal casserole dish that's already in your kitchen.

Many of my recipes are for smaller breads – these should be baked on trays, and trapping their steam is impractical. Except those buns you don't mind cramming together into a high-sided roasting tray: cover with kitchen foil for the first 10 minutes to capture the steam.

If you've no option to bake under cover, most breads could do with extra moisture, so I'd recommend adding steam by spraying the oven and tray with water, or having a tray that sits on the base of the oven that you can stick in a splash of water or a few ice cubes.

Baking takes up to 50 minutes or so for larger, darker loaves, where you're aiming for a thick crust. These will be cooked enough in about 30 minutes, though – the rest is for the crust. Bread is resilient: you can take it out at most stages to check if it's done. Lift it up and if you tap the bottom and it sounds hollow, it's done enough. If it's dull, or it's pale and soft on the bottom, give it a bit longer. If this is a recurring issue, invest in a baking stone or steel, preheating as hot as the oven goes.

I've said in the past that you can't overcook bread, but you will find that the longer and hotter you bake a loaf, the less moisture is in the final crumb. This can be a desired effect for chewy, rustic breads, and it makes them easier to cut and prevents mould over several days. For a fluffy white bread, though, or a delicate iced bun or sweet plait, where you want a tender crumb and soft crust, you can certainly overbake, so it's worth going by the timings to ensure your breads are not getting overly dark or dry.

10. Cool

Hot bread has a certain appeal, but eat it straight out of the oven and it's going to clump in your stomach, burn your mouth and form lots of annoying little lumps as you try to slice it. Let your bread cool, at least until it's easier to handle, then start slicing and enjoying it.

I almost never use a cooling rack but either prop my loaves up on the edge of my baking pot, allowing air to circulate all around, or stick them straight on the bread board. I don't have any problems with soggy bottoms.

How to Make Bread Using the No-knead Method

Y

YS

This is the most basic method – that is to say, it requires the least input from you. It does, still, require some input: learning how to shape bread and some of the basics of dough handling, but this will come with time. If you find my recipes too wet and sticky, start out by using this method. Indeed, in the drier bread doughs, you'll find this method doesn't work so well: the softness given by wet doughs really lends itself to no-knead baking.

10 Steps to Making Bread Using Yeast

1. Weigh – less than 5 minutes
2. Mix – less than 2 minutes
3. Autolyse (rest) – 20–30 minutes
4. Stretch and fold – less than a minute
5. Rest (first prove or bulk fermentation) – 60–90 minutes or 8–12 hours in a fridge set to cold
6. Shape – less than 5 minutes
7. Rest (second prove) – 45–60 minutes or 8–12 hours in a cold fridge
8. Score – less than a minute
9. Bake – 30–50 minutes
10. Cool – 30–60 minutes

***Total time**: 3–24 hours*
***Time spent in kitchen**: less than 15 minutes*

1. Weigh

Just the same as if you were kneading (page 34). Weigh your ingredients, one by one, in a large bowl on some electronic scales. Use grams and never volumes. There is no special order to weighing.

2. Mix

This bit is the same too. Mix your ingredients together. Use a wooden spoon or a blunt knife, then you can finish off with one hand if you like. Always keep the other hand clean in case the doorbell goes. Stop once all the dry flour is mixed in but it's still lumpy.

If you have an electric mixer, by all means, use this, but weigh your liquid ingredients first to make it easier on the dough hook.

3. Autolyse (rest)

This first rest isn't optional here as you'll need time for a good no-knead dough. Cover the bowl and let the dough rest. The yeast will just begin to spring into life, while the tangles of gluten in the flour relax, stick together and become more stretchy. Stretchiness is what we want: too dry a dough and it won't be stretchy and might need a helping hand with some extra working.

4. Stretch and fold

This is an essential step for the no-knead method, and when it comes to making sourdough, too. It creates the gluten network of kneading with a fraction of the effort, and by avoiding the aggressive shearing forces of the knead, with care, we can achieve an extremely light bread. The key to achieving this is to avoid breaking up your network of gluten. It's a difficult thing to describe – as you stretch the dough, you will build an innate sense of when the dough is going to start to tear. It will start to get tough, like a rubber band being stretched too much. Pull further and it will break, but fold before it hits this point, and you'll have layers of preserved gluten, and layer upon layer of beautiful structure, begging to be filled with lovely CO_2. Fold the dough at this point, and turn and repeat.

5. Rest (first prove or bulk fermentation)

As in the kneaded method, this is where you leave your dough to rise – for the gluten-walled bubbles to fill, and for the starches to be broken down into sugars. You can leave your dough uninterrupted here, but for a really light loaf, I would split this step in two, and add another stretch and fold about half way through.

Like for a kneaded dough, you can just stick your dough in the fridge overnight or while you're at work and forget about it. If doing this, make sure your fridge is set very cold (about 2°C/36°F) or reduce the amount of yeast by half. Do try and get that second stretch and fold in, still, even if it's shortly after the first, just before you go to bed or leave for work.

6. Shape

From here, the steps are identical to kneaded bread. Shaping remains the trickiest part to get your head around, if you're not used to it, and does require practice. Head back to page 38 for a full step-by-step guide on what to do here.

Stretch and fold – the tuck method

1. Use a wet dough scraper and wet hands to loosen the dough from the sides of the bowl, re-wetting as necessary
2. Grab one edge of the dough and pull it up and towards you
3. Fold it over into the middle and press down to seal. If it doesn't seal, hold it longer
4. Work your way all the way around the bowl

7. Rest (second prove)

As detailed on page 43, this is the second rest to allow your dough to inflate to its maximum stable potential. If you like, you can use a tin, a couche (folded cloth), a proving basket, or let smaller doughs rest directly on a baking tray.

8. Score

As detailed on page 43, score down the length of your loaf to release maximum tension. You can score with your dough directly on your baking surface, a piece of baking parchment, or on a semolina-dusted peel. Use something serrated or something very sharp. Many smaller doughs, anything plaited or buns, don't require scoring.

9. Bake

See page 44 for full details. If making a large loaf, bake within a cast iron pot, a Dutch oven or a special bread cloche. You can improvise one of these by placing a stainless steel or Pyrex bowl – anything that creates a dome – upside down on a baking tray. The lid stays on for the first 15–20 minutes, then it comes off to crisp the crust until you hit your desired colour.

If making smaller breads, either cover with kitchen foil for the first 10 minutes, or add a few spritzes from a spray bottle full of water, and/or add some water or ice into a tray that's been preheated on the base of the oven.

If baking in a tin, I like to slide the loaf out of the tin for the last 5–10 minutes of baking to allow the sides to properly crisp up.

10. Cool

Cool on your baking surface, a cooling rack, your bread board – wherever. Don't worry about it, but make sure your bread is mostly cool before slicing.

Stretch and fold – the coil method

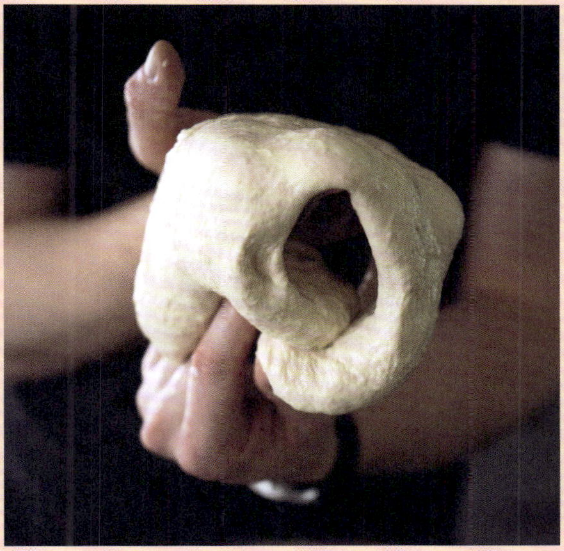

1. Use a wet dough scraper and wet hands to loosen the dough from the sides of the bowl, re-wetting as necessary
2. Place both wet hands underneath the dough and lift it up, allowing the weight to stretch the dough.
3. Place your hands back down, tucking the curls of dough underneath
4. Rotate by 90 degrees and repeat up to twice more

How to Make a Sourdough Starter

First, catch the bug, then grow some bugs.

You don't have to read any further if you don't want to get started with sourdough. This book can be read and enjoyed using only yeasted breads and you'll have awesome results, I'm sure. I recommend, if you're new to bread, becoming familiar with a yeasted approach before considering sourdough.

Sourdough is not made from commercial yeast. Instead, it's made from a sourdough starter: a mixture of flour and water that's left to ferment. This microbiological marvel is a symbiotic concoction of yeast and bacteria that takes the starches of the bread, breaks them down into an abundance of sugars, and churns out plenty of carbon dioxide to make the bread rise, as well as imparting interesting flavour compounds, and a notable acidic tang.

You do not need to buy a sourdough starter. While dried and fresh starters are available online, they are ridiculously expensive and will take a few days to get going anyway, so just now make one. The fastest way to start a starter is to 'borrow' a little of someone else's: even a teaspoon is enough to give you a fully functioning starter within about a day. If you're wanting to start your own unique starter, though, then this symbiotic relationship is achievable with almost any flour – especially 'good' flour. Flour that has been stoneground, that is organic and is wholemeal has the best chance of having the right bugs to create a sourdough starter. Using these three rules, I've never failed, and I've made hundreds of starters from scratch – I've killed a fair few too, and there's no shame in that.

Some people – especially internet influencers who feel bread needs to be done in a very rigid, complicated way – use various different terms for starters at different stages: mother, starter, leaven, levain. Disregard this. They can all mean the same thing. I recommend having one starter, and you'll likely never need to throw any of it away if you follow the tips I'm about to give you.

You might have heard you need to go to great lengths to keep your starter alive; to feed it like a pet. This is true, but the effort involved is tiny. So long as you keep it at the back of the fridge, once you've got it going, it will stay alive for weeks or months without a feed of fresh flour and water, nourishing the yeast and causing them to burst into life. If it's been a long time since its last feed, though, you might need to give it an extra feed and rest at room temperature to get it going again. If you're new to this and the repeated referrals to 'feeding' a jar slurry seems like the author has gone mad, all will become clear.

In the recipes, if you are going for the full sourdough experience, you will need a recently fed, active sourdough. Any starter made with any flour will work. Where I recommend a starter made with a particular flour – such as a rye starter – it means that I have given my starter a final feed of that flour. Again, I do not recommend having multiple starters because that is a faff.

7 Steps to Making a Sourdough Starter

1. Measure and mix – less than 2 minutes
2. Wait – 24 hours
3. Mix – less than a minute
4. Wait – 24 hours
5. Mix – less than a minute
6. Repeat – 48–96 hours
7. Feed – less than 2 minutes

Total time*: 4–7 days*
Total time spent in kitchen*: less than 10 minutes*

1. Measure and Mix

Into a container, such as a Tupperware, glass kitchen jar (seal removed) or a re-used yogurt pot, measure 50g of your wholemeal, stoneground, organic flour (I prefer rye, but you can use wheat, spelt, whatever you want). Add 50g water, then mix them together. Scrape down the sides, as these are most prone to getting mouldy.

Do not use a sealed container. Sealed containers explode under pressure. Yours might not explode yet, but it will, and it will be messy.

Do not worry about mixing in air, as many guides suggest – all the bugs needed for getting your fermentation going are in your flour already, they're not in the air around it.

Note: I've previously recommended using fruit juice instead of water, which makes the starter more acidic from the off. This is helpful because it avoids an early fermentation that can cause people to think their starter is ready too soon. So long as you know about that, you've got nothing to worry about. Using fruit juice does increase your chances of a mouldy starter if you don't stir it as often as specified, and not everyone has it to hand, so water is fine.

2. Wait

Cover your starter but don't seal it. You won't get an explosion at this point but get into good habits: a loose lid, kitchen foil, loose clingfilm (plastic wrap) or a plastic bag all work well.

Put your starter somewhere that will remain at a consistent temperature, warm if possible, but not hot. Do not put it in direct contact with a radiator. I like to use on top of the fridge, at the back, which is a good 5 degrees hotter than the rest of my kitchen and around the perfect 25°C (77°F) mark.

If you don't have anywhere this warm, it will still work at anywhere from about 18°C (64°F), but it will take significantly longer, and probably over a week to get going.

3. Mix

It's about a day later, and starter-starting guides will suggest feeding your fledgling starter with more flour and water. Don't, there's no need. All you're doing is diluting the few lovely bugs you've got growing; they've got loads of food left to keep them going.

Just mix everything thoroughly. You might notice a bubble or two before you start: these are probably from the dough settling and don't mean anything. Keep those hopes contained.

4. Wait

Cover your starter again, stick it somewhere warm again for 24 hours.

5. Mix

At this point, a couple of days in, you might notice quite a few bubbles have formed. This is not a sign that your starter is even remotely ready. These tend to be from an initial fermentation of *Leuconostoc* bacteria, that thrive in an early starter, and are later killed by acid. It's nothing to worry about, but don't get your hopes up yet, just mix it through, re-cover and leave your starter another day. Some breads use this little fermentation for their lightness, including idli and dosa (page 275).

If you use fruit juice instead of water, or add a squeeze of lemon to your water, you won't have the uncertainty of these bubbles, but if you forget mixing for a day, you'll have a mouldy mess.

6. Repeat for 48–96 hours

Mix and leave, mix and leave. The initial fermentation will settle down, and then you'll notice a gradual increase in bubbles until suddenly, usually 5–7 days after first mixing, your starter will be at least twice as big as it was, full of gas, and smelling slightly beer-ish, slightly funky and a lot like sourdough. Well done. Now your starter is ready for its first feed.

If you're unsure, and there's been a modest rise, still give it a feed, as described below. If it then doubles in size over the 8–12 hours, you're golden. If it doesn't, leave it longer and get it a bit warmer. Heat, or lack of it, makes a huge difference, and if you're in a cold, draughty house, then you could be waiting 7–10 days for this big jump.

If you've forgotten to mix at any stage during this process, mould can form on top of your starter. Don't worry about this. Scoop it off and mix everything thoroughly. If you've left it several days and the top is completely dense with blue or pink or black, start again, and just be more conscientious next time, or set an alarm on your phone.

7. Feed

You generally want to feed your starter with the same flour that you used to start it, or the change in environment can make the yeast a bit stressed out. Things will take a bit longer but they'll adapt eventually.

Measure another 50g of flour and 50g of tepid water, and mix these into your burgeoning starter. You want it as smooth as possible. If you're using good wholemeal rye, as I recommend, this will be very thick. That's OK.

Now, as confirmation that your starter is happy and ready, check on it occasionally over the next 6–12 hours. It should rise considerably in response to the feed. Don't put arbitrary limits – such as doubling or tripling in size – as these depend on flour type and the container used. If it puffs up well within a few hours and smells sweet and not overly acidic, it's ready to use.

If its response is lacklustre, or you're just unsure, don't use it for sourdough, yet. The thing that puts people off making sourdough is failure, and success helps you catch the bug. By all means, add a spoonful of the starter to yeasted breads for a bit of flavour, feed if necessary, leave it another 12–24 hours, and try again. Watch for the big rise. When you have it, stick it in the fridge, and follow my guide for how to keep it alive, coming up next.

How to Maintain a Sourdough Starter

The key to success in sourdough bread is using an active, fresh starter. It should have been recently fed, show clear signs of activity, and the gap between feeds kept to a week or less, if it's been kept in the fridge. The only difference between sourdough and regular, yeasted breads is the raising agent used, and so I guarantee that if you're having trouble with sourdough when you didn't have trouble with yeasted bread, it's your starter that's causing it.

I really recommend sticking to keeping one starter at a time, unless you're making different breads with serious regularity. My solution is to care for my one starter well, and keep it in the fridge between bakes. Then, if I'm making a white bread and my recipe specifies a 'white sourdough starter', I take it out about 6–8 hours before I'm going to bake, feed it with white flour and warm water, and leave it somewhere warm. When I use it, there's going to be a little bran left in there from the last time I fed it with rye or wholemeal, but it's so little it's not going to have any significant effect on the eventual white loaf.

By feeding using a different flour to what it's used to, it can stress out the yeast a little. It can be lacklustre until the bugs have become used to the new flour. For that reason, my one healthy starter is kept as a mixed flour sourdough starter. Usually, this is half strong white, and half wholemeal rye. Whenever I decide to feed it with either pure white or pure rye, for example, the change in environment is much gentler, and it kicks in straight away.

The following steps are carried out every time you make a loaf of sourdough.

6 Steps to Maintain a Sourdough Starter

1. Let your starter come to room temperature – 30 minutes

2. Feed – 2 minutes

3. Wait – 4–8 hours

4. Use – 2 minutes

5. Feed and fridge – 2 minutes

6. Repeat or refresh after inactivity

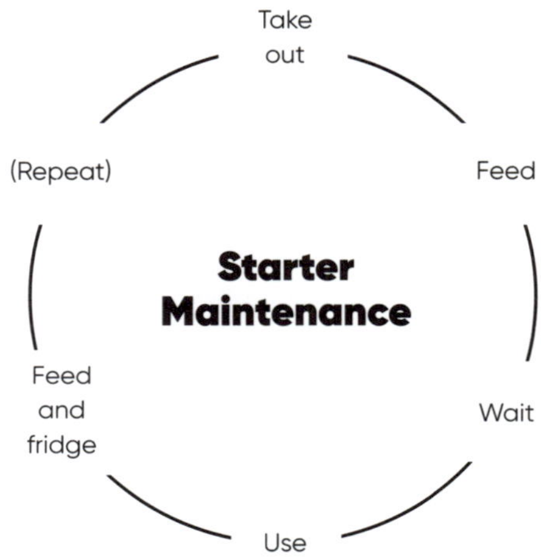

1. Let your starter come to room temperature

Your starter will be kept in the fridge the vast majority of the time and having a small volume helps – we're talking perhaps 25g total size, or less than a tablespoon each of flour and water. This takes up less space, means you almost never waste or discard any, and it means that it will warm to room temperature more quickly.

Take the starter out of the fridge and let it adjust to your room temperature for about 20–30 minutes, ideally. You can feed it straight away if you're in a rush, but sudden temperature changes stress yeast out, and so it can get going a bit slower.

2. Feed

Add fresh flour and water to your starter to at least triple its size. Ideally, a ratio of 1 part starter : 2 parts flour : 2 parts water (1:2:2).

Each time we feed a starter, we make it bigger by adding flour and water. A crucial thing to understand is the ratio of old starter to new flour and new water.

For example, you might feed at a ratio of 1:1:1, so 1 part old starter to 1 part flour and 1 part water. A ratio of 1:1:1 means that if you start with 25g of old starter, you add 25g of flour and 25g of water and end up with 75g of new starter.

The problem with that is, a whole third of your new starter is actually old starter. Almost all of the energy in that old flour will have been used up already, and it means that the starter is already quite acidic from the outset, and gets more acidic as it swells, leading to extra tang. Enzymes made by the older bugs break down the protein and give a more unstable structure to your dough. Then there are huge numbers of bacteria and yeast relative to the amount of new 'food' being provided for them, and so they'll munch through it very quickly, then head back into rest mode. I hope you can see why starter care is so important.

1:1:1 is the absolute minimum ratio I would now recommend using, and only if you've got an already fresh, regularly used starter. Instead, for most, I recommend 1:2:2. This would mean feeding 25g of starter with 50g flour and 50g water, leading to a new starter weight of 125g. This gives you at least 100g of fresh, active starter for most recipes in this book, and a little left over to stick in the fridge for next time.

Want to make a double batch? Just double your feed. Your starter will take just an hour longer to hit the dizzying heights it needs to, will be super-fresh and you'll still have the same 25g left over for fridging for future breads.

In time, you might do what I do, and simply guestimate your feeds. I just cannot be bothered to get the scales out to feed my starter, usually while I'm in the middle of making breakfast. I know what looks right based on using the same container time and time again. You will too.

3. Wait

Stick your starter somewhere warm, such as on top of the fridge at the back or in your oven with the light on, for about 6 hours.

If you've got a fancy modern oven that can go as low as 25°C (77°F), then use that. Just make sure anyone else in the house knows there's starter in there, and remember yourself. I've had many pictures sent of starters baked in innocently preheated ovens, asking for my help in reviving them: there's no hope.

As a rough guide, a starter is ready to use when it hits peak rise. In reality, how big it gets depends on flour and water and temperature, so don't obsess over it hitting twice, three times or even four times its original volume. These markers are just for the breadfluencers to brag about how active their starters are.

About 6 hours is usually a sweet spot, but in summer this could be 4–5 hours, and, in my house, kept no higher than 18°C (64°F) through the winter, it can be 8 hours or more. But don't worry about it: if you feed your starter before work and are gone all day, returning 10 hours later, and your plan is to make your dough through the evening, that's fine. Your starter will work, even if it looks like it's already collapsed.

Similarly, overnight, if you fancy a lie-in and feed it the night before, it will be fine 10 hours later. The bread will be a little bit tangier, and the dough a little bit stickier, but it will still work fine. This is how I tend to make my sourdough, and my sourdough ain't bad.

4. Use

Measure out the required amount of starter for your recipe, leaving some behind for future doughs.

If you've miscalculated how much you need, or mis-guessed in my case, then you might either not have quite enough starter for your recipe, or far too much starter left over. Either is fine: your dough is going to behave just like a really big, salty starter. Adding not quite as much as the recipe wants will mean it ferments a bit slower but will get there eventually. Adding too much starter to your recipe will make the dough a little wetter and stickier and tangier, and things should move a bit quicker.

When my recipes call for 'active sourdough starter', it means going through the above processes to prepare your starter every time. Having said that, if you feed your starter, then forget that you were going to make bread, or something more important comes up, don't chuck it away.

Fridge it for up to a maximum of 24 hours, then take it out, allow it to warm for half an hour, and you can use that starter straight from the fridge. Your dough will behave a bit like you've used too much starter, but it will be fine. Longer than this, and you're looking at crumpets (page 88) or rye breads (page 143), or keeping it to add to yeasted doughs for a bit of extra flavour and texture.

5. Feed and fridge

To your remaining starter, add a tablespoon of your chosen flour or flour mix, and enough cold water to make a paste, then cover and stick this in the fridge.

You've used almost all your starter – but even the scrapings that remain in your jar are enough to maintain it. You're about to chill your starter again, and while you can stick your jar straight in the fridge, adding just a little bit of food for your bugs helps them stay happier for longer.

I never measure this second feed, because I'm done on measuring by this point, having just measured my dough. I add about a teaspoon each of wholemeal rye and strong white flours, and enough water to make a paste-like consistency, and mix this with my remaining starter. This gets covered and stuck in the fridge for usually between 3 days and a week until I get it out and start the whole process again.

6. Repeat or refresh after inactivity

Repeat this cycle for eternity. If it's longer than a week between feeds, your starter may require an extra, interim feed prior to use.

Contrary to many people's belief, a starter isn't inactive while it's in the fridge. It's certainly slowed down, but it's still munching through that starch in a slightly different way.

Leave it too long, and several things start happening. The starches it needs are used up, so different kinds of fermentation start. These further increase the acidity (it will smell vinegary) and don't produce any gas. The inactive, starved yeasts start to die. Enzymes, called proteases, that can break down the gluten of any potential future dough, are produced in abundance.

A neglected starter is the only time, then, that I ever discard any of my starter. And even then, this can still be dosed into yeasted breads in small quantities. This is called a 'type 2' sourdough, and is used industrially to give yeasted breads some of the characteristic flavour without the effort. And it's a bit naughty because they call them sourdoughs.

So, post-holiday or bread-sabbatical, I discard the vast majority of my old sourdough, down to a teaspoon, or 5g or so. Then I'll feed with a 1:2:2 ratio, bringing us back up to 25g. This gets an 8–12 hour rest somewhere warm, usually overnight. Then the next morning, I'll give it another 1:2:2 feed to bring it up to 125–225g, ready to use later that day. If your starter has been left in the fridge for months, it might not be worth saving, but it's worth giving this method a go. It will be slower: that first refresh with just a teaspoon of the old starter might take 24–36 hours before it's properly going.

How to Make Sourdough Bread

Many recipes in this book have both a sourdough and a yeasted option. The lack of separation is intentional because I want to highlight that the only difference between the breads is what makes them rise. As such, if you can make a yeasted loaf, you are perfectly capable of making sourdough. It just takes a bit longer, and you have to make sure your starter is happy before you start. If it's not rising and falling reliably and impressively with each feed, don't use it. Revert back to yeast and enjoy awesome bread.

Still, sourdough is awesome. It has longevity, thanks to the acid and alcohol content. It has a unique flavour. It has a unique texture, and your personal sourdough is unique in a world of many breads.

If you've not read it, please go back and check out my guide for yeasted breads first (page 34) as I'll be brushing over some definitions. Then you'll need a sourdough starter, and for it to be healthy and happy (page 50).

12 Steps to Making Sourdough Bread

1. Weigh – less than 5 minutes
2. Mix – less than 2 minutes
3. Autolyse (rest) – 20–30 minutes
4. Knead (optional, but recommended) – 5–15 minutes
5. First prove with stretches and folds – 4–6 hours or 2 hours plus 8–12 hours in a fridge set to cold
6. Lamination (optional, if adding fillings, nuts or seeds)
7. Split, pre-shape and bench rest (optional, if multiple loaves) – 15–30 minutes
8. Shape – less than 5 minutes
9. Second prove – 1½–2 hours (or 4–24 hours in a fridge set to cold)
10. Score – less than a minute
11. Bake – 30–50 minutes
12. Cool – 30–60 minutes

***Total time**: 5½–36 hours*
***Time spent in kitchen**: less than 25 minutes*

1. Weigh

Flour, water, starter, salt. Weigh using electronic scales; only use volumetric measurements for salt. Use only an active starter that's at peak height, generally following being fed 6–8 hours before. After weighing your dough's ingredients, remember to feed and fridge your starter again.

If you're in a very cold house, or your starter is a bit suspect, one variant to this (sorry for complicating things already) is to delay adding the salt until after the autolyse. Salt inhibits yeast of all kinds, including those in your starter, and can have an effect on how quickly your dough kicks off. Don't bother with this unless you're finding things are taking far longer than stated.

2. Mix

Here, we're bringing the ingredients together into a rough dough. Nothing special. It doesn't need to be super-smooth, it just needs to be together. For sourdough, I tend to just use my electric mixer and leave the dough in there for the next steps, but you can equally use a wooden spoon or a blunt knife to create your dough.

3. Autolyse (rest)

As explained on page 35, autolyse means the short rest before kneading. It allows the starch to hydrate properly, the gluten to relax and begin to form smooth layers, allowing you to bring your dough together into a strong amalgamation.

If you choose not to knead your sourdough (which is fine), this step basically becomes an extension of the next few hours of intermittent resting, with stretches and folds in between.

I recommend an autolyse with all your ingredients added – with the possible exception of your salt, as noted previously. Many recommend an autolyse with only flour and water, extending it for hours, and even starting it when you first feed your starter. I don't, as it's generally not necessary, but you can if it works for your schedule.

4. Knead (optional)

Kneading isn't essential in sourdough, but can be helpful to build the strength that's inherently lacking in these tricky doughs, and for avoiding huge, unruly bubbles and tunnels through your final dough. The difference between a kneaded dough and one that has had three to four stretches and folds (page 47) over the first prove isn't huge, and if you're finding your sourdoughs are 'splats' that simply flow everywhere and never seem to hold together, kneading probably won't be your saving grace (that comes with a healthier, more vigorous fermentation).

I knead because it's easy in an electric mixer, or fun by slapping and folding (page 36). The stretch and roll (page 37) will be of limited use, as sourdoughs tend to be on the sticky side. The other clear indication to knead is if you have to be away from your dough during your first prove: a well-developed dough will only need perhaps a single stretch and fold during its prove to keep its strength. Of course, you could just take your bowl with you wherever you go, like me.

5. First prove with stretches and folds

Sourdough is slow. You have to wait. As you wait, that gluten relaxes, the dough splays, and you end up with a bowl containing a flaccid lump that turns into a pancake if you tip it out. This is not a strong dough. Stretches and folds (page 47) with an active fermentation give it strength.

The same principles apply as when making no-knead bread. You want to stretch gently so as not to break the gluten already formed, and then fold.

Most of the time, I recommend two to three stretches and folds during the first prove for a sourdough. As the dough gets puffier, you want to take some care not to damage its structure, but you'll be surprised at how light it remains even after a good handle.

The time range I've given on page 58 is approximate. If you're in a heatwave or a hot country with nowhere to store your dough below 30°C (86°F) or so, then your first prove will be done within 2-3 hours. And in a cold Scottish flat in winter, it's more like 6-8. A little bit of warmth to drive that fermentation and keep the structure taut, really does help.

You can fridge the first prove of sourdough, but it does require at least a couple of hours out of the fridge first for the fermentation to get going. Otherwise, if you just stick it straight in the fridge after mixing, it never really rises, and you'll end up with a pool of sagging, unfermented and slightly sour starch soup.

After 2 hours of warm proving, stick it in the fridge for as long as you need until you've got time to carry on. Bear in mind, the dough will be cold, and after shaping it will take a wee while to heat back up again, so add 30–60 minutes on to your second prove. See step photography opposite.

6. Lamination (optional, if adding fillings, nuts or seeds)

This is an optional extra step that I tend to use only if I'm really struggling to build strength into my sourdough, or if I'm wanting to incorporate a filling that would interrupt my kneading or stretching and folding. You can see a lamination as an alternative to stretching and folding, and it's usually carried out 1–2 hours after kneading.
It's extremely effective at developing dough strength, preventing any future sagging or flopping issues with loaves, and allows you to incorporate fillings very well. It might seem strange using just water to stop the dough sticking, but it really works: if you do find any bits stick, just get under them with a dough scraper.

7. Split, pre-shape and bench rest (optional, if multiple loaves)

You don't need to think about any of this if you're just making one loaf – all that stretching and folding has built up your strength and your dough can be shaped directly.

But if you're making big batches, by doubling or tripling any of the recipes here or beyond, this involves cutting your dough into bits and slicing straight through that structure you've strived to create. Pre-shaping is a gentle, flourless shape to prepare these rough lumps for their final shape. The bench rest is there just to allow the gluten to relax a bit, or the final shaping ends up involving some frustration.

This is a method I've settled on after trying many: it's extremely quick, rough and easy. I've broken it right down on page 62 so you can see exactly what I do. Whatever you choose to do, don't go for tightness at this stage. Don't force the dough, be very gentle, and preserve all those lovely bubbles.

Lamination

1. Lightly dampen a clean work surface by rubbing it with wet hands and turn your dough out onto it
2. Using wet hands, lift and stretch it out from the centre into a very big rectangle and add any fillings
3. Using a damp hand and damp dough scraper, scrape underneath one side and lift it from the surface
4. Fold one side of dough into the middle, as if folding a letter for an envelope
5. Work your way down the other side of the dough and fold this over too
6. You should now have a long folded dough, with little or no filling visible
7. Roll this dough towards you like a Swiss roll, using your scraper to release it from the surface
8. Once you've got a tight roll, place it into a bowl, cover and rest. It's not a problem if it splits

Split, pre-shape and bench rest

1. Lightly rub a little water onto a clean work surface, just to dampen it
2. Using slightly wet hands and a wet dough scraper, scrape your dough onto your surface
3. Using your scraper, divide into however many lumps you need
4. Work out which is the smoothest side of a lump and turn this so it's facing down
5. Gently roll up the dough in a spiral like a Swiss roll
6. You've now got an oblong dough
7. Turn it and roll the other way gently
8. Place seam-side down and repeat with the rest

8. Shape

Most sourdoughs involve using a proving basket or couche, but it's also fine to use a tin. I start by flouring my basket, or greasing my tin. Then you can shape, and shaping is no different than on page 38.

Except. In yeasted breads, you can happily knock back your dough and expect it to refill with gas; in short, you can shape with heavy hands. In sourdough, if you want that characteristic sourdough open crumb with large bubbles, you want to be careful. Do everything to preserve as much lightness as possible. Gentle hands. Gentle fingertips.

Create tension, yes, but using the inherent tension that's in the dough. Gently fold it and press only to seal each fold. Don't press so hard that the thing loses any volume. If you feel your hands sticking, get them cleaned and floured.

9. Second prove

The vast majority of the time, I recommend sticking your dough straight in the fridge once it's shaped. As it cools, it continues to ferment, before slowing to a crawling pace over the next couple of hours. The cold stabilizes the gluten and your proving basket supports the sides, so that even as it ferments a bit, it maintains its shape. This approach gives you flexibility as to when you can bake it: that might be 4 hours later, 8 hours later or even 24 hours later. If your fridge is really cold, you might be able to go longer.

If you're in a rush, you could leave your dough at room temperature for as little as 30 minutes after shaping, so long as it was nice and puffy when you popped it in the basket. You'll have a slightly tighter crumb with mind-bogglingly irregular bubbles, but that's fine. If you've got time but not enough to chill, I'd give it a rest at room temperature, usually an hour or two.

10. Score

Scoring is the same as with yeasted breads, but possibly even more important, as sourdough breads tend to have such pronounced oven spring – or the rise that takes place within the oven. Following the instructions on page 43, score down the length of your loaf to release maximum tension.

You can score with your dough directly on your baking surface, a piece of baking parchment, or on a semolina-dusted peel.

11. Bake

Baking sourdough isn't any different, except that you can usually push it a bit further and the lines between 'caramelization' and 'burnt' are somewhat blurred.

If making a large loaf, I recommend you bake within a cast iron pot, a Dutch oven or a special bread cloche. You can improvise one of these by placing a stainless steel or Pyrex bowl upside down on a baking surface: anything that creates a dome. The lid stays on for the first 20 minutes, then it comes off to crisp the crust.

If making smaller breads, either cover your tray with kitchen foil for the first 10 minutes, or add a few spritzes from a spray bottle full of water, and/or add some water or ice into a tray that's been preheated on the base of the oven. If baking in a tin, bash the loaf out of the tin for the last 5–10 minutes of baking to allow the sides to properly crisp up.

12. Cool

Cool on your baking surface, a cooling rack, your bread board; wherever. Don't worry about it, but make sure your bread is mostly cool before slicing. This is especially important in sourdough, which is a nightmare to cut if hot.

A Note on the Recipes

I want you to love baking bread as much as I do – and part of that is getting hooked. There may be a certain sort of person who falls in love following back-to-back disasters, but most people are not that person. Most of us get hooked when things go well and we feel good about what we've created. If you're new to bread baking, it's best to start by making yeasted breads, to get a sense of the dough with a reliable rise. There's less to go wrong, many breads are better with yeast, and you can still enjoy nearly every bread in this book, and they will be as good as the best bread that exists. When starting out, you can just ignore the sourdough starter.

Then, once you get the hang of things, nearly every recipe offers you two more options. You can add some sourdough starter as well as yeast, to add longevity and complexity of flavour; this is regardless of whether it's been freshly fed or left at the back of the fridge for weeks. Or, as long as you're using fresh starter at peak rise following a feed, you can leave out the yeast and go full sourdough.

The icons on each recipe show you at a glance whether you have one, two or three options, and the methods will give you the yeast instructions, followed by the two alternatives. And any time you need to brush up on the details of techniques, just turn back to the step-by-step techniques. Plus there are some breads that don't fit into these categories as they use bicarbonate of soda (baking soda) or other raising agents, so they go in a group of their own.

Y yeasted bread

YS yeast with sourdough for extra flavour

S full sourdough

BP other raising agents

U unleavened

Troubleshooting Bread

This is a list of what can go wrong – and it isn't exhaustive. Often, common sense will prevail when this guide won't: I once found these strange crusty brown bits within a slice of sourdough. Curious, I tasted it, and I realized that my toddler had filled my sack of flour with pieces of dried dog food. It's also worth remembering that if you're making sourdough and have previously had no trouble with yeasted breads, there are almost no problems that can't be solved by refreshing your starter, ensuring it's rising well after feeds, warming it to 25°C (77°F) or so, and adding an extra stretch and fold during the first prove. If anyone asks me how to fix their failed sourdough, that's almost always my answer.

'My dough hasn't risen'

Yeast, whether that's commercial yeast or sourdough, makes bread rise. If the dough hasn't risen, it means the yeast isn't active. This could be due to cold, so first try warming it up. I'm assuming you've tried this.

For dried yeast, this usually means it's out of date, or it has been stored next to something hot that's killed it. Fresh yeast must be stored in the fridge and used within a few weeks or the vast majority dies. Sourdough starters must be cared for and must be reliably rising and falling before use (page 54).

'My bread is dense'

Commonly, it's because the temperature of your dough is too low, or your yeast is unhappy (see above). Try using warmer water or proving somewhere warm.

Traditional English low-hydration doughs do require some kneading, or they will be dense. Give them a pummelling until stretchy and smooth. The final reason may be that your dough is overproved: it's got too big, it's collapsed when you've tried to shape it or score it and your gluten matrix is destroyed. Cooler or shorter next time.

'My dough is wet, sticky and unmanageable'

If you're not used to them, many of these doughs may seem very wet. You'll get used to them. I recommend becoming familiar with the slap and fold (page 36) or sticking to a no-knead method until you've got the hang of how they feel. Using wet or floured hands will stop them sticking.

Low-gluten flour, especially from independent local flour mills, or featuring biodiverse wheat blends, often can't handle the hydration I recommend. The gluten is low quality and doesn't stretch so well. This can cause a sticky, wet dough and you may need to reduce your water to compensate.

If your dough is sticky late in the fermentation, and sticks to the basket, it's usually because it lacks strength. This tends to be because of inadequate rise, so back to healthier yeast or a more active sourdough starter. Less likely, it's poor flour, as above.

'My dough never passed the "windowpane test" no matter how much I knead'

Most won't. I don't recommend the 'windowpane test' (where you stretch some dough to see if you can see through it) any more as it's rarely achievable or desirable. So long as you've given your dough a bash around, it'll be fine. You can add a stretch and fold (page 47) if you're not sure.

'My dough deflates when I score it'

Your dough's second prove is too long – it's 'overproved'. There's not much you can do except prove it less, or colder (such as in the fridge).

'My dough spreads like a splat when I turn it out of the proving basket'

Common in sourdoughs that use old, acidic starters and have inadequately vigorous fermentation – refresh your starter, and get that first prove plenty warm, with plenty of stretches and folds to keep dough strength.

If we're talking yeasted, this is rare (that says a lot about the power of a vigorous fermentation) but usually means it's overproved or you've got too much water in the dough for the strength of your flour.

'My breads or buns stick together'

They're too close together – you've got to remember oven spring when baking. But don't worry, just claim they were meant to stick together.

'My pizzas or flatbreads break when I try to shape them'

Yeasted flatbread doughs that are shaped by hand, such as pizzas, require the dough to be very stretchy and extensible. If your dough is tough and tenacious, it breaks, and it usually means you've not left it to rest for long enough. If you've rested it for ages in the fridge, you've got to take it out of the fridge to warm up a little before shaping, too (this only applies to flatbreads).

Poor, low-gluten flour is another reason, as is the incorporation of too much wholemeal, where the bran gets in the way and doesn't allow you to stretch very thinly.

'My dough doesn't rise in the oven'

A dough with a second prove that's too long will have poor oven spring, because the gluten has already been stretched as far as it can go. This does lead to a gummy texture, web-like crumb with denser patches around the bottom and the sides.

If this isn't the case, another problem can be not enough steam – your crust forms too fast and stops the dough rising. Bake in a pot or covered with a cloche, or add plenty of steam. Sometimes, shallow scoring can cause a similar effect, restricting growth.

'My bread has weird lumps and tumours'

Usually a combination of your dough being underproved AND not scored deeply enough, so you get uncontrolled growths in odd directions. Common in sourdough in winter: get that first prove warmer, then stick it in the fridge for the second.

'My crust is pale and thick despite a long, hot bake'

This is a sign of poor caramelization, and usually means not enough proving during the first prove, and so your dough has an abundance of starch and not much sugar.

A pale, dry crust can also be caused by a lack of steam during baking: common in outdoor clay ovens that give a very dry heat. Try a spritz of water in the oven next time.

'My bread is burnt'

While it might be easy to blame this on your oven being too hot or you leaving it in too long, it can also be due to overproving in either prove: you get too much starch breakdown into sugar, and so your bread burns easily.

'My bread is doughy in the middle despite having a dark crust'

It's not baked enough. Turn your oven down and go lower and slower. Make sure, especially with tin loaves, that your bread isn't getting too close to the heating elements.

Some ingredients can lead to a doughy centre – too much sugar, salt or honey will all cause a sticky, doughy, dense middle.

'My bread goes mouldy quickly'

You don't eat your bread fast enough, obviously. Slice and freeze some for instant toast.

Mould is often due to moisture levels where your bread is stored. I recommend storing it in a bread bin, in a paper bag, or even out on the bread board (if you've no problem with vermin).

'My slices have a few very big bubbles and tunnels'

Often, this is due to poor strength, and can be remedied with a stretch and fold late in the first prove to give your dough a real tightness. Still, if you've got poor yeast or an inactive sourdough starter, then this might be inevitable: a lack of activity leads to a lack of structure.

'My crust is covered in little bubbles on the outside'

These are 'bird's eye bubbles' and are a sign of a prolonged, dry and cold second prove followed by a steamy bake. I think they're beautiful. If you don't, you can avoid them by proving inside a plastic bag to keep the skin moist.

'My scores don't open up'

If you've been tentative with your scoring, they won't open. But more likely, your dough doesn't have the underlying tension needed to spring open in the oven. This can mean poor shaping, inadequate dough strength due to a poor fermentation, or that you've left things far too long and you're scoring a far too fragile, flaccid dough.

'I've got a dense line of dough at the bottom of my tin/tray'

When making hand-shaped loaves, this shouldn't be a problem because you'll be using proving baskets and flipping before baking. In a tin, especially if it's too small, your dough can push up against the sides and bottom and the bubbles can collapse under the pressure.

Good dough principles, strength and stopping before you reach overproved are important.

'I've got big bubbles under the crust'

This is a sign of poor strength, usually, and due to inadequate yeast activity (or an unhealthy starter – page 54). In yeasted breads with a vigorous fermentation, this can happen due to inadequately deep scoring, or missing scoring out of a certain area of the top.

THE UK & IRELAND THE UK & IRELAND

Soda Farl

BP

Soda breads involve no yeast – instead, they rely on chemical raising agents for their lightness. Usually, this is achieved by using bicarbonate of soda (baking soda) in combination with something acidic – such as buttermilk – to create a reaction. The most famous undoubtedly come from Ireland – great wholemeal loaves adorned with a cross – they are delicious eaten fresh.

When it comes to competing soda breads I've been known to display favouritism towards the bannock. Being from the Northern Isles of Scotland, where I've judged hundreds of them at agricultural shows, I have a fondness for this white, light staple I grew up with. I can bore you with endless variations and the controversies involving the inclusions of extravagances such as butter or, Heaven-forbid, an egg.

But in the interests of inclusion, I thought I'd start with a shout-out for a bread of the same lineage – the soda farl. I was introduced to these delights by a Northern Irish relative, and at once scorned for my ignorance of its separate (identical) identity. This was the first time I could see how fierce allegiances could be formed towards indistinguishable recipes with twinned lineages. Maybe there are certain minor aesthetic differences, but a farl is essentially a bannock, and vice versa. Spread with thick, soft butter and eat fresh with a cup of tea.

Makes 16 large soda farls

400g self-raising (self-rising) flour, plus extra for shaping and frying
100g wholemeal flour
½ tsp bicarbonate of soda (baking soda)
½ tsp table salt
280g buttermilk
180g whole milk

1. Into a large bowl, weigh your flours, bicarbonate of soda and salt. Mix to combine.

2. Add your buttermilk and whole milk, then use a wooden spoon to mix everything into a sloppy dough. At this point, it helps to get a heavy-based frying pan (skillet) or smooth griddle pan onto a low–medium heat.

3. Very generously flour a work surface, and turn your dough out onto it. Then liberally cover your dough in flour. If you're finding things too wet, then add more flour to stop it sticking. You can't use too much flour here, unlike with most other breads.

4. Cut your dough into four roughly equal balls. Using plenty of flour, press one into a disc about 2cm (¾in) thick. Use a palette knife or metal spatula to get under it and place it on your hot pan. I then use the palette knife to cut it in half, on the pan as it starts to cook, and then half again, into quarters.

5. After about 3 minutes and once they have risen as tall as they're going to get (be very careful with them as they rise, they are fragile), flip them over carefully and, if necessary, divide them if they're too stuck together for your liking. The dough should have areas of golden brown as photographed, but the flour should remain white. If the flour is turning brown, turn the heat down.

6. After another 3 minutes, remove each farl from the heat and place between two dish towels to finish cooking (they will continue cooking off the heat). Repeat with your remaining balls of dough. Give each round of farls at least 10–15 minutes before tucking in – but don't worry, you can still have them warm.

7. Alternatively, you can oven-bake your farls: shape and separate your rounds in the same way, but place on a baking tray and bake for 20–25 minutes in a preheated oven at 160°C (325°F) fan (180°C/350°F/gas 4).

Scottish Batch Bread

Y

This is a large, oblong version of the Scottish plain loaf, a much loved 'batch' style loaf, still popular in much of central Scotland and among nostalgic expats. It's characterized by its shape, and the comparative darkness (near burnt) of its top and bottom crusts, with a pale, near-crustless finish down its sides. This is my ode to it.

A batch loaf is achieved through proving and baking loaves close together, so that each loaf first touches, then supports the ones next to it as it rises. Then, after baking, they are torn or sliced apart.

Given us home bakers only tend to bake one loaf at a time at home, or a couple at a push, I've copied a method used by the wonderful Campbell from Rackmaster, who created a wooden frame that he soaks beforehand and then bakes batches of eight loaves at a time inside. We can do the same at home for a couple of loaves, but it requires a little DIY. If you want a perfect batch loaf, you'll have to go to these lengths. If you want an otherwise well-fired white loaf, just bake in a tin.

Makes 1 large loaf – for batches, scale the recipe appropriately

For the frame

8 woodscrews
a length of untreated timber, at least 10cm (4in) in height and 1cm (½in) thick. Do not use treated timber, plywood, MDF or OSB

For the loaf

500g strong white flour, plus extra for dusting
1½ tsp table salt
2 tsp instant yeast
15g salted or unsalted butter (or vegetable shortening, for austere authenticity)
280g tepid water

1. First, build your wooden batch loaf frame. Saw your length of timber into four pieces – for example, for one loaf, you're aiming for dimensions of about 30×15cm (12×6in) so you'll need two lengths of each. If you want to make a frame for baking two loaves side by side, make it roughly 30×30cm (12×12in). That means you'll need four 30cm (12in) lengths, if a square that big fits in your oven. Please check.

2. Get someone else to hold your pieces of timber at right angles so the corners abut, and drill pilot holes with a 2–3mm drill bit. Screw your screws to create an L shape using a simple butt joint. Repeat with remaining lengths to create a rectangle or square. It doesn't need to have much structural integrity. Your frame is complete.

3. I recommend you soak your frame in water for 10 minutes before baking to avoid burning. You can fill a sink partially with cold water during the proving stages and turn your frame occasionally so that all of it is submerged for a time.

4. To make the bread, start by weighing your flour, salt and yeast into a large bowl. If you are planning to leave the dough overnight in the fridge, reduce the quantity of yeast to 1 teaspoon. Mix the ingredients together to distribute, then add your butter and give it a rub to create something akin to breadcrumbs. Then add your tepid water and combine to a dough – this one's dry by my usual standards, so it might take a bit of work to get rid of all the dry flour.

5. Leave it to autolyse (rest) for 10–15 minutes if you've got time, as this will make your job of kneading it much easier.

6. Otherwise, just crack on and get kneading – an old-fashioned English knead (page 37) is best to build up a strong gluten network. Otherwise, use a mixer and keep going until the dough is soft and elastic. It's really important to give this bread a good pummelling: 10 minutes of hard work. It's very dry, so should keep your hands very clean.

7. Leave your dough to rest at room temperature for about 90 minutes or so. Alternatively, you can leave it overnight in the fridge, in which case you will have reduced the yeast quantity.

8. Place your soaked wooden frame on a baking tray. Turn your dough out onto a floured surface, then knock back your dough until it's a flat rectangle. Shape for a baton by rolling this up into a spiral like a Swiss roll, then place in your prepared bread frame. Allow the dough to rise for about an hour until it is filling most of the frame. About 15 minutes before it's ready to bake, preheat your oven to 210°C (410°F) fan (230°C/450°F/gas 8).

9. Bake for 45 minutes at that temperature until very dark on top, nearly black. Once done, it should slide out of its wooden frame with ease. If you've got a bigger frame and baked a batch of loaves, split them once they are nearly cooled by tearing them apart.

Milk Loaf

Y

YS

S

This is a departure, and a hybrid recipe, of sorts. In my previous books, I've been evangelical about the virtues of the *pain de mie* – a soft everyday bread found throughout France. It's the sort that children and adults love equally, that makes the best buttered ham sandwiches or jammy toast the next morning. It's subtly enriched with butter, milk and often a little sugar or honey, and it has a texture and crust that remains just on the acceptable side of savoury.

The milk loaf is the English equivalent – it tends to be a far drier dough, leading to a taller shape and bulbous rise, and rarely will it be quite so enriched, instead following a simple white bread recipe with the liquid portion made up of milk rather than water. This is a slight variation on both – we're using milk here, and plenty of it, to create a wetter dough, and we're adding a tiny amount of both butter and sugar. Make sure that your tin is well greased with plenty of butter, even if the tin is supposed to be non-stick, as the butter flavours the crust. And we're making this in a traditional 900g English loaf tin for that classic round top, perfect for fitting in the toaster.

Dust the top with flour before baking and it'll look authentically English, but with an extra sweetness, soft breakable crumb and a buttery crust.

Makes 1 large loaf

500g strong white flour, plus extra for dusting
1½ tsp table salt
15g caster (superfine) or granulated sugar
2 tsp instant yeast (optional)
100g sourdough starter, fed with white flour (page 50) (optional)
15g salted or unsalted butter, plus extra for greasing
350g whole milk

1. Start by weighing your flour, salt and sugar into a large bowl. For a yeasted loaf, mix in the yeast. If you are planning to leave the dough overnight in the fridge, reduce the quantity of yeast to 1 teaspoon. For extra flavour, you can add some sourdough starter with the liquid ingredients. For a full sourdough, leave out the yeast and add the sourdough starter, instead, although I wouldn't recommend this one for a full sourdough. Mix your chosen ingredients together to distribute. Add your butter, then rub this in roughly so that it's mostly combined.

2. Weigh your milk in another bowl or jug, then warm it in the microwave or by placing it in a sink with some hot water. You want it tepid – neither hot nor cold. Add this to your flour, with the starter, if using, and combine to a dough.

3. Leave it to autolyse (rest) for 10–20 minutes if you've got time, as this will make the next stage easier.

4. Get with kneading. This is a sticky dough that will quickly come together with a bit of work, so the slap and fold method (page 36) will work well. You can use a mixer, or use a no-knead method (page 45).

5. Leave your dough to rest at room temperature for about 90 minutes or so. Alternatively, you can leave it overnight in the fridge – in which case you'll have reduced the yeast quantity.

6. Grease a 900g loaf tin with plenty of butter – make sure you smear it right down into the corners of the tin to prevent sticking. Scrape your dough out onto a lightly floured surface, then shape into a baton shape by rolling it up, and place this in your tin, seam-side down. It would be traditional to knock back this dough to remove the bubbles, but this just gives you a very closed structure.

7. Dust the top of your dough with a sprinkling of flour, then prove your dough for another hour. Overnight or all day in the fridge is fine as long as you've got a very cold fridge. About 15 minutes before it's ready, preheat your oven to 200°C (400°F) fan (220°C/425°F/gas 7).

8. You could score the top, but if it's had a good second prove and risen plenty in the tin, it shouldn't need it. It does benefit from a little steam, though, so add some ice or water onto a tray at the bottom of the oven as you slide it in. Bake for 40 minutes or so, or until a deep golden brown and cooked through. I like to bash the loaf out of the tin after 30 minutes, then return it to the oven for the final 10 minutes to crisp up the walls. Cool before slicing.

Soft Baps and Morning Rolls

Y

It's time for a confession. When it comes to what to put your bacon in, I'm going to upset some people, and probably downright puzzle far more. Lest I be judged for lacking some nationalist pride, I'm forced, in any kind of social situation, to opt for the crispy Scottish 'morning roll'. It's a Glasgow thing, really – the unbelievably light crumb, crispy exterior and slight tang are undeniably good.

But if left to my own devices, I'd opt for the quintessential soft and floury English bap any day of the week. The shame. It's comfort. Once sliced, each half is a pillow of buttery softness, cradling two or three slices of dripping, ketchuppy bacon. Squeeze the whole lot together, take one bite and repent any lingering thoughts of ever becoming a vegetarian. I could eat three back to back.

Crispy rolls and soft rolls can be made with the same dough. If you do prefer the crisp, I'd try to start them the day before you're planning on using them. Then, baked fresh the next morning, following a long overnight prove in the fridge, they're at maximum lightness and have developed the sugars needed for that crackly crust. When it comes to soft rolls, we're going to bake them hot and fast, but also sprinkle a little flour on top before baking to stop that crust.

Makes 12 baps or rolls

500g strong white flour, plus extra for dusting
½ tsp table salt
2 tsp instant yeast
330g tepid water
a little semolina, for dusting (optional)

1. Into a large bowl, weigh your flour, salt and yeast and rub them together until combined. Then add your tepid water. Mix everything together until roughly combined.

2. You can knead at this stage, or you can autolyse (rest) for 10–20 minutes before continuing and cut how much kneading you need to do.

3. Knead your dough – you want it smooth and lump-free and so that it forms a ball that removes excess dough from your work surface and from your hands. If you've autolysed, give it a minute or so. If not, give it 10. Alternatively, you can use a no-knead technique (page 45).

4. Cover your bowl and leave your dough somewhere warm for 90 minutes or so.

5. Get a roasting or baking tray and cover it in a sheet of baking parchment. If you don't have any, lightly sprinkle over some semolina if making crispy rolls, or flour for soft rolls. Add some flour onto your work surface, then use a dough scraper to scrape the dough out of the bowl. Roll your dough into a sausage shape and divide it into 12 roughly equal lumps. Shape these into rough rounds and place in your baking tray. They shouldn't be touching at this point, and will rise to be closer together and eventually touch.

6. Prove your rolls for at least another hour, or until they're noticeably puffed up. If they're sluggish, give them a little longer. Alternatively, prove them overnight in the fridge – especially for crispy rolls. About 15 minutes before you plan on baking, preheat your oven to 210°C (410°F) fan (230°C/450°F/gas 8).

7. If you're aiming for soft rolls, sprinkle a little flour on top, then bake for 15 minutes, or until just blushing golden brown. Remove and cool for as long as you can before tearing open. If you're having to store them for more than a few hours after cooling, pop them in an airtight container.

8. If you're wanting crispy rolls, these are a bit more forgiving. Spray or splash the tops of your rolls with some water, turn the oven down by 10°C (32°F/one gas mark) and bake for 20–25 minutes, or until golden brown. If you want proper Scottish 'well-fired rolls', just keep on baking until nearly black.

Chelsea Buns

Y

YS

S

You could, and I may, write an entire book on the regional bun variations within the British Isles. They are all good things. I'm left with some difficult decisions, though, in choosing only a few recipes representative of the world for this humble little cookbook. And that means picking one bun. One.

My affinity with the Chelsea bun began during the photography for my very first book, back in 2013. I met the wonderful Tim Hayward, and he was kind enough to introduce me to the wares of his newly acquired bakery: Fitzbillies, in Cambridge. Any connoisseur of the bun knows these buns.

Sliced and served in boxes of four, with a syrup so sticky it can't help but coat every interdigital web and bring the inevitable type 2 diabetes one day closer, stuffed with currants and with a spiral so tight that you have to wonder how they manage to get the dough that thin before rolling it up.

I'm now 10 years older and several thousand buns down, and I am on intimate terms with the Chelsea bun. And while a recipe approximation of the Fitzbillies bun is now in the public domain by the bakery itself, I don't want to quite go down the route of imitation. Instead, here's an in-between – inspired by Fitzbillies, but also aiming for something approaching the lost 18th-century recipe of the bun that made the original Chelsea Bun House a sensation. The earliest Chelsea was conceived before the advent of commercial yeast, so it would have been a sourdough. It's said to include both honey and lemon, so I've incorporated them both.

Makes 12 buns

For the dough

500g strong white flour, plus extra for dusting
30g unsalted butter
1½ tsp table salt
50g caster (superfine) sugar
2 tsp instant yeast (optional)
300g whole milk
1 egg
100g sourdough starter, fed with any flours (page 50) (optional)

1. Start with the dough. In a large bowl, weigh your flour, and then add your butter. Rub them together until the butter has mostly disappeared and what's left looks like breadcrumbs. It doesn't need to be perfect. Then add the salt and sugar. For a yeasted loaf, add the yeast. Heat the milk in the microwave until it's a little warmer than tepid, then add this, along with your egg. For extra flavour, also add the sourdough starter with the wet ingredients. For a full sourdough, leave out the yeast and use a sourdough starter, added with the liquid ingredients. Mix everything together until you've got a dough.

2. Leave it 10–15 minutes to autolyse (rest), then give the dough a good knead for 10 minutes. You could use a mixer but this works with any method of kneading (page 35).

For the filling

75g unsalted butter, softened
75g caster (superfine) sugar
2 tsp ground cinnamon
250g currants
grated zest of 1 lemon

For the sticky, sticky glaze

150g golden (light corn) syrup
juice of ½ lemon
50g honey, set or runny – doesn't matter
1 tsp ground cinnamon

3. Put your dough back in the bowl and cover with clingfilm (plastic wrap), a dish towel or a plastic bag. Leave it for 60–90 minutes until it's noticeably puffy and about doubled in size.

4. Next, flour a work surface, and scrape your dough out onto it. Add some more flour on top, and use the edges of your hands to make it a rectangle shape. Use a rolling pin to roll it out into a large rectangle, at least 60×40cm (24×16in).

5. Now, for the filling. If your butter isn't soft, give it a buzz in the microwave so that it's almost melted. Spread this over your dough, then sprinkle with sugar, cinnamon, currants and lemon zest. From the short edge, roll this up to create a tightly wound spiral of curranty dough.

6. Line a roasting tray with baking parchment. Use a scraper to slice your buns into 12 equal shapes, then place them in the tin so they've got plenty of room to rise. Cover again, this time with a sheet of kitchen foil, and leave to rest for another hour. About 15 minutes before you plan on baking, preheat your oven to 180°C (350°F) fan (200°C/400°F/gas 6).

7. Bake your buns for about 25–30 minutes, taking the foil off after 10 minutes of baking. The buns should be blushing golden brown, but not too dark; if they are crusty, they are not so delicious. If you can see currants burning, get them out.

8. As they begin to cool, make the glaze. Place all the ingredients in a saucepan and heat over a low heat until they are homogenous. Spread over the still-hot buns, and use all of it. Don't go easy on those buns. Allow them to cool before tucking in.

Tattie Scone

BP

The tattie scone – or potato scone, if one is feeling posh – completes the Full Scottish Breakfast and, in its simplest form, is a mixture of cooked potato and flour, fried – the gnocchi of the Highlands, so to speak. And indeed, it exists across the Irish sea, too, in the form of the potato farl, which completes the equally delicious Ulster Fry.

Puzzled? Well, don't be, just roll with it and whip up some tattie scones, which are amazing if made fresh. While this recipe starts with cooking the potatoes, the best opportunity comes when you've got leftover potatoes from the night before. Then, if you own this book, I'm sure you've got some spare flour and butter to hand. There's no excuse not to.

Makes 16 scones

500g floury potatoes, peeled and uncooked weight (or about 400g leftover cooked potatoes)
a generous pinch of table salt
50g unsalted or salted butter
100g self-raising (self-rising) flour, plus extra for dusting
a little oil, for re-frying

1. Start by cooking your potatoes, if you're not using leftovers. Peel them, weigh how much you need, then place them in a pan of water and bring to the boil. Boil until soft, about 20 minutes. Drain, and let them cool. You want to use them as cool and as dry as possible – if they're sitting in their own water, you'll have soggy scones. Arguably, that's why leftover is best.

2. Put your potatoes, salt and butter into a large bowl. Use a masher or balloon whisk to mash them together. Then add your flour and stir together to create a dough – I like to use my hands as it can get a bit tough.

3. Flour a work surface, then turn your dough out onto it and split it into four. Then, with each lump, you can either press it out into a circle shape about 5mm (¼in) thick or use a rolling pin. I like to just ease it into the right shape using the palm of my hand. This will be a rough circle; you can then cut this into four quarter-circles using a scraper.

4. Preheat a large, cast iron griddle pan or heavy frying pan (skillet) over a medium heat. If you're serving them fresh, then I suggest frying them in oil from the off; otherwise, if you're storing them for later, cook them on the bare flour only, then you can fry them in oil just to heat up when serving.

5. Fry for about 3 minutes on each side, or until golden brown – if the flour is starting to burn, you've gone too far, but they do need to be cooked enough to eliminate the risk of raw flour. If storing, store in the fridge in an airtight container for up to a couple of days.

Welsh Cakes

BP

The thing that's taught me to be sensitive when writing recipes for breads or dishes from other countries is that I know what a minefield it can be even within our own British Isles. Even mentioning the word 'scone' I know I'll be met with scoffs and scowls.

And in truth, Welsh cakes are somewhat odd – they're almost as though a sweet pastry, a fruit scone and a pancake had some kind of lovechild. The texture of the dough is pastry-like, but cooked like a dropped scone or Scotch pancake on a cast iron griddle or high-sided pan. Through the use of the baking powder, they puff up, lose their biscuit-like quality and remain soft. Sprinkled generously in sugar, they keep remarkably well, but they're best eaten fresh, in the afternoon, with a cup of tea out of a floral mug. They're dead easy and perfect for making with kids.

If you're not familiar with mixed spice, this is a traditional British ground spice mix, usually of ginger, cinnamon, clove and nutmeg. Most of us have a jar that's years old and has lost much of its potency, and this is a perfect time to use it.

Makes about 12 Welsh cakes

225g plain (all-purpose) flour, plus extra for dusting
2 tsp baking powder
85g caster (superfine) sugar, plus extra for dusting
½ tsp mixed spice or ground cinnamon (optional)
100g salted butter, cold
1 egg, beaten
30g milk
50g currants (alternatively, use raisins or sultanas)

1. Start by sorting the dry ingredients. Put the flour, baking powder, sugar and mixed spice (if using) into a large bowl. Weigh the butter, then rub it in with your fingertips until the mixture looks like breadcrumbs (a few lumps are fine).

2. Break in the egg, add the milk and currants and mix with a butter knife or wooden spoon to form a dough. If the dough is too dry, you can add a touch more milk.

3. Turn your dough out onto a lightly floured surface, then sprinkle with some more flour. Roll out the dough to a thickness of about 5–10mm (¼– ½in) – thicker than pastry, thinner than a scone. Use a cutter to cut out rounds however big you like, and if you don't have a cutter, use the rim of a mug or glass. As you're cutting, I would stick a heavy high-sided pan or cast iron griddle over a medium–low heat to get it up to temperature.

4. Cook the Welsh cakes for about 3–4 minutes on each side until golden brown and cooked through. Be sure to flip them carefully so they don't break apart. Once cooked, I put them between the folds of a dish towel so they keep warm and continue to cook through. Then you can dust with caster sugar and serve them warm, or let cool and keep them in an airtight container or cake tin for when neighbours come knocking for a cup of tea, if you're fortunate enough to live somewhere that still happens. Wales, maybe.

Sourdough Crumpets

S

Go get yourself a set of crumpet rings. My previous misguided suggestion that you can use empty tuna cans, with both ends removed, will work for a while, but crumpet rings make your life a lot easier. Go for non-stick if you've no objection to the coating.

While this recipe might be labelled as sourdough, it isn't your average convoluted and hours-long recipe. This is something you can use (virtually) any sourdough starter for – whether it's old and separated or fresh and bubbling. We don't require it to be active, but rather acidic – the reaction between the acid in your sourdough starter and the alkali of the bicarbonate of soda creates huge bubbles, more than adequate for rising your very wet dough.

I used to recommend this was made with no new flour added – for example, with only sourdough starter. But you can imagine, if this starter was days or weeks old, the flavour could be quite intense. This recipe will be more stable and more reliable.

Makes 4 crumpets

50g strong white flour
½ tsp table salt
2 tsp caster (superfine) sugar
50g tepid water
100g mature sourdough starter, fed with any flours (page 50)
½ tsp bicarbonate of soda (baking soda)
plenty of butter, for greasing, frying and serving

1. Start by preheating your heaviest-bottomed high-sided pan over a low heat on a medium ring. Let this come up to temperature slowly as you get the batter sorted. Grease your crumpet rings with lots and lots of butter.

2. In a bowl, weigh your flour, then add the salt and the caster sugar. Stir these in gently to combine. Add your water and starter and stir the thing into a paste. It should be able to be poured in a gloopy way – if it doesn't run from a spoon, mix in another tablespoon of water.

3. Add your bicarbonate of soda and stir. It will begin to bubble vigorously if all is well. As soon as it has combined, add a good knob of butter to your pan and tilt the pan to spread this around. Place your crumpet rings in the pan, then add enough batter to fill each ring to the halfway point and no more.

4. Cook on a low heat for about 6–8 minutes. You'll notice the crumpets beginning to get a waxy tinge and the sides just loosening away from the rings. Gently pry the rings away and lift off using a spatula or gloved hand. Flip your crumpets over.

5. Fry for another 2–3 minutes on the other side before removing from the pan to rest. If you've got some more mix left over, re-grease your rings, wipe the pan clean using some kitchen paper and add some more butter. You can then do the next batch. Cooked, they'll keep in an airtight container for a few days – toast before using and spread generously with butter.

FRANCE
FRANCE
FRANCE
FRANCE

Baguette

Y

YS

S

This is French Bread, as my father called it on the Breton holidays of my youth. The baguette: an iconic, spindly baton, and a bread that's all about the crust. Indeed, a good chunk of it is crust, meaning it's quick to stale. To be loved, it has to be eaten within hours of baking. And thus, the unrivalled supply chain of bread throughout France is the envy of every dough-lover on the planet.

Any bread labelled as *pain de tradition Français* – including the baguettes of most local bakeries – are governed by *Le Décret Pain* (Bread Law). This states that bread must be made on the premises, not frozen, and only from the four traditional ingredients of bread: flour, water, salt and yeast. This lack of preservatives ensures baguettes stale quickly and so need to be made fresh; the bakery, then, is enshrined as an essential part of the community. That's the plan, anyway, but sadly many are still closing.

While you might imagine a baguette as a strictly white affair, this is only through modern convention and the tastes dictated by the consumer culture. It's traditionally made with Type 55 flour, which is pretty white in the French system of flour categorization, but it can easily be made with Type 65 or Type 80, which have more bran and therefore more flavour, but can have a heavier structure. You can substitute this yourself by sifting wholemeal flour with a fine sieve, and keeping back the majority of the bran and germ for use elsewhere.

Variations
You might see some called a *ficelle* – a longer, thinner baguette, and difficult to make in a home oven without them coming out like bread sticks. A fun alternative, though, is the *pain d'epi* – where you use a pair of scissors to 'score' the baguette multiple times at an angle, down its length, creating a spiked pattern.

Makes 4 demi-baguettes

500g strong white flour, plus extra for dusting
1½ tsp salt
320g tepid water
1 tsp instant yeast (optional)
150g sourdough starter, fed with white flour (page 50) (optional)
a little semolina, for dusting

1. In a large bowl, mix together your flour and salt. Add the tepid water and combine into a wet dough, along with the yeast, if you are making a yeasted version. For extra flavour, add some starter. For a full sourdough, leave out the yeast and use the starter.

2. Let the dough autolyse (rest) for 30 minutes, if you like, until it feels stretchy and smooth, then give it a quick knead, or knead for 10 minutes by hand or machine.

3. If you've used yeast, cover your bowl and stick it in a cold fridge for 12–24 hours or overnight – this long slow fermentation is a substitute for the traditional poolish. If you've used sourdough, you'll first have to let it prove for a couple of hours at a warm room temperature (22–26°C/72–79°F) to let the wild yeast take off, before sticking it in the fridge overnight or all day.

4. The morning or evening you want your fresh baguettes, scoop your dough onto a floured work surface and cut it into four roughly equal pieces. Shape each piece into a long, thin baton shape (page 42).

5. Transfer each baguette to a dish towel or stiff linen couche, which has been rubbed generously with flour and placed on a baking tray or other hard board. Make folds in the material to separate the baguettes and so they support each other. I often use a book or a wine bottle (ensure it's French wine) placed on its side to support the baguettes on the end.

6. Cover loosely with a dish towel. Prove a yeast dough for about 1 hour at room temperature; a sourdough will need 2 hours. You don't want them really puffy and fragile, but rather robust enough to be turned out and handled a bit. They should spring back when pressed. When you're nearly at this stage, preheat your oven to 220°C (425°F) fan (240°C/465°F/gas 9), preheat a baking stone, if you have one, and dust a baking tray with semolina.

7. When ready to bake, turn the loaves out on to the baking tray, leaving room between them for the bread to rise. Score, making long scores down their length. Do not score in horizontal slashes as these won't open up.

8. Either bake on the tray, or slide the baguettes onto the preheated baking stone. Place some ice cubes on the tray with them, or pop some water onto another tray to create some steam. Bake for 30 minutes, or until the crusts are golden but not overly dark. Leave to cool, but eat fresh.

Pain de Campagne

Y

YS

S

(Country Loaf)

The country loaf, or *pain de campagne*, is a history lesson in a loaf. These loaves were prepared in awesome size by individual families, the doughs carted to the local, communal, wood-fired bread oven and baked in the dry heat, all together. This one large loaf was designed to feed a family for as long as possible, as firing up the oven was an expensive and laborious process.

The flour is where this gets interesting: this would once have been a lightly sieved wholemeal, with some of the bran and germ still left in. It wouldn't have been the wheat monoculture of today, but rather a biodiverse mix of wheats of previous years and some rye, all combined.

Then, in the late 18th century, the cumulative poor harvests, population expansion and mismanagement by the old monarchy led not just to grain shortages but increasing grain inequality: the rich took the white flour for themselves, leaving bran-heavy maslin bread for the poor. Enough to spark some sort of revolution, apparently.

Variations

Miche is now the common term for the huge variations in the country loaf, but this word has come to be a distinct bread in itself, featuring a darker colour and a higher proportion of rye or ancient grains. It tends to be sourdough only but, to be honest, you can make it either with a slow yeast fermentation or sourdough and you'll still get good results. For preservation, though, the acidity of the sourdough helps keep things fresh.

Makes 1 large loaf

200g strong white flour, plus extra for dusting
250g strong wholemeal flour (sifted weight)
50g wholemeal rye flour (sifted weight)
20g table salt
1 tsp instant yeast (optional)
375g tepid water
100g sourdough starter, fed with any flours (page 50) (optional)

1. Sift your strong white and strong wholemeal flours and then your rye flour into a large bowl. The weights stated are the sifted weights. You can keep the bran for later. Add your salt. For a yeasted loaf, add the yeast and mix everything together. Combine some warm and cold water in a jug until it feels just warmer than tepid, about 25°C (77°F), then add this too. For extra flavour, add your active sourdough starter with the water. For a full sourdough, leave out the yeast and add the sourdough starter, again with the liquid. Mix using a wooden spoon, a dough hook or your hands, until you've got a lumpy dough.

2. Ideally, let your dough autolyse (rest) for about 30 minutes. That means you have to knead very little – just for a minute or so, enough to make the dough smooth and pliable. If you opt to miss this step, you'll find you have to work a lot harder to bring the dough into a ball that's smooth and doesn't stick to everything.

3. Cover your dough and leave for 1½–2 hours, or double this if you're opting to avoid commercial yeast and using only sourdough. Timings will vary depending on temperature, and especially if going sourdough, make it warm. The dough should swell noticeably and be aerated when scooped out, but shouldn't collapse.

4. Use your bran to coat a proving basket and sprinkle some flour on a work surface, then turn out your dough. Shape your bread – trying to preserve as much of that aerated structure as possible. A boule is traditional (page 39) but the shape is really up to you.

5. Stick your proving basket in the fridge, ideally. If you have your fridge set really cold (1–2°C/34–36°F), you can leave a yeasted dough overnight in the fridge. A sourdough can be left for up to 24 hours in most fridges set to a colder setting. Alternatively, leave the dough at room temperature and get ready to bake within 1 hour of shaping for a yeasted loaf; 2 hours for sourdough.

6. Preheat your oven to 220°C (425°F) fan (240°C/465°F/gas 9) – this loaf works best at home using a covered cast iron pot (page 44), but you can bake on a tray with some added ice or water.

7. Once proved, turn your loaf out into your cast iron pot. Score – an overlapping square works well for this one – and bake for 20 minutes with the lid on, then 20 minutes with the lid off. Alternatively, bake on a tray or stone with some water or ice on the floor of the oven to create some steam.

Fougasse

(French Flatbread)

Y

YS

S

Fougasse hails from Provence, in south-eastern France, bordering Italy. It is a flatbread and fulfils the role of the Italian focaccia. Even the etymology is the same (from the Latin for 'focus', referring to the intense heat used at the heart of the fire).

But the breads can be very different – usually there's no olive oil in a *fougasse*, the dough is much less hydrated and therefore more manageable, and it is often shaped into an impressive-looking but easily achieved leaf shape. But the closer to the Italian border you go, and depending on who you talk to, a *fougasse* and a focaccia can sometimes look a lot like one another.

We've got to thank the legend that is Richard Bertinet for the popularization of this bread in the UK, with his conscientious attempts to teach us, through his bread academy, about the utter superiority of French bread culture to our own. And he's right, of course.

Variations

A *fougasse* has infinite variations. It can be covered in any topping you wish, just about, and I've tried to show a few variations I like, all made in a single sitting and from the same dough: olives, rosemary, sundried tomatoes, hard cheeses, anchovies. You can easily make a wholemeal version by subbing out half the white flour for wholemeal, and the dough works well with a couple of teaspoons of dried *herbes de Provence* mixed through.

Makes 4 loaves

425g strong white flour, plus extra for dusting
1½ tsp table salt
2 tsp instant yeast (optional)
280g tepid water
150g sourdough starter, fed with any flours (page 50) (optional)
a little semolina, for dusting (optional)

1. Into a large bowl, weigh your flour and salt. For a yeasted loaf, add the yeast and rub the ingredients together until combined, then add your tepid water. For extra flavour, add the sourdough starter with the water. For a full sourdough, leave out the yeast, pour in the water and add the sourdough starter on top. Mix everything together until a rough dough forms.

2. Autolyse (rest) the dough for 20–30 minutes, if you wish, which will cut how much kneading you need to do. Then knead your dough until smooth and lump-free and so that it forms a ball that removes excess dough from your work surface and from your hands. If you've autolysed, give it a minute or so. If you've not, give it 10.

3. Cover your bowl and leave your dough somewhere warm. For yeasted breads, this will be 90 minutes or so. For sourdough, 4–6 hours at 18–20°C (64–68°F).

4. About 30 minutes before you are ready to bake, preheat your oven to 230°C (445°F) fan (250°C/480°F/gas 9) – that's as hot as possible. Heat up a baking stone or a cast iron slab, if you can, but you can bake them directly on a tray. You can check if the stone is hot enough using an infrared thermometer, if you have one. If not, flick a drop of water onto the stone; it should instantly fizzle away.

5. Sprinkle some flour or semolina on your work surface and use a dough scraper to scrape the dough out of the bowl. Careful, you don't want to knock back this dough; those bubbles should stay. Add more flour on top.

6. Cut your dough into four equal lumps. Use floured hands to work on one at a time: flatten them gently to rough triangles about 20cm (8in) across, then put them on your baking tray. Use your dough scraper to make a cut right down the middle, but not quite end to end. Then make four short, angled cuts on each side of your central cut. Spread your dough out to open up the cuts, and move it around, adding more flour to ensure it's not sticking.

7. Repeat with as many as you can fit in the oven at a time (usually one to two to each tray), then add whatever toppings you like. If using a stone, slide the *fougasses* onto the stone, being careful to maintain their structure. Alternatively, bake directly on the tray. Feel free to re-arrange your *fougasses* on the stone if the pattern collapses as you slide it in, but be careful as it's easy to burn yourself trying.

8. Bake for 15–20 minutes – this means you can leisurely shape your next couple and have a coffee while you wait. It's OK to open the oven to add another tray or slide another one onto your baking stone. These breads should be a deep dark brown. Enjoy while still warm and crusty as this bread stales quickly.

Brioche

Y

YS

S

Ask 100 people from 100 countries to describe a brioche and you'll get 100 different answers. And the truth is, they're probably all right. This bread has had years of refinement and personalization by generations of international bakers.

Brioche has, of course, evolved. It has had the Church claim ownership and attempt to proscribe its ingredients – unsuccessfully. It has, at various times, required milk, cheese, then butter (but no egg), then eggs, eggs and butter, and eventually morphed into the sweet-savoury borderline bread that we know today. I'm sure all evolutions were delicious; combining refined white flour with lots of rich and sweet ingredients is, almost always, delicious.

But, after a thousand years of history, we get the little plastic-packeted chocolate-chipped monstrosities that my daughter so loves. They are not what this recipe will produce; far from it. My version will create something flaky, crusted, a little spongey, not particularly sweet and that makes the most intense jam-covered toast you'll ever eat.

It was once hypothesized in *Larousse Gastronomique* that the inclusion of all the enriching ingredients was to mask the 'stench' of a sourdough starter, but adding some starter or extending the prove gives you a complexity that I love. You can definitely make this without, and I'd even recommend this if you value lightness and softness above all else. But if you want something firmer and flakier and more interesting, go the other way and omit the yeast altogether.

Makes 2 medium-sized brioches or 12 sizeable brioche à tête (as pictured)

500g strong white flour, plus extra for dusting
1½ tsp table salt
30g caster (superfine) sugar
1½ tsp instant yeast (optional)
5 large eggs, at room temperature
100g whole milk
100g sourdough starter, fed with white flour (page 50) (optional)
200g unsalted butter, at room temperature, plus extra for greasing
1 egg, beaten with a pinch of salt, for brushing

1. Into a large bowl, weigh your flour, salt and sugar. For a yeasted loaf, add your yeast, then mix everything together using your fingers. Break in your eggs. Warm your milk until it is tepid (too cold for a bath), then add to the bowl. For extra flavour, add your sourdough starter with the liquid. For a full sourdough, leave out the yeast and add the sourdough starter with the liquid ingredients. Mix everything together until you've got a very rough dough.

2. It really helps to let it autolyse (rest) for 20–30 minutes here.

3. Knead your dough – preferably in an electric mixer (page 35). If you decide to use your hands and find it sticky, that's OK; use your dough scraper to unstick your hands or the worktop. Once you've got a soft, stretchy, pliable, smooth dough, you can add the softened butter. If it isn't, give it a blast in the microwave (it doesn't matter if it's a bit melted). Keep working until the dough is shiny, smooth and consistent.

4. Cover your bowl with a plate or damp dish towel and leave it at room temperature for 2 hours, or up to overnight in the fridge for a more complex flavour. If you're making a pure sourdough brioche without any commercial yeast, prove it for a couple of hours, then stick it in the fridge.

5. Following your first prove, grease either two 900g loaf tins or 12 small brioche tins. You'll find that if you cold-proved, you'll have a rather solid lump, and this is fine. Divide your dough into how many loaves you're making, and roll into batons (page 42) if shaping for tins or into little balls (page 40) for rolls depending on your use. To make the *à tête* shape, you can pinch a little of the ball nearly off by rolling your ball of dough beneath an outstretched finger.

6. Leave to prove in a warm place for another 1 hour or so for yeasted brioche; 2–3 for sourdough – you want to see them noticeably rise again. If you see little activity, move them somewhere warmer – on top of the back of the fridge or in an oven with the light on are good places. About 20 minutes before you think they will be ready, preheat your oven to 230°C (445°F) fan (250°C/480°C/gas 9).

7. When they're noticeably plump, whisk your remaining egg with a fork and brush the egg wash over the top of your risen brioche. Stick your tins in the oven and turn it down to 200°C (400°F) fan (220°C/425°C/gas 7). Bake for about 40 minutes for large loaves or 20–25 minutes for smaller rolls. Leave to cool in the tins for at least 30 minutes, then turn them out to finish cooling on a rack – and they must cool completely before slicing.

Pain d'Épices

S

(Spiced Bread)

Spiced bread, or *pain d'épices*, has historic integrity that's largely unknown today; now, it's a cake. It was once a supremely difficult and interesting sourdough bread, risen from the spontaneous fermentation of rye flour, exotic spices and honey. Each batch would have taken days or weeks to create.

I have tried to make 'original' *pain d'épices* and have found that over the fermentation, even just a little too much honey can cause the thing to clump into a dense mess of dough. I had to cut the honey right back, so basically had something akin to a spicy rye sourdough with mild honey sweetness, rather than the cakiness people might expect. And while the bread was delicious, especially spread with hot melted butter, it's not what we know, so in order to conform to convention, here I'm sticking to the cakey version – but with a historic and scientific twist.

Most modern recipes make use of modern raising agents, particularly, bicarbonate of soda (baking soda), an alkali. Combine this with an acid and it releases loads of CO_2 for a very light loaf. A convenient way of getting that acid is a sourdough starter – this can be one that's being discarded and is a bit neglected, or it can be fresh. My best results actually come from the latter – where there's added complexity, but not too much to distract from the inherent warmth of the bread.

And of course, that honey. Use the best honey you can find. Though not authentic, heather honey from Scotland or Scandinavia in this loaf is astounding.

Makes 1 large loaf

250g good set honey, plus extra for glazing
200g water
zest of 1 unwaxed orange
zest of 1 unwaxed lemon
½ star anise (optional)
2 cloves
a pinch of salt
130g salted or unsalted butter, chopped, plus extra for greasing
150g plain (all-purpose) flour, plus extra for dusting
50g wholemeal rye flour
½ tsp ground cinnamon

1. Preheat your oven to 160°C (325°F) fan (180°C/350°F/gas 4). Grease your 900g loaf tin and line it with baking parchment, unless you've got absolute confidence in your tin's non-stick abilities (I don't).

2. In a saucepan, weigh your honey and water. Grate in your zest, add your whole spices and your salt. Place over a medium heat and stir gently until it's barely simmering and the honey has dissolved. Remove from the heat and add the butter to melt. Set aside to cool for about 10 minutes, giving you ample opportunity to sort the dry ingredients.

3. In a bowl, weigh your flours, cinnamon, nutmeg and bicarbonate of soda. Pour your wet ingredients onto your dry ingredients, sieving out your spices as you do, and mix until lumpy. Only at this point, add your sourdough starter and mix together. Your final mixture can still be a touch lumpy, but no raw flour should be visible.

¼ nutmeg, grated

1 tsp bicarbonate of soda (baking soda)

40g sourdough starter, fed with any flours (page 50) – doesn't need to be fresh

For optional decorations

1 orange or lemon (the remaining one from your zest will do)

100g water

100g caster (superfine) sugar

4. Scoop the dough into your baking tin and smooth it out. Bake for 25–30 minutes, or until golden brown, it doesn't wobble when gently shaken, and when you press the top, it springs all the way back. If in doubt, another 5–10 minutes won't do this one much harm.

5. While still warm, remove from the tin and brush some extra honey over the top. I don't think anyone will pour scorn on the simplicity of your glazed loaf but if you want an extra edge, you can decorate it with glazed fruit. Take either your orange or lemon from your zest, and slice thinly. Place in a saucepan with your water and sugar over a low heat. Simmer for about 10 minutes, or until a little liquid remains but it hasn't yet begun to caramelize. At this stage, turn your fruit out onto some baking parchment laid out on a work surface, being careful not to burn yourself. Leave to cool completely before lifting with a knife and placing on your glazed loaf.

Pain aux Noix

Y

YS

S

(Nut Bread)

You can't summarize French bread philosophy in a few recipes. It's impossible, it's disrespectful. It's damn cultural appropriation. But when you've got to pick your favourite breads from across the world, it's important to pick the ones that are interesting, and that represent techniques or aspects or ingredients that are relevant to breads from a wide range of origins. Bread is of such national and regional importance in France, and so, so many of the other breads I've written about are derived from French practices and traditions, that we've got to do little justices where we can.

So with the *pains aux noix* – simply nut breads – which exist in various forms up and down France (and anywhere France has had influence across the world) and with my recipe, I'm sure I won't please anyone. Except you, if you decide to make it.

This recipe uses the 'scalding' technique to allow you to create a bread that is easier to handle and not weighed down and stodgy, like lots of wholemeals. It's also a little enriched, giving it a spongy lightness that just makes the most excellent toast for days on end.

This proves these approaches are not mutually exclusive and that introducing an earthy character into your sweeter breads can be a positive – not just for health and planet but for flavour.

Makes 1 large loaf

200g strong wholemeal flour
50g just-boiled water
300g strong white flour, plus extra for dusting
1½ tsp table salt
2 tsp instant yeast (optional)
40g salted or unsalted butter
150g whole milk
175g tepid water
100g sourdough starter, fed with any flours (page 50) (optional)
200g whole hazelnuts

1. Into a medium bowl, weigh your wholemeal flour. Then sieve this into a larger bowl, separating the white-ish flour from the bran. Place the bran back into your smaller bowl and add the just-boiled water to make a kind of thick paste. Mix together using a spoon and set aside.

2. To your sieved flour, add your white flour and salt, and distribute. For a yeasted loaf, add your yeast, then your butter, and use your fingertips to rub the butter into your dry mix until it disappears into ever-smaller clumps, a bit like when making pastry dough. Weigh in your milk and water. If your milk is cold from the fridge, a zap in the microwave will help. For extra flavour, you can add your sourdough starter to this mixture. For a full sourdough, leave out the yeast and use your sourdough starter instead. Mix everything together until it forms a dough.

3. If you can, knead for a few minutes – this will help with the overall lightness and evenness of the loaf. Then place back in your bowl and set aside for 30 minutes for a yeasted dough or 1 hour if sourdough.

4. Turn your dough out onto a wet surface. Consider the lamination method as on page 61. Using wet hands (and preferably a dough scraper), stretch your dough out into a large flat 50cm (19½in) square. Spread your bran paste over the dough and scatter with your hazelnuts, saving a few for your proving basket. Then, like you're folding a letter for an envelope, fold your dough into thirds, and roll it up. Place the dough back into the bowl to rest for another 1 hour if yeasted, or 3 hours if sourdough. If the latter, try to keep it above 20°C (68°F). If it's winter, on top of the fridge towards the back or in the oven with the light on are good places.

5. Turn your risen dough out onto a floured work surface. Sprinkle any leftover hazelnuts into a proving basket after the flour. Shape into a boule (page 39) and place in your basket, seam-side up, for another 45 minutes if yeasted, or 2 hours if a sourdough. You can fridge to delay your fermentation, but it depends how cold your fridge is. You can do this overnight if it's a sourdough in nearly any fridge, but a cold fridge of about 2°C (36°F) will be required if you're using yeast. Fifteen minutes prior to baking, place a cast iron pot inside your oven and preheat to 200°C (400°F) fan (220°C/425°F/gas 7).

6. Turn your dough out into your cast iron. Or if you're having to lower it into the pot and don't want to get burned, turn out onto some baking parchment first. Score the loaf, and bake with the lid on for 20 minutes, then with the lid off for another 20 minutes or so. Leave to cool before slicing.

ITALY

A Pizza Masterclass

Y

YS

S

Bread, tomato, cheese. How can there be so many different ways of doing it? But in this book, you've got one recipe inspired by the best sort of pizza in the world: the Neapolitan style. And while making it might be governed by a city and even a designated regulatory body, this is the way I suggest you get there.

This has changed from my previous iterations because I've refined this dough every time I've made it, and I've made it literally hundreds of times. It's not quite what the *Associazione Verace Pizza Napoletana* say it has to be in their very specific guidelines – their rules are designed to showcase local Italian ingredients.

For example, it's said you must use fresh Italian mozzarella, 0 or 00 flour, and San Marzano tomatoes. But unless you're in Italy, those ingredients won't be local to you, nor necessarily the best quality you can find. While choosing to use these can be a useful (and recommended) exercise in making 'authentic' pizza, whatever that means, it's better for your pocket and the planet to find local flour, local tomatoes and local mozz.

Then there's the baking. I use a fantastic Ooni pizza oven most of the time, but if it's dark and wet outside (as it often is in a Glasgow winter), I'll use the classic skillet-broiler method. Not that the oven doesn't work in the wet, it's just that it's not fun standing outside on your own making everyone else dinner as they drink and be merry in the warm and dry.

However you bake it, the key here is to be organized – have a Pizza Standard Operating Procedure (Pizza SOP), the basis of which I'll try to provide over the following pages. Each pizza may take as little as 90 seconds to bake, and that means everything has to be set for the next one, and for people to eat it. A sit-down meal with a pizza each and some side salad doesn't work – this is hands-dirty, sharing food. It encourages and enhances any social situation. It is magnificent.

Makes 4 large pizzas

600g strong white flour, plus extra for dusting
1½ tsp table salt
1 tsp instant yeast (optional)
390g tepid water
150g sourdough starter, fed with white flour (page 50) (optional)
a little semolina flour, for dusting

For the toppings
400g tin of good tomatoes, whole or pulped
300g mozzarella, drained weight
good extra virgin olive oil
salt and freshly ground black pepper
a bunch of fresh basil
any other toppings you'd consider

To make the dough

1. You can start the dough anywhere from 2 days before you plan to bake to a minimum of 2½ hours ahead, if you're using yeast. A pure sourdough will take at least 4 hours, so if it's a last-minute decision then you'll need to use yeast.

2. Begin by weighing your flour and salt into a large bowl. For a yeasted loaf, add the yeast and then the water. For extra flavour, you can then add your sourdough starter at the same time. For a full sourdough, leave out the yeast and use your sourdough instead, added with the water. Mix to a dough.

3. I'd suggest kneading, especially if you're in a rush and don't have time to give it some extra stretches and folds in lieu of kneading (page 47).

4. Prove a yeasted dough for at least 1 hour at room temperature, or you can put it in a cold fridge at this stage for up to a day or so. If you're using sourdough only, prove for about 4 hours in a warm place, with a couple of stretches and folds during the prove (page 47).

5. Find a dish or roasting tray with plenty of space to hold your individual pizza doughs, and cover it in a mixture of flour and semolina – be generous. Turn your dough out onto a floured surface, and cut it into four pieces (there are more opposite as I'm making a double batch). Shape each into a loose boule (page 39) but don't be too tight, then place each in your dish, spaced as far apart as you can. Cover with more flour and semolina, making sure the sides are coated.

6. Cover your doughs with kitchen foil, clingfilm (plastic wrap) or a plastic bag, and stick them in the fridge. So long as your fridge is set to cold, they can stay in there for up to 2 days. Then 30 minutes before you're going to bake, take the doughs out of the fridge – if they're too cold, they can be difficult to shape.

To prepare the tomatoes

Prepare the tomatoes any time before baking. If you're using pulped tomatoes ('polpa') you can just stick a spoon in the tin and it's ready. If whole tinned tomatoes are being used, pour the tin into a bowl and use the fingers of one hand to crush the tomatoes into pulp. I wouldn't bother with fresh – but if you do, make sure to blanch them and remove the skins, remove any tough bits of the core and then crush them in a similar way.

To prepare the cheese

Unless you're using a pre-drained block of mozz (I recommend you don't), drain the liquid from your mozzarella at least half an hour before you plan on baking. Slice your mozz into rounds each about 5mm (¼in) thick, then cut these into strips. Drain off any more liquid, then place on two pieces of kitchen paper.

To prepare the toppings

Wet vegetables – such as mushrooms, aubergines (eggplants), courgettes (zucchini) or peppers – you must fry or oven bake first to remove the vast majority of the moisture and to cook them through. I tend to fry them as it's quickest, and they absorb the oil from frying, which gives extra flavour.

For sliced meats, such as salami or prosciutto, make sure the packet is open and ready, and there aren't bits of plastic in between that are fiddly when trying to top your pizza in a hurry.

Mise en place

Have the open oil, salt and pepper all to hand, next to where you're going to build. Semolina should be available at all times for stopping things from sticking.

Pizza oven preparation – at least 25 minutes before baking

For this, you'll obviously need a dedicated pizza oven. Pizza ovens, including the Ooni, are supposed to be able to get up to temperature in 15 minutes. If they burn any kind of solid fuel, take this claim with a pinch of salt. Give them about 25 minutes.

It might be controversial, but I use a mixture of charcoal – which gives a really good base heat to the oven and the stone – and some dry kindling that gives the intense dry flame you want. You could use only wood, but make sure it's super-dry and measure the temperature.

Before lighting, flip the stone over, scraping off any heavy debris. By flipping it each time you light it, any residue burns off the bottom of the stone during the bake and you're left with a clean stone every time.

Light the oven with a blowtorch if you have one – it makes getting it going super-easy. If not, matches and a firelighter will have to do.

The temperatures you're aiming for are frankly shocking. You want the stone to be up to about 450°C (840°F) and at a minimum of 400°C (750°F). This super-intense heat is required for the proper Neapolitan bake.

Skillet-broiler preparation – at least 5 minutes before baking

You'll need a working grill (broiler), a cast iron pan (skillet) big enough to take your doughs and a working hob. Make sure the pan fits under the grill with a bit of room to spare. You'll also need a palette knife or steel spatula to get the pizza out.

Equipment checklist

Infrared thermometer
A near-essential if you're using wood to bake your pizza, but can also be really helpful to check your cast iron pan is hot enough.

Peel
A thin, solid metal peel is the best do-all peel, great for building your pizza on, turning your pizza in the oven and removing it when it's done. If using the skiller-broiler method, you don't need this as you build in the pan.

Serving boards
I'd recommend two heat-safe, food-safe boards for serving on. Wood is best.

Pizza cutter
Can't be without, obviously.

Dough scraper
You will need it to divide and scoop the dough.

A cloth or sponge
For any spillages or leakages.

Drinks
Because what's a pizza party without some kind of beverage to hand?

Pizza oven – method

1. Use the titles on pages 110–112 (dough, tomatoes, mozz, toppings) alongside the equipment list as a checklist. Make sure they are all to hand before you start and you are ready. Check your oven is up to the required temperature – at least 400°C (750°F).

2. Scrape out a lump of dough onto a work surface coated in semolina – be generous. Add more semolina on top. Use the tips of both sets of fingers together, as pictured overleaf, and spread the dough out into a disc, maintaining the crust all the way around. If you ever get a hint of sticking, add more semolina.

3. When you've got a disc with a crust around it, lift the dough up, place it over your knuckles and gently stretch it out, working your way around the dough. If it feels as if it might tear, it probably will, so set it down. Patch any tears by making a little fold in the dough – this is fine, and a sign your dough should be given longer out of the fridge, or be better developed next time.

4. Don't worry if the dough isn't pizza-sized yet. Place it on your peel. Spoon on 2–3 tablespoons of tomato and spread it out thinly – it might look like not enough, but don't worry – it is.

5. Add a quarter of the mozzarella, followed by any toppings, and don't forget the seasoning and a drizzle of oil.

6. Check your flame is roaring. If it isn't, add a little dry kindling into your oven for some roar.

7. Give your peel a little shake to make sure the pizza isn't sticking. If it is, scatter some semolina under any stuck bits. Quick. Then it's time to stretch out the dough to the full 30cm (12in) size. Just grab opposing edges and pull. Work your way around and adjust toppings if necessary.

8. Open the oven door and slide it in. Check after 30 seconds, and if the side closest the flame is beginning to burn, turn it, quick.

9. Slice and eat. **Caution** – these are hot hot hot from the oven. I've got into the habit of sticking the first one in a low conventional oven at about 90°C (195°F) to keep it warm as I build a second pizza and get the pizza oven back up to temperature. That way, I can serve two pizzas almost simultaneously, I can eat with everyone, then we can go back to make another two.

Skillet-broiler – method

1. Use the titles on pages 110–112 (dough, tomatoes, mozz, toppings) alongside the equipment list as a checklist. Make sure they are all to hand before you start and you are ready.

2. Preheat your grill (broiler) on a high heat. Place your cast iron pan (skillet) on the hob on a high heat – you want it at the 'very hot' stage, where any seasoning is starting to smoke just a tad. This is about 200°C (392°F) on your infrared thermometer, if you have one. You can let it heat up while you build your first pizza.

3. Scrape out a lump of dough onto a work surface coated in semolina – be generous. Add more semolina on top. Use the tips of both sets of fingers together, as pictured on page 116, and spread the dough out into a disc, maintaining the crust all the way round. If you ever get a hint of sticking, add more semolina.

4. When you've got a disc with a crust around it, lift the dough up, place it over your knuckles and gentle stretch it out, working your way around the dough. If it feels as if it might tear, it probably will, so set it down, or move to a different bit of the dough. Patch any tears by making a little fold in the dough – this is fine, and a sign your dough should be given longer out of the fridge, or be better developed next time. Keep going until it's slightly bigger than your pan.

5. Place the dough into the hot pan, on the heat: it's OK if the crust is riding up the sides a little. Working quickly, build your dough, adding your tomatoes, cheese and toppings. Once your pizza is topped, use a palette knife or spatula to check the underside – you want it to be speckled light brown. If it's getting dark, get it straight under the grill. If it's all white still, give it 1–2 minutes longer.

6. Grill until the cheese is melted and turning golden, and the crust around the edge is speckled.

7. I like to keep one pizza warm in a warm oven at 90°C (195°F) while I get the pan back up to temperature and make the next one, so I can serve two pizzas at once. If your grill is a function of your oven, then you can just place your first pizza on a tray at the bottom of the same oven while you make the next one.

Fancy Bruschetta with Burrata

The pedants among you will point out that bruschetta can be made with any bread – it's just chopped tomatoes on bread, maybe some garlic and oil and salt. Right? Right.

Yet this bruschetta is taking things a bit further. It's a variation on a garlic bread I make using my Ooni as an indulgent first course to test my dough before the pizzas start flying, or using the skillet-broiler method (page 118) as a starter or accompaniment to an indoor Italian meal.

Push the boat out. With a bit of prep and, of course, the right ingredients, this is a fancy thing indeed.

Makes 2–3 pizza-like breads

½ quantity pizza dough (page 110)
15g olive oil, plus extra for drizzling
30g salted or unsalted butter
4 garlic cloves, peeled
30g basil, about 40 leaves and stalks
400g ripe heritage tomatoes
1 burrata, drained
sea salt and freshly ground black pepper
a little flour and semolina, for dusting

1. Start, ideally the day before but at least 2½ hours before you want to bake, by making your pizza dough. You can make the full quantity and leave half in the fridge for another day, use the rest for pizza, or just make a half quantity. You want it pre-shaped into two balls, ideally, as previously.

2. If you have a pizza oven, get that lit while you do your prep. In a blender or food processor, place your olive oil, butter, peeled garlic cloves and basil. Blend into a green paste.

3. Chop your tomatoes finely with a very sharp knife – using a very sharp knife and being careful really makes all the difference, as you don't want to release much of their liquid. Place in a bowl, and add salt and pepper and another glug of olive oil.

4. Place your burrata on a piece of kitchen paper to dry out a little.

5. **To bake in a pizza oven**, make sure the oven is hot, ideally 400°C (750°F) or more. Dust your work surface with flour and semolina and scrape out a portion of dough. Use your hands to shape it into a large round, similar to Neapolitan pizza, with a lip around the edge to contain your butter. Use a fork to prick the flat central portion of your dough several times, then make sure it hasn't stuck and transfer onto a pizza peel dusted with semolina. Scoop on half your garlic and basil butter and spread this over. Bake for about 90 seconds, turning halfway through, until the edges are speckled.

6. **To bake using the skillet-broiler method**, preheat your cast iron pan over a high heat on the hob. Scrape a portion of dough out onto a flour and semolina dusted surface, and use your hands to shape into a large round, similar to Neapolitan pizza, with a lip around the edge. Transfer onto your hot pan, then use your fork to prick the central portion to stop it puffing up. Cook until the base is starting to go a speckled golden, lifting up to check. Once it's nearly there, after a minute or two, spread over your basil butter and stick it under the grill. Cook until speckled and golden.

7. Place your hot fresh dough on a serving board. Top with your chopped tomato mixture, then tear over your burrata. Drizzle with yet more olive oil, then crack over more black pepper.

Focaccia Four Ways

Y

YS

S

I've gone full circle on my focaccia. I maintain it is about the single most accessible bread for those sceptical of the value of making it yourself, and it is therefore with regret that I have encouraged evermore enthusiastic bread makers to push what is possible, in terms of the incorporation of both water and oil, to tackle recipes that are achievable, but difficult.

I'm therefore going back to basics. The focaccia – analogous to the French fougasse (page 97) – is a flat, dimpled Italian bread, known for its big holes, oil and toppings. It's the ultimate dinner accompaniment. It's not just unbelievably delicious, but just so easy.

Note, it's not my intention you see this recipe as one for a focaccia with four different toppings (bringing four different focaccias to a dinner party takes you to the level of 'smug bread-baking git'). Instead, use it as inspiration. Each topping quantity will coat an entire focaccia.

Makes 1 large or 2 small focaccia

500g strong white flour
1½ tsp table salt
2 tsp instant yeast (optional)
400g tepid water
100g sourdough starter, fed with white flour (page 50) (optional)
30g extra virgin olive oil, plus at least the same again for drizzling and baking

For the topping options

1 punnet of cherry tomatoes, sliced in half, and a scattered handful of green olives

~~~~~

200g new potatoes, very thinly sliced, layered over your bread, and a scattering of fresh rosemary

~~~~~

1. Into a large bowl, weigh your flour and salt. For a yeasted loaf, add the yeast and rub the ingredients together until combined. Then add your tepid water. For extra flavour, add your sourdough starter with the water. For a full sourdough, leave out the yeast but include your sourdough starter instead. Mix everything together until roughly combined.

2. If you wish, you can autolyse (rest) the dough by leaving to rest for 20–30 minutes before continuing, which will cut how much kneading you need to do.

3. Knead your dough – you want it smooth and lump-free and so that it forms a ball that removes excess dough from your work surface and from your hands. As it comes together, add your oil, and work this into the dough until it is completely incorporated.

4. Cover your bowl and leave your dough somewhere warm. For yeasted breads, this will be 60–90 minutes. For sourdough, 4 hours at 20°C (68°F) if you've an active starter.

5. Line a roasting tray or baking tray with baking parchment, cover it in oil, and scrape your dough out onto it. Grab one end, and fold it in half like closing a book. Give it a shoogle to make sure that it's not sticking; if it is, unstick it and add more oil under there.

1 large red onion, thinly sliced and slowly fried in some oil over a low heat, with a splash of balsamic as they start to stick, then cooled and spread across with some pitted kalamata olives and perhaps some thyme

2 ripe pears, thinly sliced, skin-on, with 150g Gorgonzola broken over the top

some fresh sea salt and rosemary is fine, too, if you're not feeling fancy

6. Spread your focaccia out to the edges of your tray, flattening it as you do. A little more oil won't go amiss. Leave it to prove for another 1–2 hours for yeasted, at least 2 for sourdough. If you're making it early, stick it in the fridge for up to several hours or overnight.

7. It's topping time – these can actually be added at any point from when you finish the shaping, and if you're leaving it out uncovered, it can help to get the toppings on sooner rather than later, or they will struggle to stick to the dough. Follow the mini instructions here for your chosen toppings. Beware if using fresh tomatoes or soft cheese: they can ooze off the bread and cause sticking, hence the baking parchment.

8. About 15 minutes before you want to bake, preheat your oven to 210°C (410°F) fan (230°C/450°F/gas 8). If you've got a baking stone, give it a bit longer so it's properly hot.

9. Bake for about 35 minutes, but check the oven after 25 minutes and turn it down by 20°C (68°F) if you notice any toppings getting too dark. In the worst situations, where the toppings are at risk of burning and the dough isn't cooked, you can make a cover using kitchen foil to trap steam and prevent burning.

Durum Ciabatta

Y

YS

S

Ciabatta – which means slipper – is a modern bread. Be sceptical of cultural allegiance: these traditions go back a generation, no more. It can be a tricky bread. Or rather, we bakers make it tricky by introducing so much water into the dough to make it completely unachievable. We think that the key to that light, open, airy crumb is adding more and more water. It can help, but it can also lead us to push too far, with sticky doughs that become completely unmanageable for most bakers.

This recipe does indeed have a lot of water – perhaps a shocking amount if you're not that familiar with high-hydration doughs. But it should be manageable, because of the semolina.

I should clarify: when I'm specifying semolina, I'm meaning Italian semolina, which is durum flour – any semolina marketed for pizza or pasta-making is perfect. What I don't mean is British semolina, a waste product from the production of white flour. The germ of the wheat is separated from the bran and the starches are ground down and packeted as semolina. Check the packet if you're not sure.

Durum flour is strong and hard. It has a good gluten content, and those wee crystalline grains absorb a lot of water. Not only that, but it takes a while for the water to be absorbed, forcing you to work the dough through an extended proving, creating a beautiful and strong network. This, when handled with extreme care to avoid deflation when shaping, creates that wonderfully light dough.

Makes 4 ciabatta

300g durum flour (semolina)
200g strong white flour, plus extra for dusting
1½ tsp table salt
2 tsp instant yeast (optional)
440g tepid water
100g sourdough starter, fed with white flour (page 50) (optional)

1. In a large bowl, weigh your flours and salt. For a yeasted loaf, add your yeast and mix to combine, then add about three-quarters of your water. For extra flavour, add your sourdough starter with the water. For a full sourdough, leave out the yeast and add three-quarters of the water with the sourdough starter. Mix everything into a dough, adding a little more water if it won't come together.

2. Once you've got a rough dough, let it autolyse (rest) for about 15 minutes for the flour to absorb the liquid.

3. Add your remaining water, and start to work it into your dough. It helps if you have an electric mixer for this (page 35) but you can also do it within the bowl using a dough scraper and the stretch and fold (page 47) method. Work around the bowl until the water is completely incorporated and your dough is feeling wet and elastic, almost batter-like. Good. Now mix it some more – 10 minutes is good.

4. Leave your dough for 30 minutes, then give it another stretch and fold – either more stretching and folding (page 47), or turn your mixer on until the dough is starting to come away from the sides of the bowl.

5. Now, for pure sourdough, your dough will take another 3 hours resting at a warm room temperature, with another stretch and fold half way through. For yeasted, it will be another 45–60 minutes, no more folding required. You want a puffy, pillow-like, strong dough.

6. During the next steps, it's important to be very careful – you do not want to burst all the bubbles you've worked hard to create. The worst thing that can happen to a ciabatta is it is overproved and the structure collapses. Prepare a dish towel or linen couche by dusting with plenty of flour.

7. Carefully scrape your risen dough out onto a very well-floured surface. Before it spreads out too much, gently grab one edge and fold it over, like closing a book, so you've got both flour on top and the bottom of your dough.

8. Using floured hands, pat your dough down to flatten it slightly, then use a dough scraper to slice it into four lengths. Use your hands to lift each one up and transfer it to your floured cloth for their final rest, stretching each out as you move them, as much as you dare. Dust them with some semolina, and leave them uncovered for a final 30 minutes for yeasted breads, or 1½ hours (up to 3 in the fridge) for sourdough. Your doughs should look very wobbly and full of bubbles.

9. About 15 minutes before you plan on baking, preheat your oven to 210°C (410°F) fan (230°F/450°F/gas 8). If you've got a baking stone, preheat it for 30 minutes. Otherwise, we're baking on trays.

10. Wedge your baking tray at the edge of a ciabatta, and carefully roll the dough onto the tray. You should be able to get a couple on each tray. Don't score, but do add a bowl of water or ice to the bottom of the oven to create some steam. Bake for 30 minutes, or until a dark golden brown. You want a good crust on these.

11. Ciabatta are excellent for par-baking and freezing, or storing for up to 3–4 days in an airtight container. Just bake them initially for only 20 minutes, store and bake them for 15 minutes to order.

Colomba di Pasqua

(Tuscan Easter Doves)

Y

YS

S

This is probably the most complicated and involved recipe in the book. You have been warned. Unless you're an experienced sourdough baker already, with an extremely reliable starter, and good dough-handling skills, and the ability to prove a dough warm for a sustained time, then just please please do the yeasted version. The full sourdough may make the best bread on the planet, but it's a kick in the gut if it doesn't come out right after all that work (and cost).

This is a Tuscan Easter bread, and dates to somewhere between 1000 and 1500 years ago, depending on which legend you believe. Perhaps it was this dove-shaped bread, given as a peace offering, that ended a war? Does it mark the victory of Lombardy over the Holy Roman Empire after the miraculous appearance of doves on the battlefield? Or was it just one clever baker's way of selling panettone twice in a year? I know which my money's on.

This is made in a very similar way to panettone. The first stage gets the fermentation going, then the next adds fresh gluten and fuel for fermentation. The full sourdough version of this gives a bread of unparalleled longevity and lightness. I prefer this to panettone as the moulds aren't so tall and, as here, you can even bake without.

Makes 2 medium colombas

For stage 1

360g strong white flour
110g caster (superfine) sugar
1 tsp instant yeast (optional)
90g tepid water
6 egg yolks (120g)
80g sourdough starter, fed with white flour (page 50) (optional)
120g salted or unsalted butter, softened

1. In a large bowl, mix together your strong white flour and caster sugar. For a yeasted loaf add your yeast, water and egg yolks and mix until they form a dough. For extra flavour, include the sourdough starter. For a full sourdough, leave out the yeast but include the sourdough starter. It helps if you have an electric mixer (page 35) because this dough needs working. Only a true martyr would knead by hand.

2. Knead your dough vigorously for 10–15 minutes, or until it feels smooth and almost silky. Only then, add the butter and beat until totally smooth and combined – at least another 5 minutes. At times it will feel gloopy, like it won't come together. It will.

3. Give your dough a long prove – for a sourdough, this will be 6–8 hours at 24–26°C (75–79°F). A prover, an oven with the light on or even a low oven is really required in the cold of Scotland. If you're using yeast, it can still take a while: 3-4 hours at a cool room temperature. If it's going faster than that, fridge it and leave it for 12 hours or so before continuing.

For stage 2

120g strong white flour
80g caster (superfine) sugar
1 tsp vanilla bean paste
1 tsp orange blossom water
30g honey
1 tsp table salt
60g tepid water
6 egg yolks (120g)
130g unsalted butter, softened
200g dried fruit of your choice, or chocolate chips
200g Italian mixed candied peel (optional)
50g flaked or blanched almonds
neutral oil, for shaping
granella di zucchero (sugar logs), for decorating

You'll also want two medium colombas paper cases, but you could bake them in tins without the shape to create panettones

4. Once tripled in size, it's time to add the stage 2 ingredients to your proven dough. Add the flour and sugar, then mix to combine into a new, drier dough. Add the vanilla, orange blossom, honey, salt and water, incorporating them into the dough. Finally, add the egg yolks, and again mix into a coherent dough. This will be a strange dough, both kneaded and not.

5. Then it's time to knead again. And again, knead vigorously, for a good 10–15 minutes at least. Only then, start incorporating the remaining softened butter. Continue to work until this is totally smooth and incorporated, probably another 5 minutes. Finally, add the fruit (or chocolate) and peel. Keep working the dough until the fruit is as evenly distributed as it can be.

6. Lightly oil a work surface and turn your dough onto it. Using oiled hands and a dough scraper, slice your dough in half, if you like, for two doves. Each piece, you'll want to split into three – one large piece and two small. The large you should shape as for a baton (page 42) – this is the body of the dove. Each smaller one can be shaped for a boule (page 39), and placed next to it for the wings. Repeat with your other dove, then sprinkle with your almonds.

7. Lie a piece of well-greased clingfilm (plastic wrap) over the top of the dough, then prove for about another 6–8 hours, preferably on the warm side. If it's too cold, this can take 12 hours or more. You want the dough to swell considerably – to be at least two-thirds up. At this point, it's ready to bake; 20 minutes before baking, preheat your oven to 200°C (400°F) fan (220°C/425°F/gas 7). In an ideal world, you'd preheat even longer with a baking stone inside for maximum bottom heat.

8. Just before you bake, turn the oven down to 170°C (340°F) fan (190°C/375°F/gas 5). Sprinkle over your sugar logs, if using, and bake for 50–60 minutes on the bottom shelf of the oven. If the loaves are becoming very dark after 30 minutes, turn the oven down. Steam can be useful here to maximize oven spring. Allow to cool slowly and do not even think about cutting into it until it's completely cool.

EASTERN
EUROPE
EASTERN
EUROPE

Bubliki

Y

YS

S

(East European Bagels)

I did think about including a traditional bagel recipe, as you'd find in modern-day New York City, but I've done that before. These are *bubliki (bublik* is the singular), and are equally exciting. They co-evolved from the precursers to the bagels we know today, throughout modern-day Ukraine, Belarus and Russia.

These are much bigger than the ring-shaped breads of the West and are designed to be torn and dipped, rather than sliced and stacked with fillings. They're sharing size, and an excuse for you to break bread with family across borders and divides. Come together, over bread.

These have far softer crumbs than bagels due to their enrichment, and they have a certain stability thanks to the addition of egg white. Their deep, dark colour is thanks to both boiling in an alkaline solution of bicarbonate of soda in water, but also brushing with the remaining yolk.

***Makes 6* bubliki**

450g plain (all-purpose) flour, plus extra for dusting
1½ tsp table salt
25g unsalted butter
2 tsp instant yeast (optional)
100g sourdough starter, fed with white flour (page 50) (optional)
200g milk
2 eggs, separated

For boiling
2 tsp bicarbonate of soda (baking soda)
poppy seeds or sesame seeds, for topping

1. In a large bowl, weigh your flour and add your salt. Add your butter and rub it in with your fingertips so that it's mostly distributed. It doesn't need to be perfect. For a yeasted loaf, add your yeast and rub that in too, then add the milk. For extra flavour, add the sourdough starter with the milk. For a full sourdough, leave out the yeast and just use the sourdough starter, adding it with the liquid.

2. Add your milk, warmed in the microwave if necessary. Add the egg whites; no worries if a little yolk gets in, but keep the yolks covered in the fridge for later. Mix together your dough with a wooden spoon, a dough hook or your hands until you've got a solid lump.

3. Let your dough rest for approximately 30 minutes – this autolyse (rest) really helps you manage such a dry dough. Cover the bowl with a damp dish towel or a plate to stop the dough drying out further.

4. Once rested, knead your dough for 10 minutes, or until the dough is properly shiny and smooth. I think an electric mixer makes this far more palatable, to be honest, but otherwise the English stretch and roll knead (page 37) will work well. This firm dough does benefit from some working, and doesn't work as well with the no-knead method. If you don't have such a firm dough (though it's not as firm as bagels), then the *bubliki* tend to end up quite flat after baking.

5. For yeasted, cover and leave it for 60–90 minutes; sourdough will need 3–4 hours near a source of heat. Your proving time will vary depending on temperature. This dough swells – you do indeed want it to nearly double in size. If making sourdough, don't add any extra stretches and folds here.

6. Lightly flour a work surface, then use a dough scraper to scoop your dough out onto it. Use floured hands to gently roll it out into a big doughy sausage, then use your scraper to cut this into six roughly equal lumps.

7. You want to start shaping your *bubliki* almost like you're making them into baguettes (page 42). You won't need much or any flour as your dough is so dry, I think. Start by flattening your lump slightly, then roll it up tight. Using flat hands, rock this backwards and forwards against your work surface to create a long sausage – and keep going until it's about 30cm (12in) long. Taper the ends slightly, and then curl your dough into a ring shape, overlapping the ends. Place a flat palm over this overlap with your fingers through the ring, and rock back and forth to seal. Repeat five more times. You're aiming for a larger hole than with bagels.

8. Your *bubliki* can be left to prove for the second time on a floured couche (or dish towel) or just a tray or board as long as you're happy to gently unstick them using a dough scraper later. Prove uncovered for 45 minutes at room temperature for yeasted, or 1–2 hours at a warm room temperature for sourdough. Alternatively, you can fridge this dough at this point to extend this prove.

9. The next step is boiling. First, preheat your oven to 200°C (400°F) fan (220°C/425°F/gas 7). You'll need two baking trays, but if you want to stone bake, then this is a great opportunity. Bring a large pan of water – with enough space to fit each *bublik* – to a rolling boil. Add your bicarbonate of soda. Scoop or scrape one ring into the water, and boil for 1 minute. Use a slotted spoon to turn over, and boil for a further minute.

10. Remove this ring, and pop it on a piece of baking parchment to sit and steam. It will dry as you boil the rest, and that is fine. Once they have all been boiled, remove your egg yolk from the fridge and give it a mix, just using a brush is fine. If it's too thick, cut it with a splash of milk or water. Brush this equally over your six doughy rings, then sprinkle with sesame or poppy seeds. Bake for 20–25 minutes, or until they have a deep, dark golden shine.

Kolach with Honey

Y

YS

S

(Braided Festive Bread)

When you've been making a recipe for a long time, it seems to become yours, rather than whose it was before. It turns out that, if you're doing this, it's important to avoid appropriating something with religious or cultural significance, as I did inadvertently with *challah*, a similar braided bread with common etymology and cultural origins to *kolach*. I included butter and milk. I made some passing suggestion of serving it during Passover. I plaited it wrong. Thankfully, those who educated me treated me with good grace.

So when treading the world of bread, one has to be careful. *Kolach* (or *kalach*, in Russia) exists in various guises across Eastern Europe, and has equal religious and cultural significance. This is a bread baked when good fortune is sought and made to be gifted: at baptisms or weddings. It's served at Christmas, too, and it sits with pride, with a candle lit inside it, not to be eaten until Christmas Day due to the traditional Nativity fast.

Note that this recipe is Kosher, I'm assured, and can also be used to make a mean *challah*; just don't form the braid into a ring.

***Makes 1* kolach**

450g strong white flour, plus extra for dusting
1 tsp table salt
2 eggs
1 egg yolk
30g honey
160g tepid water
40g vegetable or sunflower oil
2 tsp instant yeast (optional)
100g sourdough starter, fed with white flour (page 50) (optional)

To finish
1 egg mixed with a pinch of salt, for egg wash
a little icing sugar, for dusting

1. In a large bowl, weigh your flour and salt. Add the eggs, egg yolk, honey, water and oil. For a yeasted loaf, add the yeast and mix to combine. For extra flavour, add the sourdough starter to that mixture. For a full sourdough, leave out the yeast and use the sourdough starter instead. Combine everything to form a rough dough.

2. Cover the mix and leave to rest for at least 20 minutes – the autolyse (rest) will really help when it comes to the plaiting.

3. Knead your dough for 5–10 minutes, or until it's feeling smooth and stretchy. Cover and leave to prove for 1–2 hours, or until it's noticeably big and domed. This dough can take a little longer to get going due to the honey, but by all means stick it in a cold fridge to delay things by up to 8–10 hours.

4. Lightly flour a work surface, then scrape your dough out onto it. Use your scraper to cut the dough into three equal pieces, and then shape each piece into a baguette shape at least 30cm (12in) long with tapered ends (page 42). These are your strands.

5. Lay the strands out like an arrow pointing away from you, with the ends coming together to form a point. Squeeze this point together hard. Now, it's just like plaiting hair: take the left strand and fold it gently over the middle, and then do the same with the right. Pull each strand snug, and as you reach the end it will become tighter.

6. You can bake this in a greased *kugelhopf* or *bundt* tin or a baking tray with baking parchment. Take your plait and stretch it out gently before forming it into a ring shape. Overlap the ends slightly, then tuck the narrower end under the wider end to make the plait look continuous. Place in the lined tin or on the tray.

7. Make your egg wash, then brush half of it generously over the bread, reserving half for later. Prove for a final 1 hour at room temperature, or 8–12 hours overnight in a cold fridge.

8. At least 15 minutes before you're going to bake, preheat your oven to 190°C (375°F) fan (210°C/410°F/gas 7). Then, once proved, brush with the remaining egg wash and bake for 30–35 minutes until a dark and shiny golden brown all over. Let cool, and dust with a little icing sugar to finish.

Khachapuri

(Georgian Boat-shaped Bread)

Y

YS

S

I'd have been ignorant of the wonders of Georgian bread if there wasn't an excellent Georgian bakery in the east end of Glasgow (if you want to find it, it's handily called 'GEORGIAN BAKERY', all caps). There, you can get *khachapuri* like this one. This is the Adjarian version: you'll never forget that Adjara is on the coast, because this bread is shaped like a boat.

At the time of writing, I'm quite amazed this bread hasn't gone viral through the Western bread-centric social media channels I enjoy, because it's such a beautiful and ingenious thing. It's elliptical, with soft crusts stuffed with cheese, then topped with more cheese. And once it's baked, like all the best things, it has an egg cracked on top of it. Return to the oven until the egg is soft, et voilà. A meal. A really delicious cheesy, bready, eggy meal.

And like the best ideas, and not to take away from one of Georgia's national dishes, other people thought very similar ideas: I've had traditional *fougasses* in northern France shaped exactly the same way, just filled with comté and ham instead of zingy curds and egg.

It's traditionally made with a brined, soft cheese curd that's quite difficult to find where I am. If you've any Eastern European supermarkets, you're after some *suglini*, or Polish *twarog* is close. Like most, I've used a mix of feta and mozzarella to get that combination of soft, stretchy meltiness and zing.

***Makes* 4 khachapuri**

For the dough

500g strong white flour, plus extra for dusting
1 tsp table salt
2 tsp instant yeast (optional)
150g whole milk
1 egg
100g tepid water
100g sourdough starter, fed with white flour (page 50) (optional)

1. Into a large bowl, weigh your flour and salt. For a yeasted loaf, add the yeast and rub together until combined. Then warm your milk in the microwave until tepid, and add this with your egg and water. For extra flavour, also add your sourdough starter at the same time. For a full sourdough, leave out the yeast and include the sourdough starter. Mix everything together until a rough dough forms.

2. You can knead at this stage, or you can autolyse (rest) for about 20–30 minutes before continuing so that the dough comes together easily.

3. Knead your dough for 5–10 minutes: you want it smooth and stretchy and so that it seems to absorb excess sticky dough from your hands and worktop. The slap and fold method (page 36) works well for this one. Alternatively, use a mixer or a no-knead method (page 45).

For the toppings

100g mozzarella, drained and finely chopped
100g *suglini*, alternatively feta or *twarog*, crumbled
4 eggs
freshly ground black pepper
a handful of chopped parsley, to garnish (optional)

4. Cover your bowl and leave your dough somewhere at room temperature. For yeasted breads, this will be 90 minutes or so. For sourdough, it will be 4–6 hours as long as it's over 20°C (68°F).

5. When you're about to start shaping, preheat your oven to 220°C (425°F) fan (240°C/465°F/gas 9) and line two baking trays with baking parchment. This is a good time to get your cheeses ready.

6. Scrape your dough onto a floured work surface. Add a little dust of flour on top, then press down gently so it's easier to divide. Use your scraper to cut it into four roughly equal pieces.

7. Flour well and use floured hands to press and stretch each piece gently into a larger, flatter piece of dough. Then use a rolling pin to flatten them some more, until it's at least a 20cm (8in) oval. Sprinkle with your cheese, then make a fold down both long ends, by about 2cm (¾in) to create a stuffed-crust ellipse. Then just pinch both ends together, twisting them round as you do so they stick. Set this on the prepared baking tray, then repeat with the remaining dough.

8. Bake for 15–20 minutes – you want your edges to be golden and fully cooked and the cheese to be fully melted, but not quite as dark as you'd want them to end up.

9. Then you've got two options. You can serve immediately or set them aside to cool and store them in an airtight container for up to a day. Either way, when you are ready to eat, crack the eggs into separate small cups. Remove your tray from the oven briefly, and add an egg on top of each boat. Stick back in for another 2 minutes, and repeat for your other tray. It's fine to open the door to check that the white is cooked and the yolk is just still a bit runny. Add salt, pepper and chopped parsley, if you like, to taste.

Bialy

Y

YS

S

(Polish White Rolls)

Though the two are often confused, these aren't bagels. There's no boiling, meaning they're crusty rather than chewy, and, crucially, they don't have a hole in them. No, that's not a hole, that's a depression, in the nice, undulating sense of the word. It's used to cradle delicious things that don't, therefore, get all over your baking tray.

The word *bialy* (roughly pronounced 'be-oway') means 'white' in Polish, but this isn't any reference to the whiteness of the bread, but rather shorthand for *bialystok kuchen*, or bread from the eastern Polish city of Bialystok. A significant emigration occurred from here, for obvious reasons, and it's fair to say that much of the *bialy's* current zeitgeist hails from New York City, and the popularity of its bakeries on social media. You could stick whatever you want in a *bialy*, and the hipster bakeries of today do. This recipe is a fairly traditional one, though: with fried onions and poppy seeds.

***Makes 12 wee* bialys**

500g strong white flour, plus extra for dusting
1½ tsp salt
2 tsp instant yeast (optional)
310g tepid water
100g sourdough starter, fed with white or mixed flours (page 50) (optional)

For the filling
2 brown onions
a good glug of oil (I use olive)
1 tbsp poppy seeds, plus more for topping
sea salt and freshly ground black pepper

1. In a large bowl, weigh your flour and your salt. For a yeasted loaf, add the yeast and rub together so that they are mostly combined, then add your tepid water. For extra flavour, add the sourdough starter to the mix with the water. For a full sourdough, leave out the yeast and include the sourdough starter. Mix everything together until roughly combined.

2. Leave to autolyse (rest) for 20 minutes before continuing.

3. Knead your dough – this is a dry dough, by comparison to most of mine, and therefore really loves a good pummelling. Give these a good working using the stretch and roll method (page 37) and keep going until the dough is soft and stretchy, about 10 minutes. Use a mixer with a dough hook, by all means.

4. Cover your bowl and leave your dough for 60–90 minutes if you used yeast. For sourdough, you're talking 4–6 hours at a warm room temperature or 2 hours at room temperature first, then stick the dough in the fridge.

5. While your dough is resting, you can make your filling. Finely slice your onions into thin lengths, then place them in a high-sided pan over a low heat with a glug of olive oil. Stir occasionally and keep reducing until they are golden and just starting to catch here and there on the bottom. Season well with salt and pepper, remove from the heat and stir in your poppy seeds. Set aside.

6. Scrape your dough out onto a lightly floured surface – you don't need much, and I actually prefer not to use any. Gently roll into a large sausage, just to make it easier to cut it into 12 equal pieces. Cut the sausage in half, then each piece in half again, then each of these should be cut into three pieces.

7. Shape each piece into a roll shape (page 40). Then, holding the lump in both hands, stick your thumbs into the middle, but not all the way through, and stretch out the sides gently, working your way all the way around, to create a depression. Repeat with the other pieces of dough. Arrange your *bialys* over two baking trays.

8. Fill each divot with your onion mixture. Use a wet finger just to dampen the exposed dough, and sprinkle some extra poppy seeds on top.

9. Leave them to prove for another 45–60 minutes for yeasted, or 2 hours for sourdough. Alternatively, cover with loose, oiled clingfilm (plastic wrap) and stick in a cold fridge for up to overnight or all day.

10. About 15 minutes before you plan on baking, preheat your oven to 200°C (400°F) fan (220°C/425°F/gas 7).

11. Transfer your trays to the hot oven, adding steam by putting a tray of ice or water in the bottom of the oven, for 25–30 minutes. The *bialys* should be golden, but your onions should not be so dark as to be burnt. Delicious warm, but the filling can take the skin off the roof of your mouth.

Borodinsky Bread

S

(Russian Rye Bread)

This beautiful dark brown slab is an explosion of earthy flavours: caraway, coriander and heavy, earthy rye, combined with a long, complex sourdough fermentation. It's also a bread with a great, if very sad, story, which – like most great stories – may not be true. Allegedly invented by the widow of a Russian general killed by Napoleon at the Battle of Borodino, the seeds signify the shot from the rifles of the enemy while the blackness of the loaf symbolizes her grief.

This bread is traditionally made with part of its dough pre-cooked, or scalded. This adds a stability and moisture-retaining property that we see in highly processed white breads, where it's often known as the Tangzhong method.

I'm going to combine this approach with a technique for making very light 100% wholemeal wheat breads, which is to sieve out the bran and scald this separately from the starch, similarly adding structure but also hydrating the bran well. Then the whiter dough is kneaded to develop the gluten without all that bran in the way; it's a win-win.

Makes 1 large loaf

400g rye flour
100g wholemeal wheat flour, plus extra for dusting
150g just-boiled water
50g cracked rye flakes or coarsely milled rye (optional)
1½ tsp salt
150g sourdough starter, fed with rye flour (page 50)
300g tepid water
40g treacle (molasses)
2 tsp caraway seeds
2 tsp coriander seeds
butter, for greasing

1. Start by weighing your rye flour and wholemeal flours into a large bowl – or do as I do, and weigh directly into a sieve that sits on top of the bowl. Sieve the flour to remove the vast majority of the bran, and tip the bran into a smaller bowl. Add your just-boiled water from the kettle to the bran, and stir to hydrate. Stir your cracked rye, if using, into the bran for a bit of extra texture, then set aside. Add your salt to your flours in the larger bowl. Add your starter, water and treacle, then mix with a wooden spoon into a dough. It might feel quite wet.

2. Give the dough an autolyse (rest) for 20–30 minutes and it will come together.

3. You will find kneading this dough in a traditional sense impossible – it won't stretch but will break. Having said that, give it a go; a mixer helps, but get your hands in it to feel what a really tenacious dough feels like – it's the opposite of elastic. With a few minutes of working, you should notice this becomes less so.

4. Rest for another hour somewhere warm, but not hot.

5. Lightly dampen a work surface, then turn your dough out onto it. Use a wet hand to spread the dough out as thinly as you can before it starts breaking. Use your hand to spread your bran paste over the top, distributing it as evenly as you can. Then sprinkle over your caraway and most of your coriander, leaving a little for the top. Use your scraper to roll everything up, like the lamination method (page 61). Then stick it all back in the bowl to rise for another hour.

6. Give it a stretch and fold (page 47), really just to distribute the ingredients, then rest for a final 2 hours (so 4 warm hours total).

7. It's now ready to shape (page 41). Turn the dough onto a floured surface, press it down lightly, then roll it up like a roulade or Swiss roll; try anything more elaborate and it will most likely break. Grease a 900g loaf tin, then place your bread inside. Brush the top with a little water, then sprinkle over your coriander, caraway and I like to add a bit of rye flour too.

8. Rest for a final 2 hours at room temperature, or stick in a cold fridge for 6–12 hours.

9. At least 15 minutes before you plan to bake, stick the oven on to 200°C (400°F) fan (220°C/425°F/gas 7). This one works well with a baking stone for some bottom heat, so make sure to preheat an extra 15 minutes, if using.

10. Don't score the top, just place directly in the oven for 30 minutes, adding steam at the beginning by adding some ice cubes or water to a baking tray in the bottom of the oven. Then bash out of the tin and bake another 10 minutes to crisp up the sides. Let cool completely before slicing. Serve with cream cheese and chopped chives, pepper and oil.

Proziaki

BP

(Polish Soda Rolls)

This is a quick bread to make. It's very much like the Scottish and Irish soda breads, but made from sour milk or, for the last century at least, kefir.

Kefir and I have a difficult relationship. I used to make it religiously, topping up those wee pearls, or grains, and keeping a perpetual fermented milk always ready for probiotic emergencies. The problem came with a realization: the marriage of a time-consuming and faffy process combined to create something that, if you didn't catch it at precisely the right stage of fermentation, wasn't that nice to drink.

Kefir might not have the probiotic benefits once it's been cooked in bread, but it gives a nice tang and, crucially, gives chemical lift when combined with bicarbonate of soda to create super-fluffy bread. And if, like me, you no longer make your own kefir, you can now buy it in every shop.

***Makes about 12 large* proziaki**

500g plain (all-purpose) flour, plus extra for dusting
1 tsp bicarbonate of soda (baking soda)
1 tsp table salt
380g kefir

1. In a large bowl, weigh the flour, bicarbonate of soda and salt. Add the kefir, then use a wooden spoon to mix into a wet dough. It should be wet and sticky and difficult to handle. If it sticks to you and everything, that's good.

2. Heavily flour a work surface – you don't want this sticking, but if it does, free it with your dough scraper and add more flour. Scrape your dough out onto the flour, then cover with plenty more.

3. Press down your dough with a floured hand until it's about 1cm (½in) thick. Then use a cookie cutter to cut circles out of the dough, and set these aside, adding more flour to stop sticking, if necessary

4. Heat a griddle or heavy-based, high-sided pan over a medium heat without greasing it. In batches, cook the *proziaki* for about 4–5 minutes on each side, or until speckled golden. Do not be tempted to press on the top or do anything that could alter their fragile developing structure as they cook.

5. Place the warm buns within the fold of a dish towel to cool – they shouldn't be enjoyed straight from the pan, as they'll still be cooking in the middle. Allow them to cool slowly. They should be served fresh, even just a touch warm still, within a few hours. Serve with butter, soups and cheese. If you've got leftovers, these toast quite well.

Kulich

Y

YS

S

(Easter Bread)

This is a Christian Orthodox Easter bread, noted for its height and grand, church-like domed top. It's one of a range of Easter breads eaten throughout Eastern Europe, and while it might look like panettone, this isn't at all the same. Handily, getting *kulich* right is considerably easier. It produces a more cake-like, tighter bread. It might not keep for weeks and months like a panettone, but it's awesome eaten fresh.

Its tall, slender shape can be achieved by baking in tin coffee cans, and you can certainly do this, much like Boston brown bread (page 220): just grease the bottom of the cans well, then line the sides with a roll of baking parchment, making sure it sticks out at the top. I've bought some small panettone cases, available lots of places online, and these also work well. If you like, remove them after baking, and then you can decorate and allow that icing to drip down the sides. Just don't forget the sprinkles.

Makes at least 6 small* kulich *(400g tin sized) or 2 large ones (for 500g panettone cases)

550g strong white flour, plus extra for dusting
1 tsp table salt
120g caster (superfine) sugar
2 tsp instant yeast (optional)
3 eggs
250g milk
100g sourdough starter, fed with white flour (page 50) (optional)
120g unsalted butter, softened
50g sour cream
100g raisins
neutral vegetable oil or melted butter, for shaping and greasing

For the topping
250g icing (confectioners') sugar
juice of 1 lemon
water to loosen, if required
ice cream sprinkles

1. I'll say at the start, if you fancy doing this as a full sourdough, it's a bit of an undertaking, requires lots of warmth and a very happy sourdough starter, which you should feed 6 hours before, ready for this bake. You have been warned. Yeasted works very well, and you can add some sourdough starter for flavour, if you like.

2. Weigh your flour, salt and sugar into a large bowl and combine these using your fingers. For a yeasted loaf, add the yeast, then break in the eggs. Warm your milk until about bathwater temperature and pour in. For extra flavour, add the sourdough starter with the milk. If I haven't put you off a full sourdough, add the sourdough starter instead of the yeast. Mix everything together until you've got a very rough dough.

3. It really helps to allow the dough to autolyse (rest) for 20–30 minutes.

4. Knead your dough – and it's fine to use an electric mixer (page 35). If it's sticky, that's OK; use your dough scraper to unstick your hands or the worktop. Once you've got a soft, stretchy, pliable smooth dough, you can add the soft butter – if it's hard, give it a blast in the microwave. Mix in your butter, add your sour cream and keep working until the dough is shiny, smooth and consistent.

5. Cover your bowl with a plate or damp dish towel and leave it somewhere warm for about an hour. Then it's time to laminate (page 61). We're going to turn the dough out onto an oiled surface and,

using oiled hands, spread it out as large as possible without breaking it. Sprinkle with the raisins, then roll it up.

6. Prove for another hour, or up to overnight in the fridge. If you're making a pure sourdough version without any commercial yeast, prove it in a very warm place for another 2–3 hours, then stick it in the fridge overnight, or rest it for 5–6 hours at room temperature.

7. Following your first prove, either prepare six used cooking tins by greasing the bottom and lining the sides with baking parchment, or you can use panettone cases. And if you don't mind your loaves a little squatter, just use cake tins.

8. Scrape your dough onto a lightly oiled surface. You'll find that if you cold-proved, you'll have a rather solid lump, and this is fine. Use your dough scraper to divide the dough into how many loaves you're making, then shape as boules (page 39) using oiled hands to stop sticking. Place these in your cases to prove.

9. Leave to prove in a warm place for another 60–90 minutes for a yeasted loaf. For sourdough, it will need 3–4 hours and you'll want somewhere properly warm, 25–28°C (77–82°F). You want to see a noticeable rise, and if it isn't half to two-thirds up the walls of the cases, it won't hit the top.

10. When the dough is nearly ready, preheat your oven to 180°C (350°F) fan (200°C/400°F/gas 6) for 15–20 minutes.

11. Bake for about 40 minutes for large loaves or 20–25 minutes for smaller rolls. They should be nice and golden when done. If making very large loaves, you might want to turn the oven down a tad and bake for as long as an hour to be sure they're cooked through.

12. Leave to cool. If you ice them warm, the icing will just melt everywhere. They should be completely cool before icing or slicing, not least because the centre will continue to cook once they're out of the oven, meaning that if you slice too soon, you'll have raw dough.

13. To make your icing, mix together your icing sugar and lemon juice. If it's really not coming together, add a touch of water. It should be thick and gloopy; when you lift a spoon out of it, it should gradually fall off it in clumps, rather than pour. Spoon your icing on, then scatter with sprinkles. Allow the icing to dry for a few hours before slicing.

Babka

Y

YS

S

(Chocolate and Hazelnut Loaf)

This is basically a loaf version of one of my favourite sweet buns: you'll find them at a local Glasgow bakery and patisserie, Broken Clock. It's a sweet, brioche-type dough, leavened with yeast for maximum softness and lightness (though feel free to add some sourdough for complexity). Then, the filling. It's chocolate, Nutella and whole roasted hazelnuts. Combine these, and you have the pinnacle of modern civilization.

Babka, the form that this loaf takes, is another Polish bread popularized and spread by Jewish communities across the world, especially in Israel and north-eastern USA. It has exploded in popularity today, I think, due to its Instagramability. While chocolate may not have been a traditional filling until the last hundred years or so, almost every babka made now has a chocolate filling. The reason? Cynically, I think contrast – it just looks stunning paired with the whiteness of the bread.

This pattern, one of many variants of babka, looks complex but is super-easy to achieve. Make a big rectangle, spread your chocolate filling over it, then roll it up like a Swiss roll or roulade. The bigger the rectangle, the more layers you'll have, and the more complex-looking the final shape. Then instead of slicing it into buns, you slice it lengthways, and splay it open. Twirl the two cut ends round each other, stick in a lined tin and hey presto: a babka.

Makes 1 large loaf

250g plain (all-purpose) flour, plus extra for dusting
250g strong white flour
1 tsp table salt
30g caster (superfine) sugar
2 tsp instant yeast (optional)
50g unsalted butter
275g whole or semi-skimmed milk
1 egg
zest of 1 orange
100g sourdough starter, fed with white flour (page 50) (optional)

1. Start by weighing your flours, salt and sugar into a large bowl. For a yeasted loaf, add the yeast and mix the ingredients together to distribute, then add your butter and give it a rub to create something akin to breadcrumbs. If you are planning to rest the dough overnight in the fridge, reduce the yeast to 1 teaspoon. Weigh your milk in another bowl or jug, then warm it in the microwave, or by placing it in a sink with some hot water; you want it tepid – neither hot nor cold. Add this to your flour with the egg and orange zest. For extra flavour, add your sourdough starter to this mixture. For a full sourdough, leave out the yeast but include the sourdough starter with the liquid ingredients, as usual. Combine to a dough.

2. Leave it to autolyse (rest) for 10–15 minutes if you've got time as it will make kneading easier. If you don't let it rest, it will take a bit longer to come together.

3. Get started with kneading. You can use a mixer or use a no-knead method (page 45). Kneading does help with the lightness of the dough here.

For the filling

50g salted or unsalted butter

50g dark chocolate

100g chocolate hazelnut spread (such as Nutella)

100g whole hazelnuts, roasted or blanched

4. Leave your dough to rest at room temperature for about 90 minutes. Alternatively, you can leave it overnight in the fridge. If you're planning on doing this, I recommend reducing the quantity of yeast to 1 teaspoon. Line a 900g loaf tin with a sheet of baking parchment or a paper loaf case.

5. To make your filling, heat your butter and chocolate together until just melted – I use a microwave but you could use a bain marie if you've got an aversion. Add your hazelnut spread, and mix to form a thin paste. Then gently crush your hazelnuts by bashing them with a rolling pin; just very gently so that you've still got some whole ones.

6. Turn your dough out onto a floured surface. Add more flour on top, shape into a rough square, then roll out into a big rectangle at least 30×40cm (12×16in). Spread over your filling, then sprinkle over your crushed hazelnuts, keeping back a small amount, especially any whole or nearly whole ones, for the top.

7. Roll the dough up like rolling a Swiss roll or a roulade. You should now have a long cylinder. Slice this cylinder down its length to open it in half, exposing all the cut edges. You can use a very sharp knife, a serrated knife or a dough scraper.

8. Line the two pieces up smooth side to smooth side (or back to back). Pinching or holding both ends, twist them around each other until you've got several spirals. Tuck the cut ends under to hide them, then scoop this into your tin. It can get messy and that's fine. Finally, sprinkle with more hazelnuts.

9. Prove for a final hour or so, or until it's noticeably risen. Stop the dough drying out by proving within a plastic bag or using a sheet of clingfilm (plastic wrap) placed loosely on top.

10. About 20 minutes before the dough is ready, preheat your oven to 180°C (350°F) fan (200°C/400°F/gas 6).

11. Bake for 30–40 minutes, or until you've got a deep golden colour and the chocolate is on the edge of going a bit darker than you'd like. Cool completely, if you can, before slicing, but eat fresh within 48 hours.

Ajdov Kruh

Y

YS

S

(Slovenian Buckwheat Bread)

Buckwheat's a strange one – it's not wheat at all. It's not even a cereal. It's made from the dried seeds of a plant related to rhubarb and knotweed. It's therefore not a grain and is gluten free. Yet it has a tasty, nutty flavour, and has lots of uses in breads. Personally, I use it most often for *galettes*, the savoury pancakes from northern France. Then once I've used half a packet, I'm looking for ways to use up the rest before the weevils get it.

Due to its low gluten content, it can be a struggle to get structure in your dough in a traditional sense, so this loaf is a mix of buckwheat, for soft nuttiness, and wheat for some lightness. But this does mean buckwheat makes excellent soda bread: follow any bannock or soda bread recipe using buckwheat, bicarbonate of soda and either yogurt or buttermilk, and you can have a great loaf.

This recipe is based on a traditional Slovenian staple, proposed by several people for the book. The walnuts are an addition for special occasions; a reminder of the ease with which those reading this recipe will be able to obtain walnuts, and probably not think twice about their cost or the richness they will impart to the bread.

Makes 1 large loaf

200g strong white flour, plus extra for dusting
1 tsp table salt
150g buckwheat flour
100g strong wholemeal flour
1 tsp instant yeast (optional)
300g tepid water
100g sourdough starter, fed with any flours (page 50) (optional)
60g just-boiled water
100g whole walnuts

1. Into a large bowl, put your white flour and salt, then sift your buckwheat flour and wholemeal on top. Keep the bran aside in another bowl. For a yeasted loaf, add your yeast and mix everything together. Combine some warm and cold water in a jug until it feels just warmer than tepid, about 25°C (77°F), then add this, too. For extra flavour, add your sourdough starter with the water. For a full sourdough, leave out the yeast but add the sourdough starter to the mix. Mix using a wooden spoon, a dough hook or your hands until you've got a lumpy dough.

2. Ideally, let your dough autolyse (rest) for about 20–30 minutes. This is an essential part of the no-knead method (page 45) and optional if you're planning to knead, but it really does help the dough come together. While you're waiting, add your just-boiled water to your bowl containing the bran, and mix to hydrate it.

3. Knead your main dough for 5–10 minutes, or until softer and more pliable. If going with the slap and fold technique (page 36), then you might find this one does break apart a bit, but even the action of unsticking from your surface is developing the gluten.

4. Leave your dough, covered, for 1 hour, and either do a stretch and fold (page 47) or a full lamination (page 61) to incorporate your bran and walnuts. Leave for a further 1 hour for a yeasted dough, or 3 at a warm room temperature for sourdough. Timings will vary depending on temperature. The dough should swell noticeably and be aerated when scooped out, but shouldn't collapse.

5. Flour a proving basket and a work surface, then turn out your dough. Shape your bread, trying to preserve as much of that aerated structure as possible. I like a boule for this one (page 39) but the shape is really up to you.

6. Stick your proving basket in the fridge, ideally. If you have your fridge set really cold (2°C/36°F), you can leave a yeasted dough overnight. A sourdough can be left for up to 24 hours in most fridges. Alternatively, leave the dough at room temperature and get ready to bake within 1 hour of shaping for a yeasted dough, 2–3 hours for sourdough.

7. Preheat your oven to 220°C (425°F) fan (240°C/465°F/gas 9). This loaf works best at home using a covered cast iron pan, but you can bake on a tray with some added ice or water.

8. Once proved, turn your loaf out into your cast iron pan or baking tray. Score the top (page 43). Turn the oven temperature down to 200°C (400°F) fan (220°C/425°F/gas 7) and bake for 20 minutes with the lid on, then 20 minutes with the lid off. Alternatively, bake on a tray or preheated stone with the addition of steam.

Langos

(Hungarian Fried Bread)

Y

YS

S

As a Scotsman, deep-fried bread is bound to get my attention. Then what about deep fried potato bread with garlic, then topped with sour cream and cheese? Yes, yes, yes. That's *langos* (lan-gosh). To my Scottish eyes, it's as if a tattie scone made love to a pizza in a deep-fat fryer.

This recipe wasn't always deep-fried – *langos* actually means 'flame', and up until the late 19th century, rural Hungarian households would bring their larger loaves to be baked in huge communal ovens, only once a week or so. While the oven was heating up, small pieces of the dough would be pinched off and made into flatbreads, which would be baked under the intense heat of the flames. The breads would be topped and eaten for lunch by the bakers and their families.

As one tradition has evidently faded, another one remains. And whoever came up with the idea of deep-frying them was obviously a genius. Maybe they'd been to Scotland.

***Makes 4 larger or 6 medium* langos**

400g plain (all-purpose) flour, plus extra for dusting
1 tsp table salt
2 tsp instant yeast (optional)
100g milk
150g tepid water
50g leftover mashed potato or cooked potato (optional)
100g sourdough starter, fed with white flour (page 50) (optional)
at least 300g frying oil, such as rapeseed, for deep-frying

For the topping
4–6 heaped tbsp sour cream
about 200g melting cheese, often *trappista*, but use widely available Edam or Cheddar, or torn fresh mozzarella
2 garlic cloves
2 tbsp olive oil

1. Into a large bowl, weigh your flour and salt. For a yeasted loaf, add the yeast and rub the ingredients together until combined. Then warm your milk in the microwave, or if you don't have one, cut cold milk with hot water so that the final liquid portion is warm. Add your milk and water to the flour together with your leftover mash. For extra flavour, add the sourdough starter with the milk and water. For a full sourdough, leave out the yeast and include the sourdough starter. Mix everything together until roughly combined.

2. If you want to reduce the kneading stages, you can autolyse (rest) the dough for 10–20 minutes at this stage.

3. Knead your dough, unless you want to follow a no-knead method (page 45). You want it smooth and lump-free and so that it forms a ball that removes excess dough from your work surface and from your hands. If you've autolysed, knead for at least a minute. If you've not, give it 5–10. For this one, the English stretch and roll technique works well (page 37).

4. Cover your bowl and leave your dough somewhere at room temperature for 90 minutes for a yeasted dough. If you're going full sourdough, then leave it somewhere warm for 4 hours. If sourdough, prove for 2 hours in a warm place first, then place in the fridge for up to a day.

5. There is no second prove here, so you've got to be ready with your toppings – get your sour cream out of the fridge, and grate your cheese. Crush your garlic (finely chop then scrape with the side of the knife if you don't have a crusher) and then mix this with your olive oil. Set aside.

6. Scrape your dough out onto a floured surface. Cut into four or six lumps and sprinkle with more flour. Flatten each one out with your hands or a rolling pin, until they are 5mm (¼in) thick or less and about 20cm (8in) in diameter. Make sure they're well floured and set them aside to rest as you heat the oil.

7. Get your oil into a heavy-based, preferably high-sided pan and onto a low heat. You want to bring it up to 180°C (356°F) – I would not recommend attempting this without a probe thermometer, as oil that gets too hot can lead to kitchen fires and a burned *langos*. Alternatively, use a deep-fat fryer.

8. Fry for 2–3 minutes on each side – you're aiming for deep golden. Use a slotted spoon to turn and retrieve it, and place on a piece of kitchen paper. Get the next one on, then you can top the first with your garlic oil, then a heaped tablespoon of sour cream, then grated cheese on top. Serve hot.

Potica

Y

(Slovenian Nut Roll)

How do you choose two breads from Slovenia when every country deserves its say? I tried to resist, but *potica* (po-teet-sa) ticked a few boxes: first, it's a non-breakfast-targeted enriched loaf. It fills a necessary role: serve this any time from mid-afternoon tea to a post-dinner treat with or without coffee, and it goes down exceptionally well.

The second reason is that, of the various breads baked like a Swiss roll, then sliced into stunning contrasting slices, this is my particular favourite. Alternatives might be a traditional Polish poppy seed bread, which is delicious but texturally divisive, or modern savoury bread roulades, which are just weird gimmicks written with the aim of finding the next viral video.

This bread, everyone loves because, really, it's an enriched cake. Dusting it with icing sugar while it's still warm turns the crust into something that sort of melts in the mouth.

Makes 1 large loaf

450g strong white flour, plus extra for dusting
1 tsp table salt
2 tsp instant yeast
50g caster (superfine) sugar
200g milk
1 large egg
2 egg yolks
2 tsp vanilla extract
80g unsalted butter, softened
a little icing (confectioners') sugar, for dusting

For the filling
2 egg whites
50g caster (superfine) sugar
100g salted butter, very soft
100g raisins, chopped
300g walnuts or pecans, finely chopped
50g honey
1 tsp ground cinnamon (optional),

1. Start with the dough. In a large bowl, weigh your flour, salt, yeast and caster sugar. Mix to combine the ingredients. Heat the milk in the microwave until it's a little warmer than tepid, then add this, along with your egg, egg yolks and vanilla. Mix everything together until you've got a dough.

2. Leave your dough to autolyse (rest) for 10–15 minutes, or longer if you can, which will make the next phase easier.

3. Give the dough a good knead for 5–10 minutes. You could use a mixer, but this works with any method of kneading (page 35). Once it's getting to a smooth consistency, add your butter, and work it through until combined.

4. Put your dough back in the bowl and cover with clingfilm (plastic wrap), a dish towel or a plastic bag. Leave it for 60–90 minutes until it's noticeably puffy and about doubled in size. Alternatively, you could do this in a cold fridge overnight.

5. During that prove, make your filling. First, whisk your egg whites (reserved from the yolks above) until they resemble stiff peaks, or close to them. Add the sugar and whisk again until stiff. Then soften your butter, if necessary, in a microwave, and add this with the raisins, finely chopped nuts, honey and cinnamon, if using. Combine into a lumpy paste, then set aside.

6. Next, flour a work surface, and scrape your proven dough out onto it. Add some more flour on top, and use the edges of your hands to make it a rectangle shape. Use a rolling pin to roll it out into a large rectangle, at least 60×40cm (24×16in). The bigger you go, the tighter your spiral will be and the better the final effect. Add flour as you go if you feel it sticking.

7. Line a baking tray with baking parchment. Spread your filling over your large rectangle, nearly to the edges. Working from the side nearest you, roll your rectangle up into a spiral, as tightly as you can. If the last little flap won't stick, run a wet finger down the edge, and then roll to place the seam on the bottom.

8. Lift your spiral onto your prepared baking tray, cover with a dish towel and leave to prove for a final hour or so, or overnight in the fridge as long as your fridge is set cold.

9. About 15 minutes before you plan on baking, preheat your oven to 200°C (400°F) fan (220°C/425°F/gas 7) .

10. Bake your loaf for about 35–40 minutes. The ends might leak a little, and that's OK – the sliced ends are the baker's privilege. A mid-golden brown is perfect here – once it's done, let it cool. While still a little warm, dust with plenty of icing sugar.

11. Only slice once it's completely cool, and then only cut as many slices as you need. Stored in an airtight container, it will keep for several days. You can just slice the cut-end off if it gets dry – but one nice thing I've done is to dust this dry end with extra icing sugar and blowtorched it. Awesome.

Houska

Y

YS

S

(Czech Plaited Rolls)

I'd been making *houska* for years and not knowing it: these are the ubiquitous Czech plaited rolls, perfect for accompanying a fancy dinner. They can be made using a simple three-strand plait, such as we use for my daughter's pigtails, and for *challah* and *kolach* (page 135). But these are rolls – making a batch of 12 would mean dividing your dough into 36 roughly equal pieces prior to plaiting. What? No.

Instead, there's an ingenious way to make a plaited roll with just a single strand: make a sausage, then add a loop to make a P shape. Stick the tail through the loop, twist your loop once or twice, then tuck your tail into the hole. Voilà – a single strand plait.

This can be done quickly and easily, and you've changed what is quite a basic white dough into something stunning. I've added an egg wash for a wood-like deep sheen, and given you a choice of topping: poppy seed is the obvious, but if you're a caraway fan, the traditional caraway seed and sea salt is delicious.

***Makes 12* houska**

500g strong white flour, plus extra for dusting
1 tsp table salt
2 tsp instant yeast (optional)
340g tepid water
100g sourdough starter, fed with white flour (page 50) (optional)
1 egg, for brushing
a pinch of sea salt
caraway seeds or poppy seeds, for topping

1. In a large bowl, weigh your flour and salt. For a yeasted loaf, add the yeast and rub the ingredients together until combined. Then add your tepid water. For extra flavour, add the sourdough starter with the water. For a full sourdough, leave out the yeast and use the sourdough starter instead. Mix everything together until roughly combined.

2. If you wish, leaved the dough to autolyse (rest) for 10–20 minutes before continuing. This will reduce the amount of kneading you need to do.

3. Knead your dough for 5–10 minutes. This is a relatively soft dough, so the slap and fold (page 36) method will work, or you could use an electric mixer (page 35). Alternatively, you can use a no-knead technique (page 45).

4. Cover your bowl and leave your dough somewhere at room temperature. For yeasted breads, this will be 90 minutes or so, and for sourdough, try to heat it slightly to about 25°C (77°F) and give it 4 hours, with a couple of stretches and folds (page 47) during the prove.

5. Once your first prove is done, it's time to shape. Scrape your dough out onto a lightly floured surface. Use a dough scraper to cut it into

12 roughly equal pieces – use a set of scales if you're that sort of person (aiming for about 79g each piece). Take a piece at a time and press your lump down flat, then roll it up. Use flat hands, like the last stage of baguette shaping (page 42), to roll into a sausage about 30cm (12in) long. Line a baking tray with baking parchment.

6. Follow the photos opposite to make a P shape out of the dough, then poke the tail of your P through the loop. Twist the loop twice, and then tuck your tail into the hole. You can do this in a matter of seconds – just 11 more to go.

7. Place on the prepared baking tray, and leave to prove for at least another 1 hour for yeasted bread or 2 hours for sourdough, or until they're noticeably puffed up. Alternatively, prove them overnight in the fridge, but make sure it's very cold, especially if you're using yeasted dough.

8. About 15 minutes before you plan on baking, preheat your oven to 210°C (410°F) fan (230°C/450°F/gas 8). Prior to baking, make an egg wash by whisking your egg with a little salt. Brush this carefully on your proved rolls, then sprinkle on either poppy seeds or your mixture of salt and caraway.

9. Bake for 20–25 minutes, adding steam if you can by putting a tray of ice or water in the bottom of the oven, or until a deep, dark golden brown. They will soften as they cool.

NORTHERN EUROPE & SCANDINAVIA

NORTHERN EUROPE & SCANDINAVIA

Laugenbrot

Y

YS

S

(Lye Rolls)

The pretzel in Germany is as varied as all of bread itself, it seems. It was hard to narrow it down to a single recipe: first, it made sense to go for the *laugenbrezel* – what you might think of as the traditional, deep-brown, salted, soft pretzel, served alongside a half litre or two of cold Pilsner. But simplifying this, you get *laugenbrot*, a slightly lighter roll version, and I thought it was more adaptable and an easier introduction, skipping a twirly shaping step.

The thing that links all these recipes is the process: that deep, dark hue is only achievable by dipping your dough in an alkaline solution just before baking. The alkaline speeds up the Maillard reactions, which are browning reactions between sugar and protein that create savoury deliciousness.

We're not going to use lye, which is traditional and safe in the right hands, but you'll understand I can't guarantee yours are the right hands. We're going to use bicarb, or baking soda, but we're going to bake it in the oven first. This causes a chemical reaction that turns it from sodium bicarbonate (pH 8.5) to sodium carbonate (pH 11.4), also known as washing soda. This is plenty strong enough to give a deep, dark hue. It's still an irritant, though, and you should only touch it with gloves or metal implements.

Makes 12 sandwich rolls

400g strong white flour
1 tsp table salt
1 tsp instant yeast (optional)
260g tepid water
100g sourdough starter, fed with white flour (page 50) (optional)
sea salt, poppy seeds or sesame seeds, for sprinkling

For the bath
50g bicarbonate of soda (baking soda)
1 litre cold water

1. Into a large bowl, weigh your flour, salt and yeast. For a yeasted loaf, add your tepid water. For extra flavour, also add your sourdough starter. For a full sourdough, leave out the yeast and add the sourdough starter with the water. Mix together into a very dry dough. It will take a while to form – I tend to use an electric mixer (page 35).

2. Autolyse your dough for 10–20 minutes – and you'll thank yourself when you start kneading as this one requires a good knead.

3. Knead your dough for 10 minutes, or until the dough is properly shiny and smooth. Use an electric mixer, not so slow that the motor sounds like it's struggling, but not so fast that the dough is becoming really hot in there. Otherwise, the English knead (page 37) will work well.

4. Return your dough to the bowl, cover and leave it for 90 minutes at room temperature. Or, if you're going sourdough, 3–4 hours at a warm room temperature, such as up on top of the fridge (there's no need to stretch and fold this dough). You can equally either prove overnight or all day in the fridge, but if sourdough, give it 90–120 minutes out of the fridge first.

5. This dough is so dry you probably won't need any flour for dusting. Scrape your dough out onto a work surface and ease into a long sausage shape. Use your scraper to chop this into 12 equal pieces – you can weigh them if you want, but I can't be bothered. Prepare two baking trays by lining them with baking parchment.

6. Shape your doughs. This is a dry dough and so great to practise making rolls (page 40) or little batards (page 41). Place them on your paper with plenty of space between and leave to rise for another 30 minutes, or an hour for sourdough. This gives you time to clear some space in the freezer: freezing is an optional step that helps them hold their shape much better in their soda bath.

7. As they freeze, preheat your oven to 200°C (400°F) fan (220°C/425°F/gas 7). Weigh your bicarbonate of soda (baking soda) and place this in a roasting tray, then stick it inside your preheating oven. Leave it there for 20 minutes and it will change to sodium carbonate. After 20 minutes, remove it from the oven and pour into a bowl containing a litre of cold water and stir to dissolve.

8. Using a gloved hand and a dough scraper, or a stainless steel slotted spoon or spatula, lift each frozen pretzel off the tray and into your soda solution. Let them bob around for 20–30 seconds, and then remove, letting any excess drip away. Place each back on your baking tray. You can re-use the baking parchment.

9. Use a lame or razor to make cuts in your *laugenbrot* – round ones tend to have crosses, and longer ones have many parallel slashes. Sprinkle with plenty of salt or seeds. Place your trays in the oven to bake for about 15–20 minutes. They should be a deep and shiny golden brown, with great contrast 'ears'. Let them cool until they're warm before eating.

Brussels Waffles

Y

I've thought about this a lot and decided I love waffles for three reasons ...

The tool in which we make them: a waffle iron. In its true form, it is a heavy clamp made of cast iron. It has long handles so that it can be projected over an open fire or fireplace. The deep indentations allow penetration of the heat into every part of the dough, so it cooks quickly. Waffle irons are ingenious, thousand-year-old inventions, a primitive super-fast oven of sorts. So I couldn't own a fancy modern waffle iron that breaks or starts blowing fuses within a few years, I had to get one that will still function when I am long gone.

Then the science. This is a yeasted Belgian waffle – which generally fall into two camps. The Liège-type doughs, which are indeed doughs, which you smoosh between your waffle iron and are more of a handheld snack than dessert or breakfast. Or the Brussels type, more flaky and crisp, and more familiar to most of the world. You could use a modern American quick waffle recipe using chemical agents, but if you can just have the foresight to decide you want waffles for breakfast the night before, you can make something that's incomparable using yeast (while you could use sourdough, I wouldn't here).

This batter might not seem full of bubbles, but those yeasts have been working all night to ferment it, and while the batter is too wet to hold much air in its raw state, there's still loads of carbon dioxide dissolved in it. Yes, it may be floury gloop, but it's fizzy floury gloop. As any liquid heats, CO_2 that's dissolved in it escapes. This science helps our bubbleless, bicarbless Brussels batter swell.

And finally, the deliciousness. Need I say more?

Makes 10 waffles

400g whole milk
2 large eggs
40g caster (superfine) sugar
⅓ tsp table salt
90g unsalted butter
300g plain (all-purpose) flour
1 tsp instant yeast
butter and icing (confectioners') sugar, for serving
or soft fruit, whipped cream and hazelnut chocolate spread
oil, for greasing

1. Start the night before you want to make your waffles. First, weigh your milk, cold from the fridge, into a large bowl. Add your eggs, sugar and salt and whisk to combine.

2. Warm your butter until just melted – I use a microwave – then whisk this into your liquid mixture. Finally, add the flour and yeast and whisk to combine into a thick batter.

3. Loosely cover your bowl with a plastic bag or piece of clingfilm (plastic wrap) and leave it to stand at room temperature overnight. Despite the milk being cold, it will ferment plenty by the morning.

4. The next morning, your batter might be very bubbly, or uneven, or split, so give it a gentle mix with a whisk or fork to make an even batter. If you're worried you're going to be unable to pour it, then add a touch more water.

5. Heat your waffle maker as per your manufacturer's instructions or, if going old school, like me, lightly grease your waffle iron with a little heat-stable oil (I use rapeseed) and place over a medium heat – cast iron even works with induction! Get both sides hot enough so you can't hold your hand just above them for more than a few seconds – (about 180°C/356°F) on an infrared thermometer, if you have one.

6. Pour in your batter so that it fills up one side of the waffle maker, then close the lid, and cook for 4–6 minutes total, flipping halfway through. You can open the waffle maker to ensure the waffle is golden brown.

7. Turn out of the waffle maker and repeat until no batter is left. Serve as you cook, ideally, but waffles can be stacked and re-heated in the toaster. If storing for later, refrigerate in an airtight container and toast to order.

Vollkornbrot

S

(Full Grain Bread)

Schwarzbrot (black bread) – like this full-grain bread – is a vast repertoire of deeply malty, Germanic loaves. These breads are high in rye, usually of sourdough fermentation and fairly dense things. If you're after a very typical rye- and caraway-flavoured *schwarzbrot*, I'd suggest trying my recipe for Borodinsky (page 143), but leave out the coriander seeds.

Vollkornbrot isn't 'wholegrain' but 'full grain' – meaning it contains whole, unmilled grains, giving it a real bite that goes very well with seeds. Whichever unmilled 'berries' you use will depend on what you can get: I like to combine my rye with ancient grains, but wheat, rye or others will be fine. Then, in my research for this bread, I found a variation online that contained beer, and couldn't resist giving this a go too: evidently this could go any way depending on which beer you use, but a German dunkel or English stout is a good fit for a roasty note.

Makes 1 large, long loaf

100g whole rye, wheat, spelt, einkorn or emmer 'berries' (grain)
250g cracked or crushed wheat, rye or ancient grain berries (cracked grain)
300g just-boiled water
500g wholemeal rye flour
200g sunflower seeds
50g sesame seeds
2 tsp table salt
100g sourdough starter, fed with rye flour (page 50)
250g water
500ml stout or dunkel, or another malty beer (avoid hoppy beers)
rolled oats, for sprinkling
butter, for greasing

1. Start at least 6 hours before, when you feed your starter. If your starter has been a bit neglected, don't worry. At the same time, place your whole and cracked berries in a bowl, and pour over your just-boiled water. Cover, and set this aside to absorb, up to a day ahead.

2. When your starter is happy, weigh your flour, seeds and salt into a large bowl, and mix them together to distribute. Add your starter, water, beer and soaked berries, along with the liquid, and stir everything to combine. It will feel like a batter.

3. Cover your bowl and leave it to prove for about 6–8 hours, and it should rise magnificently. At this point, I like to fridge the whole bowl, creating a more solid structure and giving me flexibility about when I want to bake. You can leave it in the fridge for 2–48 hours – the longer, the better.

4. Grease and line a long loaf tin with baking parchment. Then, depending on your grains and how much they've absorbed, you'll have something that's between a batter and a dough. If it's truly liquid, use your scraper to scrape it directly into the tin and flatten using floured hands. If it's a dough, turn it out onto a floured surface, and gently ease it into a long shape the size of your tin. Use your scraper to lift it in.

5. Sprinkle generously with rolled oats, and preheat your oven to 160°C (325°F) fan (180°C/350°F/gas 4) for about 20 minutes as your dough rests. Bake for an hour, then turn down to 140°C (275°F) fan (160°C/325°F/gas 4). Bake for a final 30 minutes, then remove, bash out the tin and let cool completely before slicing. Freezes excellently, sliced.

Suikerbrood

Y

YS

S

(Dutch Caramel Bread)

Biologically speaking, lots of sugar and dough don't typically mix that well – after a point, the concentration of sugar starts to inhibit the yeast, rather than fuel it. Then sugar in very high concentrations draws water from the yeast cells, killing the cells and not allowing the spores to grow.

It can therefore be hard to make yeasted breads very sweet. In *suikerbrood*, a Dutch bread from Friesland, in the north, the problem is solved by using sugar pearls, which are folded through the dough in a spiral shape. While they'll partially dissolve to sweeten the bread itself, they form lovely caramelly lumps during the baking process, which then become divots to fill with butter.

It's usually made with ginger, but you can leave it out if you're not a fan. It's an essential part of the flavour for me, even to the extent that this recipe contains two sorts: dried ginger, a whole different beast from the fresh stuff, and the syrup from preserved ginger. Both are optional, and you could use one without the other if you prefer.

Makes 1 large loaf

400g strong white flour, plus extra for shaping
1 tsp table salt
½ tsp ground ginger (optional)
2 tsp instant yeast (optional)
40g unsalted butter, plus extra for greasing
250g milk, plus extra
1 large egg, plus 1 egg for brushing
40g syrup from preserved ginger (optional, or substitute 20g each of water and caster/superfine sugar)
100g sourdough starter, fed with white flour (page 50) (optional)

For the middle
100g butter, for brushing
1–2 tsp ground cinnamon
150g pearl sugar (Belgian waffle sugar), plus extra for topping

1. For a yeasted loaf, start by weighing your flour, salt, ground ginger, if using, and yeast into a large bowl. If you are planning to leave the dough overnight in the fridge, reduce the quantity of yeast to 1 teaspoon. Add your butter, then rub this in roughly so that it's mostly combined. Weigh your milk in another bowl or jug, then warm it in the microwave or by placing it in a sink with some hot water. You want it tepid – neither hot nor cold. Add this to your flour, crack in an egg and add your syrup. For extra flavour, add some sourdough starter with the liquid ingredients. For a full sourdough, omit the yeast and add the sourdough starter with the wet ingredients. Combine everything to a sticky dough.

2. Leave it to autolyse (rest) for 10–20 minutes if you've got time, then get started with kneading. This is a sticky dough and the slap and fold method will work well (page 36). Alternatively, you can use a mixer for up to 10 minutes until smooth, or use a no-knead method (page 45): they're all fine.

3. Leave your dough to rest at room temperature for about 90 minutes. Alternatively, you can leave it overnight in the fridge – and you'll have reduced the yeast quantity.

4. Grease a 900g loaf tin with plenty of butter – make sure you smear it right down into the corners of the tin to prevent sticking. Scrape your dough out onto a lightly floured surface, then grab the corners and ease into a rectangle shape. Add a bit more flour on top, and roll it out so that it's the width of your tin and as long as you can bear: the longer it is, the better a spiral effect you'll get.

5. Heat your butter until just melted using a microwave (or in a pan if you don't have one) and brush your rectangle with the melted butter. Sprinkle over your cinnamon and your pearl sugar, then roll up your spiral and pop it into your greased tin, seam-side down.

6. Cover your dough with a plastic bag or a sheet of oiled clingfilm (plastic wrap), then prove your dough for another hour or so at room temperature. Overnight or all day in the fridge is fine, as long as you've got a very cold fridge.

7. About 15 minutes before it's ready, preheat your oven to 200°C (400°F) fan (220°C/425°F/gas 7).

8. Don't score this one: instead, brush with a little egg wash, and sprinkle with a touch more pearl sugar. Bake for 40 minutes or so, or until a deep golden brown and cooked through. Let cool before slicing, but it's best eaten fresh.

Oliebollen

(Dutch Doughnuts)

Y

YS

S

I feel the frustration from the pedants that I stuck English Muffins in the American chapter but these doughnuts are over here, hanging out with the rye breads and cinnamon buns. Except these aren't doughnuts in the traditional sense, but *oliebollen*, or oil balls: you can see why the Dutch settlers, who introduced them to the Americas, changed the name.

This is the original doughnut as we know it today, and was preceded by the equally squelchy sounding *oliekoek* (oily cake). If I may be so bold, I think that they demonstrate that society is the primary driver of the health of a nation, regardless of wealth or access to food: for most in Holland, these are still a treat enjoyed on occasion. They are not an aspirational part of everyday life or a daily comfort from the stresses of work or family, nor the target of multinational sales targets or the feature of a start-up business that people will only applaud. This recipe may be for the precursor to the confectionery that the creators of *the Simpsons* decided symbolized an obese culture of convenience, but that's not the doughnut's fault, nor the people who consume them (including me), but the society that envelops them. A society that the rest of the world is drifting towards.

So make these, on occasion, and really, really enjoy them, because they are delicious. But please don't proclaim they're the 'next big thing', don't start writing a business plan and don't even think about putting together the funding for a street food stall.

Makes 12 doughnuts

500g plain (all-purpose) flour
1 tsp table salt
2 tsp instant yeast (optional)
100g sourdough starter, fed with white flour (page 50) (optional)
250g whole milk
1 large egg
1 tart apple, such as a Granny Smith
150g currants or sultanas (optional)
at least 1 litre vegetable oil
200g caster (superfine) sugar, for dusting
1 tsp ground cinnamon, for dusting

1. Start by weighing your flour and salt into a large bowl. For a yeasted loaf, mix in the yeast. If you are planning to leave the dough overnight in the fridge, reduce the quantity of yeast to 1 teaspoon. For extra flavour, add the sourdough starter. For a full sourdough, leave out the yeast and add the sourdough starter.

2. Weigh your milk in another bowl or jug, then warm it in the microwave or by placing it in a sink with some hot water. You want it tepid – neither hot nor cold. Add this to your flour. Then crack in the egg. Peel and coarsely grate in your apple, and combine to a dough.

3. Leave it to autolyse (rest) for 10–20 minutes if you've got time. Then knead your dough until smooth, about 10 minutes. This is a sticky dough and the slap and fold method will work well (page 36) or you can use a mixer or use a no-knead method (page 45). Towards the end of kneading, or after your first stretch and fold if going no-knead, add your dried fruit, if using. Continue kneading to distribute it equally.

4. Leave your dough to rest at room temperature for about 90 minutes, or for a full sourdough, this will be about 4 hours. Alternatively, you can leave it overnight or all day in the fridge – and you'll have reduced the yeast quantity if yeasted, and for sourdough make sure to give them a couple of hours at a warm room temperature first.

5. Line a tray or baking tray with some baking parchment and brush over some oil. Scrape your dough out onto a lightly oiled surface, then add a little more oil and ease into a sausage shape. This allows you to easily divide your dough into 12 by cutting it in half, then each half in half again, then each quarter into three.

6. Shape each lump into a rough ball – these don't have to be exact. Then place them on your oiled, lined tray, and once they're all done, cover with some oiled clingfilm (plastic wrap) or with a loose plastic bag, and leave to prove for another hour, or 2 for sourdough. Overnight or all day in the fridge is fine, again, as long as you've got a very cold fridge: if these overprove, you'll have very flat doughnuts.

7. When your doughs are ready, mix your sugar and cinnamon in a bowl and set aside. Line a plate with a couple of sheets of kitchen paper and set this aside. Add your oil to a wide, high-sided pan and place over a low–medium heat. Heat slowly, checking regularly using a thermometer, to hit 160°C (320°F). Add as many doughnuts as you can safely fit in at a time: they should sizzle and puff, gradually turning brown under the oil. After 3–4 minutes, they'll be golden brown and may even flip over naturally, as they puff and become top heavy. Use a wooden spoon or your thermometer to give them a helping hand.

8. Another 3–4 minutes, then lift out with a slotted spoon and check that the oil hasn't got too hot or too cold before adding your next batch. Allow your doughnuts to drain on the kitchen paper for a couple of minutes, before rolling or tossing them in the cinnamon sugar. They can now be set aside to cool for as long as you can bear. Best served within a few hours.

Knäckebröd

S

(Crispbread)

Here's a sourdough-only recipe, and if you've not got a starter going reliably enough for bread yet, this is a recipe with which to build your confidence. The starter in this case can be inactive, it can be neglected, it can be straight from the fridge, split and suspect, and these crackers will still work out.

These crispbreads – *knekkebrød*, *knäckebröd*, *knækbrød* or something else, depending on your language – are about as basic and humble a cracker as you can make, but that doesn't stop modern companies profiteering on ancient tradition. These are ridiculously expensive to buy, but very simple to make. Indeed, bake large batches and gift them to people at Christmas, and you'll probably save yourself enough to buy your own knobbly rolling pin – a *kruskavel*. Despite the evidence you see here, I don't actually own a *kruskavel*. I found that one of my daughter's wooden Play-Doh toys was the perfect shape for making crispbread, and she's not even noticed it's gone.

Makes 6 tray-sized crispbreads, or over 40 little rounds

150g wholemeal rye flour, plus extra for rolling
150g unbleached strong white flour
1 tsp table salt
175g tepid water
150g sourdough starter, fed with any flours (page 50)

1. In a large bowl, weigh your two flours and your salt. Mix these to combine. Add your water and starter and mix together until you've got a stiff dough. Cover the bowl and leave for about 6 hours at room temperature. If you've got a very active starter, you could start to roll after 4 hours or so, or if you're a very bad starter parent, then give it 8 or more.

2. Preheat your oven to as hot as it goes – usually 230°C (445°F) fan (250°C/480°F/gas 9). If you've got a baking stone, now's the time to break it out and get it properly preheated for half an hour. If you don't, trays are fine.

3. Flour your work surface using rye flour, then scrape your dough out onto it. Chop your dough into six roughly equal chunks – there's no need for precision here. Dust a chunk in flour, then use a rolling pin to roll it out as big as you can – you want them really thin. Then you can either cut into rounds with a cookie cutter and place on baking parchment, or you can roll your dough around your rolling pin and unfurl it onto your baking tray for baking as one large cracker.

4. Either lift your baking parchment and slide it as a whole onto your hot stone, or slide a baking tray underneath and transfer into the oven to bake for 6–8 minutes, or until they are turning a dark golden brown – watch, as they can burn at the edges very easily. Shape the next as your last one bakes, and repeat until you've got none left.

White Kanelbullar

Y

(Cinnamon Buns)

The next two recipes go together. They are the superstar Swedish buns, and I had to give you both. They are markedly different, so I have shaped them so – this one a spiral and the next a knot – but feel free to mix and match elements of each recipe that you like to create something in between.

For this first example, I wanted to create the whitest, softest, most cloud-like bun imaginable: sweet enough to be considered a sweet bun, but without being drenched in syrup or icing like its British or American counterparts. If your only experience of *kanelbullar* – or the cinnamon bun – comes from IKEA, I'm so excited for the joy you're about to experience.

Makes 12 buns

500g plain (all-purpose) flour, plus extra for dusting
1 tsp table salt
40g caster (superfine) sugar
2 tsp instant yeast
40g unsalted butter
280g whole milk
1 large egg

For the filling
50g butter, soft or melted
150g light soft brown sugar
15g ground cinnamon
1 egg, for brushing
pearl sugar (Belgian waffle sugar), for sprinkling (optional)

1. Start by weighing your flour, salt, sugar and yeast into a large bowl. If you are planning to leave the dough overnight in the fridge, reduce the quantity of yeast to 1 teaspoon. You'll notice I don't recommend sourdough for this one. Add your butter, then rub this in roughly so that it's mostly combined, but you don't have to be super-conscientious. Weigh your milk in another bowl or jug, then warm it in the microwave or by placing it in a sink with some hot water. You want it tepid – neither hot nor cold. Add this and your egg to your mix and combine to a dough.

2. If you've got time, leave it to autolyse for 10–20 minutes. Then get started with kneading. Any method will work, including using an electric mixer (page 35) or using a no-knead method (page 45).

3. Leave your dough to rest at room temperature for about 90 minutes or so. Alternatively, you can leave it overnight in the fridge – in which case you'll have reduced the yeast quantity.

4. Line a roasting tray with a sheet of baking parchment. Lightly flour a work surface and turn your dough out onto it. Add a little more flour on top, then, using floured hands, stretch out the corners of your dough to make a square shape. Gently roll your dough out until it's at least 40cm (16in) square. The bigger your square, the tighter your spiral is going to be.

5. If your filling butter isn't soft, give it a buzz in the microwave. Brush this over the top of your dough, then scatter over your sugar and cinnamon. Roll up your big rectangle like a roulade, as tight as you can, and seal with the seam on the bottom. Use your dough scraper to cut your roulade in half, then each half in half again. Then cut each quarter into thirds: you should now have 12 buns.

6. Place your buns in your lined roasting tray, and cover with kitchen foil. Prove your buns for another hour. Overnight or all day in the fridge is fine as long as you've got a very cold fridge.

7. About 15 minutes before they're ready, preheat your oven to 190°C (375°F) fan (210°C/410°F/gas 7). Peel back your foil, brush your buns with the egg wash and scatter with the pearl sugar, if using. Stick the foil back on top and bake for about 10 minutes. Remove the foil, and bake for a final 15–20 minutes, or until a pale golden brown and set. Allow to cool completely before eating.

Einkorn Kardemummabullar

Y

YS

S

(Cardamom Buns)

Cardamom can divide, and so I wanted this Swedish sweet bun to divide further: this bun has bite. It's sweet, but complex: a bit more earthiness and just something indescribably sophisticated, or maybe that's the marketing talking. This is the bun for adults.

That'll be the powerful one-two of the cardamom, which if you're going to use, you might as well make the star of the show and use plentifully. I chose einkorn as an ancient grain here, but feel free to use spelt, khorasan, emmer or any other you see fit – we're after earthiness, but not a wholemeal graininess that gets in the way and leads to a denser loaf.

Hence we're cutting it with white and removing most of the bran from the dough, but reintroducing it in the filling to hold it together. And unlike the last recipe, you can use some sourdough for a bit of flavour, if you like.

Makes 12 buns

250g strong white flour, plus extra for dusting
200g wholemeal einkorn or other ancient grain, sieved
1 tsp salt
1 tsp cardamom seeds, crushed (or ground)
30g caster (superfine) sugar
2 tsp instant yeast (optional)
100g sourdough starter, fed with white flour (page 50) (optional)
250g milk
1 egg
75g unsalted butter

1. Start by weighing your two flours, sieving out the bran to save for later. Add your salt, cardamom and sugar into a large bowl. For a yeasted loaf, mix in the yeast. If you are planning to leave the dough overnight in the fridge, reduce the quantity of yeast to 1 teaspoon. For extra flavour, add some sourdough starter with the liquid portion. For a full sourdough, leave out the yeast and use sourdough starter instead.

2. Weigh your milk in another bowl or jug, then warm it in the microwave or by placing it in a sink with some hot water. You want it tepid – neither hot nor cold. Add this to your mix, add your egg and combine to a dough.

3. If you've got time, leave it to autolyse for 10–20 minutes. Then get started with kneading. Any method will work, including using an electric mixer (page 35) or using a no-knead method (page 45). As you're reaching the end of your knead, add your butter: soften it in the microwave if it's cold from the fridge. Keep working until it's completely combined.

For the filling

sieved bran from the flours
40g just-boiled water
100g butter, softened
2 tsp cardamom seeds, crushed (or ground)
100g light soft brown sugar

To finish

1 egg, beaten
50g caster (superfine) sugar

4. Leave your dough to rest at room temperature for about 90 minutes or so, or 4 hours if you've gone down the sourdough route. Alternatively, you can leave it overnight in the fridge. Make sure to leave it a couple of hours first at room temperature if it's sourdough, with a stretch and fold (page 47) before the fridge.

5. Make your filling. Take the sieved bran from earlier, pour over your just-boiled water, and mix it into a thick paste. Add your butter, cardamom and sugar, and mix everything together. The heat from the water should keep it nice and soft. Set aside.

6. Line a roasting tray with a sheet of baking parchment. Lightly flour a work surface, and turn your dough out onto it. Add a little more flour on top, then using floured hands, stretch out the corners of your dough to make a rectangle shape. Gently roll your dough out really wide, until it's a bigger rectangle, at least 60cm (24in) wide by 30cm (12in) tall. Add a bit more flour if required.

7. Try to see your big rectangle as two squares side by side. Over one of the squares, brush all your filling. Then fold your other square over the top to create a kind of square sandwich with your filling in the middle. Use a scraper or a pizza cutter to chop this into 12 long thin strips, starting at the folded edge (pictured overleaf). Like dividing Chelsea or cinnamon buns, start in the middle, then cut each half into two thinner strips. Then cut each quarter into three really thin strips.

8. The final step is to shape. Pick up the folded end of a strip and hold it between your fingers and thumb. Wrap the strip several times around all your fingers, then tuck the strip in between, wrapping it around the bundle to seal it. Repeat for your other buns.

9. Place your buns in your lined roasting tray and cover with kitchen foil. Prove your buns for another hour. Overnight or all day in the fridge is fine as long as you've got a very cold fridge.

10. About 15 minutes before it's ready, preheat your oven to 190°C (375°F) fan (210°C/410°F/gas 7). Peel back your foil, brush your buns with the egg wash and scatter over your caster sugar. Stick the foil back on top and bake for about 10 minutes. Remove the foil, and bake for a final 15–20 minutes, or until a pale golden brown and set. Allow to cool completely before eating.

Rúgbrauð

BP

(Sweet Rye Volcano Bread)

This is Iceland's most famous bread because it uses the world's simplest cooking technique: stick the batter in a pot and bury it in the ground.

If that's as far as you read, and you've tried burying a pot containing the below ingredients in your back garden, I do apologize. I should have mentioned: first, catch a geyser. You'll need an area of significant volcanic activity where the ground is literally scalding, or boiling. Sadly, this natural oven is rarely used for food any more, except for demonstrations to giddy tourists like me, but it's a wonderful demonstration of the forces of mother nature that lurk underground and the key to Iceland's abundant renewable energy.

There are three broad categories of *rúgbrauð*: the sweet rye version, which I'm featuring because it's a great example of a sweet, dense rye quick bread. Then there's the unsweetened version, most similar to an Irish soda bread (page 69) using rye. And finally there's the sourdough version, most similar to a *pumpernickel* (page 224) or *vollkornbrot* (page 170).

All these doughs will work using this cooking method, which can be emulated at home using a domestic oven. Stick it to just below boiling temperature, and bake your bread for about 10 hours, or all night long, while the electricity is cheap. Consider this, and try to do this on a windy night to take advantage of the turbines spinning. Serve fresh with butter or cream cheese, or pickled herring.

Makes 2 small loaves

350g rye flour
150g wholemeal flour
1½ tsp salt
2 tsp bicarbonate of soda (baking soda)
700g buttermilk or kefir
200g honey (preferred) or golden (light corn) syrup
butter, for greasing

1. Start by preheating your oven to 90°C (195°F) fan or as low as it will go. Grease two 450g loaf tins or 20cm (8in) cake tins with plenty of butter, then line them with baking parchment.

2. In a large bowl, weigh your flours, and then add your salt and bicarbonate of soda and mix these in to distribute. Add your buttermilk or kefir and honey, then mix it all together until it forms a grainy batter. It will seem very loose and that is fine.

3. Pour this into your tins, and then cover your tins with two layers of kitchen foil (unless you happen to be an owner of tins that have lids). Bake in the oven for 10 hours.

4. Let the bread cool in the tins, or on a cooling rack if you must. Slice it while still warm at your peril – but if you can get that perfect stage where it's warm and soft but doesn't collapse, you'll be rewarded. Freezes excellently sliced, and can be toasted and buttered as needed.

Laufabrauð

BP

(Leaf Bread)

Leaf bread is an Icelandic Christmas custom, called so as it requires rolling until so thin you can almost read through it. It was suggested for this book along with several hundred others in Instagram comments, DMs and emails, and when I first took a look I was sceptical.

But then I gave it a go, and found it rather ... meditative? There's a roller tool you can use to rapidly achieve intricate patterns, called a *laufabrauðsjárn*, but having given this a go with a scalpel from a minor surgery kit (unused), I wouldn't buy one. It somehow feels like cheating.

Traditionally made at Christmas and served with smoked lamb, this is not an everyday bread, due to the laborious process, but the dough itself is simple – with cornflour added to lower the gluten content and allow you to roll it this thin. It's a dry dough, and will dry out more as you make your intricate designs. Because each is stacked between kitchen paper before frying, you will need quite a bit of paper.

***Makes about 10 large* laufabrauð**

150g plain (all-purpose) flour, plus extra for dusting
10g unsalted butter
50g cornflour (cornstarch)
½ tsp baking powder
2 tsp caster (superfine) sugar
½ tsp salt
100g whole milk
at least 400ml vegetable or sunflower oil, for frying

1. Start by making the dough. Weigh your flour, and then add your butter and rub these together like making pastry, until it's the texture of breadcrumbs (alternatively, use an electric mixer with the paddle attachment). Add your cornflour, baking powder, sugar and salt, and then mix everything to combine. Finally, add your whole milk and mix everything until it comes together into a stiff dough. If you're using a mixer, switch to the dough hook. If it won't come together, leave it 5 minutes, then try again.

2. Knead for 10 minutes, either using your mixer (preferred) (page 35) or using the stretch and roll technique (page 37) – you want it to be supremely smooth, despite its stiffness. Then you could get on to rolling it out straight away, but you'll find it far easier to roll if you fridge it for 30 minutes first.

3. The fastest way to get a very thin dough here is to use a pasta machine, as per its instructions, to the second thinnest setting, then cutting out the largest diameter circles from the resulting length of very thin dough. The offcuts can be amalgamated and re-rolled. But this might be highly controversial, so I'll also suggest the traditional way, of cutting it into 10 lumps and, using a little flour, rolling each by hand individually into a large circle, as big as you can.

4. Trim off the edges, either using a sharp knife, a large round cutter or an upturned bowl, and get to work on scoring. Make lots and lots of parallel little 'V' shapes – the more precise you are the better they will look. Then every second 'V' can be folded over, to create a little opening. You can alternate them back and forth to create a snowflake pattern.

5. Once you've decorated one, place it on a sheet of baking parchment, and then place another sheet of baking parchment over the top, weighing down with a kitchen towel, to stop it drying out too much. Repeat with each round until you've none left.

6. Place at least 200ml of oil into the bottom of a pan (enough so that the breads can float) and place on a low heat. Monitor it until the oil hits about 180°C (356°F) on a probe thermometer. Carefully slide or tip each leaf off the baking parchment and into the oil. Cook until light golden, about 1–2 minutes on each side. Transfer them using a slotted spoon to a plate with some kitchen paper to soak up any excess oil, then leave them to cool.

MIDDLE EAST
& THE LEVANT
MIDDLE EAST
& THE LEVANT
MIDDLE EAST
& THE LEVANT

Abud

U

(Ancient Bread)

As far as I can find, this is the closest approximation to Stone Age bread – and it is still made today, using a method unchanged for the last 15,000 years. Yes, fifteen thousand years.

How do we know this? Charred remains of intact flatbreads from more than 14,400 years ago have been found in the Jordanian desert – this is the tail end of the last Ice Age, and at least 4000 years before any evidence of agriculture.

These breads were made using ancient wheat ancestors – most likely the wild emmer varieties that grew through the Middle East – mixed with the tubers of the local club rushes (reeds). These are pounded into a dough, then cooked in a pit, over hot ashes. As they cook, you can scatter more ashes on top for an even bake.

While the use of the foraged wheat and local tubers has essentially ended, bread is still made in this pit-fired way using modern flour in Jordan – and it's called *abud* (or *arbud* or *arbood* – a phonetic translation). My challenge was to create a useable recipe here, honouring both modern and ancient methods, that tastes nice, uses obtainable ingredients and is practical enough to make occasionally for interest and pleasure. An easy task.

***Makes 4 large* abuds**

100g peeled baking potatoes, yam or cassava
300g 'ancient grain' wholemeal flour, such as emmer, or a wild or biodiverse mixture of modern wheats
½ tsp table salt
180g tepid water
butter, marinated vegetables or meat kebabs, to serve

charcoal or wood, for building your pit fire

1. Start before your fire is built. You'll need to blend your root vegetables into a paste. This can be a bit tricky – I'd peel, then chop each into a fine dice first, to make it easier on your blender. Don't add any water – once the blend is going they should be just fine.

2. Add this mix to a large bowl, then add your flour, salt and water and mix into a dough. If you're finding it won't form a dough that holds together, either too dry or too wet, cover your bowl with a dish towel and come back to it in 15 minutes.

3. Once you've got a coherent dough, cover it again and leave it at least another 30 minutes until it's time to cook. There's no upper limit for how long you leave this – if you leave it until it starts fermenting, you can experience the invention of leavened bread. Use this time to build your pit fire – or you can use a barbecue, fire pit or pizza oven. So long as it involves fire, you can use it. The breads are so quick you can serve them instantly, so if you're charring marinated meat or vegetables, they can cool while you're making the breads. If you've got a flat piece of stone that is unlikely to crack in heat (such as granite), then place this within the fire to avoid the risk of ashy bread.

4. Wait until your fire is at the stage where there's no obvious flame rising from it, but it's evidently still very hot – this is the same stage as the white-charcoal stage if you're preparing a barbecue. If the fire is just ash, it's not hot enough and you're just going to get ashy bread.

5. Turn your dough out onto a floured surface, divide into four and roll out until it is less than 2mm thick. Alternatively, you can gently push and stretch it with your hands, as is more traditional. Place the dough directly on to the hot coals or your very hot stone, and watch it turn a lighter white as it cooks. You can use a pair of tongs to place some coals on to any of the bits that are slower to cook.

6. This will only take a minute or so. Once you can see the edges are cooked, you can use your tongs to lift up the edge and check whether the bottom is cooking. Because it's unfermented, it will go from white to black quite quickly – so if it's starting to burn, flip it over as soon as you can, and cook for another 30 seconds or so until cooked through.

7. Stack each one as you cook the next, or serve immediately. I strongly suggest coating in butter or creating a kebab using your pit-fired meat, and savour the experience.

Spinach Fatayer

Y

YS

S

(Hidden Spinach Parcels)

These little bread parcels – often filled with spiced, minced meat – are just unbelievably delicious. They also make a super-easy snack or light lunch – similar to an *empanada* but baked rather than fried – and have become a staple at many a Western hipster bakery.

Fatar means 'to split' or 'to open' in Arabic, in reference to the hidden nature of the fillings – if you didn't recognize the characteristic seams, these little buns might look like any other bread roll. A surprise for the ignorant traveller, I assure you. A wonderful surprise.

I like spinach with cheese – and due to local availability rather than authenticity, I tend to use feta, creating a filling you'll be familiar with if you've ever eaten *spanakopita*. If you can get Persian feta or *akkawi*, these would be more traditional.

I use a mixture of plain and strong flour here for maximum fluffiness – the cooked dough should not be chewy, but be easily broken apart, and this mixture seems to give the best results.

Makes about 6 fatayers

For the dough

250g plain (all-purpose) flour, plus extra for dusting
250g strong white flour
1½ tsp table salt
2 tsp instant yeast (optional)
150g milk, plus extra for brushing
150g tepid water
20g olive oil
100g sourdough starter, fed with white flour (page 50) (optional)
1 egg, beaten, for finishing (optional)

1. Into a large bowl, weigh your flours and salt. For a yeasted loaf, add the yeast and rub the ingredients together until combined. Then warm your milk until tepid in the microwave, and add this with your water and oil. For extra flavour, add your sourdough starter to the liquids. For a full sourdough, leave out the yeast but include the sourdough starter. Mix everything together until roughly combined.

2. You can autolyse (rest) the dough now for 10–20 minutes to reduce the amount of kneading, if you wish.

3. Either follow a no-knead schedule (page 45) or knead your dough – this is a dry dough by my standards and works well with an English stretch and fold technique (page 37), or you could use an electric mixer (page 35). If you've autolysed, 2–3 minutes should do. If you've not, give it as long as 10 minutes.

4. Cover your bowl and leave your dough somewhere at room temperature. This should be about 90 minutes or so. Alternatively, this works well in the fridge overnight or all day.

For the filling

2 tbsp olive oil

1 onion

2 garlic cloves

4 tsp za'atar (or 1 tsp each sumac, cumin, sesame seeds and dried oregano)

500g fresh spinach

juice of ½ lemon

200g feta, goats' cheese or other heat-stable, tangy cheese

sea salt and freshly ground black pepper

5. During this time, make your filling, which can be chilled and stored until needed. Place a large frying pan (skillet) over a low heat, and add your oil. Finely dice your onion as this heats, then place in the pan. Stir occasionally; you want your onions to slowly soften but you don't want to worry about any colour. As they do, finely chop or crush your garlic. When your onions are soft, add the garlic and stir to combine, continuing to cook for another minute or so.

6. Then add your za'atar, spinach and squeeze of lemon. Turn the heat up to medium–high. Stir until the spinach is wilted (sticking a lid on for 30 seconds will speed this up), and any liquid left in the bottom of the pan has evaporated, then you can turn the heat off.

7. Line a couple of baking trays with baking parchment. Flour a work surface, and scrape your dough out onto it. Add some more flour on top, then roll gently into a long sausage to allow you to easily cut the dough into 12 roughly equal pieces.

8. One by one, coat a piece of dough with flour, then roll it out into a flat circle, turning it regularly and checking it's not sticking (add more flour if it does). You want the circle to be about 15cm (6in) in diameter – really quite flat. If the spinach mix is very wet, squeeze out any excess liquid. Dollop a heaped tablespoon of your spinach mix on to the dough, then crumble over some feta or other tangy cheese. Brush around the edge of the circle with some milk, and then fold the edges over in thirds to pinch in a triangle across the top of the dough. Pinch hard to seal, then set your finished *fatayer* on your tray. Repeat with the remaining dough and filling.

9. I'd let your finished *fatayer* prove just while your oven preheats to 180°C (350°F) fan (200°C/400°F/gas 6); 15 minutes will be plenty. During that time, you can brush your dough with milk for a shine, or if you're feeling fancy use an egg wash.

10. Bake for 18–20 minutes, turning the trays halfway through if they're browning unevenly. Check the bases before taking them out – they should be golden brown. If they're pale and soggy, stick them in for another 5–10 minutes. Serve warm by all means, but not straight from the oven. If cooled completely, they are still delicious, but you can re-warm them by sticking in a hot oven for 5 minutes if you prefer.

Maalooga

Y

YS

S

(*Khubz Mulawah* – Yemeni Brown Butter Loaf)

Whatever you've got going on in your life, wherever you are, I think it's important to give some thought to the people of Yemen. These families have suffered a decade of civil war and famine, in one of the biggest humanitarian disasters of modern times. Many will not have access to breads such as *malooga*, through no fault of their own. The people suffer, and a culture is near destroyed.

It wasn't through bread that I developed an interest in the country and people, it was actually through coffee, and I even came quite close to organizing the export (read: smuggling) of several sacks of green coffee beans out of the country at the height of the conflict, but eventually decided against it once the deal was in place as I couldn't guarantee the proceeds would reach the growers. Yemeni coffee is still difficult to get hold of, and while reports of how the farmers are doing are hard to come by, you can guess things are not good.

While coffee was my hook, bread might be yours, and this layered, laminated flattish bread is awesome with almost anything, sweet or savoury. While it may be baked in the traditional clay *tannur* (emulate with a pizza oven), it works just as well in a modern oven. The butter is pre-darkened, just like making the *beurre noisette* of French cuisine, to give a nutty flavour through the loaf from the off.

Makes 2 large* maloogas*, or you can split into thinner, flatter breads

120g salted or unsalted butter or ghee
400g strong white flour, plus extra for dusting
1 tsp table salt
2 tsp instant yeast (optional)
280g tepid water
100g sourdough starter, fed with white flour (page 50) (optional)
nigella seeds (optional)

1. Start by weighing your butter into a saucepan. Prepare your sink by filling it with about 2.5cm (1in) of cold water. Place the pan over a low–medium heat so that the butter melts, then begins to brown. Once it's getting a dark, pecan-coloured brown, but not burnt, remove the pan from the heat and place it in the water to stop it browning and burning, being careful not to splash water into the butter. Remove from the sink and set aside.

2. Into a large bowl, weigh your flour and salt. For a yeasted loaf, add your yeast and rub the ingredients together until combined. Then add your tepid water. For extra flavour, add your sourdough starter on top. For a full sourdough, leave out the yeast but include the sourdough starter. Mix everything together until a rough dough forms.

3. You can autolyse at this stage for 20–30 minutes, if you wish, and cut how much kneading you need to do. Knead your dough for 5–10 minutes until smooth and stretchy.

4. Return the dough to the bowl, cover with a dish towel or clingfilm (plastic wrap) and leave somewhere warm. Give it at least 90 minutes if using yeast or 4–6 hours for sourdough. It doesn't matter if this one goes a little overproved.

5. There are so many ways to laminate this kind of bread. I like a fairly untraditional method similar to lamination (page 61). Rub your work surface lightly with water and turn your dough out onto it. Using wet hands, stretch your dough out as thinly as you can; making it a full 60×90cm (24×36in) is ideal but make it as big as possible. Then brush your dough with the brown butter (warming in the microwave if too firm). Fold your dough in half, and brush the new butterless side too. Repeat, folding and buttering your dough until you've got one square lump of dough. You can cut this in half for smaller *maloogas*. If you have any butter left, butter the top and roll out each dough, then fold and butter again. Repeat until you've just enough butter left to brush before baking.

6. Ease into a round shape, and press down or roll until about 20–25cm (8–10in) in diameter. Place on a baking tray or within a cast iron pan and leave to rest for a final 20–30 minutes while you preheat your oven to 200°C (400°F) fan (220°C/425°F/gas 7).

7. Brush with your final remaining butter, then sprinkle lightly with nigella seeds, if using. Bake for 10–15 minutes, or until a light and speckled golden brown.

Markook

U

(Shrak, Saj, Tava Bread)

I love making this bread because of the absurdity of trying to do it in my own home kitchen. This is a big flatbread. Sure, you could just make it in the largest pan you've got, but I've been drawn to re-create the impressive size using the traditional *saj* – a dome-shaped, convex cooking griddle – by using an upturned wok over a gas ring. If your wok is meticulously seasoned, or has a non-stick coating, don't risk damaging it under the intense heat, and just use a flat pan.

You can make this bread with any combination of wholemeal or white flour – but consensus seems to stick to about half and half, or similar to using all wholemeal and passing it through a coarse sieve to remove the largest bits of bran. Because this is unleavened, it can be quite dry, so I've added a little sugar to help with colour, caramelization and moisture retention.

***Makes 6 large* markooks**

150g strong white flour, plus extra for rolling
150g wholemeal flour
1 tsp table salt
2 tsp caster (superfine) sugar
200g tap water
15g vegetable oil, plus extra for seasoning the wok

1. In a large bowl, weigh your flours, salt and sugar and combine them. Add your water and oil, then using a wooden spoon or your hands, mix until you've got an even dough and no flour is visible. Cover the bowl, or wrap in clingfilm (plastic wrap), and stick in the fridge for at least 15 minutes and up to 2 days, or until ready to use.

2. Turn your dough out onto a floured surface. Divide it into six roughly equal lumps. Add more flour, and use a rolling pin to roll one out as thin as possible – as thin as you can bear.

3. Then let it rest a few minutes as you preheat your pan over a medium–high heat. As I mentioned, I use a wok, upside down, over my largest ring. Use a touch of oil on a dry cloth or piece of kitchen paper to lightly rub over the surface of the pan, to prevent sticking. Alternatively, use your largest frying pan (skillet) or griddle pan.

4. Stretch out your bread a little more as you lift it up – you want it almost the thinness of filo pastry – and place it on your upturned wok. Watch for the colour change, lifting up the edge to check how it's getting on. You want it to be turning a subtle golden brown. It's only cooking on one side, so make sure it looks cooked all the way through before taking it off the heat.

5. Once cooked, fold it in half, then half again, and either serve immediately or stack up tall, as you make the rest.

Ancient Pitta

Y

YS

S

Pitta breads work best with lower-gluten flours, otherwise the strength provided by strong flour can cause the top and bottom to stick together and you don't get the pocket forming. If you're still not getting the required puff, try baking in the hottest oven you can manage, on a preheated baking stone or thick steel tray.

If you're after a pitta for your dinner and don't have fancy flour to hand, don't worry. Just substitute the spelt or khorasan with plain white flour, or a mix of half and half strong white and plain white flour. If you've only got strong white to hand, you'll get perfectly nice flatbreads, but it's unlikely they'll puff.

This recipe utilizes ancient grains, like many in this book, which I thought was a particularly good fit for pitta. Pitta is the obvious evolution of ancient unleavened flatbreads – it really doesn't take a leap to see how a dough that was left for a few days before cooking was a bit tastier, and that if you added some of this old dough to a new dough, it sped up the process.

Makes 8 pittas

400g 'ancient grain' wholemeal flour, such as emmer, khorasan, spelt, or a mixed biodiverse flour (sieved weight), plus extra for dusting
1 tsp salt
1 tsp instant yeast (optional)
300g tepid water
50g sourdough starter, fed with any flours (page 50) (optional)

1. Start by sieving your flour into a large bowl – depending on how conscientiously you sieve, that will alter how much bran reaches your final pitta breads. More bran will give a rougher texture, and if there is too much (or the grind has been too coarse), then they won't puff up so well. For a yeasted loaf, sieve the flour into your bowl until you reach 400g, and keep the bran back to use for shaping wholemeal doughs. Add your salt and yeast, then distribute these so they disappear before you add your water. For extra flavour, add the starter with the water. For a full sourdough, leave out the yeast but include the starter with the water. Mix everything together until it forms a dough. It might be a little wet and sticky, or it might seem quite dry – this will depend on temperature and on your flour – no matter.

2. Cover your bowl with a dish towel and leave it to autolyse (rest) for 10–15 minutes.

3. Give your dough a stretch and a fold (page 47) – or even just a push and a prod. It should come together much more easily. This delay in absorbing moisture is a feature of most ancient grain or stoneground flours, and if you're finding it difficult to handle, just take some time.

4. Cover your dough again. For a yeasted dough, rest it for another 1 hour at room temperature. For sourdough, give it 2–3 hours.

5. Once you've got a noticeably puffy dough, preheat your oven as hot as it goes, or 230°C (445°F) fan (250°C/445°F/gas 9) if unsure. If you've got a baking stone, get this in there and get it very hot.

6. Scrape your dough out onto a floured surface. Add some flour on top, then use gentle rolling motions to ease it into a sausage shape. Then use this to cut it in half, each bit in half again, then each bit in half again. This should give you eight lumps of dough.

7. Add some more flour, then roll each lump out into a disc. I like to roll four out at a time, placing each one on a peel or a baking tray. Then slide them into your hot oven or baking stone, and bake for 5–6 minutes, or until they're puffed up and the bottom is blushing light brown. Roll out your next batch while they're baking.

8. Once you've removed your first batch of pittas from the oven, try not to handle them, or at least squeeze them too hard, until they've collapsed back down – those air pockets are, in fact, full of scalding steam. As you load up your next batch, let the oven heat back up for a few more minutes, then repeat.

9. Use as soon as you can, but if you'd like to store them, stick them in an airtight bag and keep at room temperature, or in the freezer. I like to spray them with some water and then stick them in the toaster to fluff them back up on demand.

Lavash

Y

(Middle Eastern Flatbread)

Lavash can't be characterized as pertaining to any particular country, and even by sticking it in this region I'm being controversial. Lavash is most commonly associated with Armenia – and indeed, was described by UNESCO as an 'expression of Armenian culture' – sparking protests across former-Soviet Asian states and the Middle East.

Food historians have debated its origins, but let's face it – it's a flat white mix of wheat flour, yeast and salt, then cooked quickly, usually on a piece of hot steel, but if you've a clay oven to hand feel free. In short, there are variations in nearly every country in the world and, like all good ideas, probably originated in lots of different places.

Regardless, this probably makes up one of the most useful recipes in this entire book. It's my go-to flatbread for almost any Mediterranean or South Asian dish that requires one, so long as I've remembered more than an hour in advance that I'm in need of bread – that's how quick you can prove it. It's rolled very thinly and, after cooking, you can allow the breads to dry out, stack them up and store them in a dry place. Simply use a spray bottle of water, give it some spritzes, let it soak in, then heat in a pan or the oven.

***Makes 8 large* lavash**

300g plain (all-purpose) flour, plus extra for dusting
1 tsp instant yeast
1 tsp table salt
200g tepid water

1. Weigh your flour, yeast and salt into a bowl large enough to take them. Add your water, and use one hand, a wooden spoon or an electric mixer to mix together into a dough.

2. Once all the bare flour has been incorporated, cover with a dish towel and let it autolyse (rest) for 5–10 minutes.

3. Give the dough a stretch and fold (page 47) or even just a poke and prod; it should be very noticeably stretchier and smoother.

4. Cover and leave it again for at least 40 minutes, or up to 2 hours at room temperature. If it's going to be longer than this (up to 2 days is fine), then stick it in the fridge.

5. Turn your dough out onto a floured surface and roll gently into a rough sausage shape to make it easier to cut into eight equal pieces.

6. Preheat a large, heavy-based pan or *tava* over a medium heat – it should be hot but not smoking. Between the breads, if the flour is burning on the pan, it's too hot.

7. Using plenty of flour, roll each lump out into a flat disc – you want it as thin as possible, and the size should be dictated by the size of your largest pan! If rolling becomes difficult, next time consider making them further in advance. Regardless, you can stretch out the dough with your hands between rolls to get to the shape you'd like.

8. Cook over your medium heat for up to 2 minutes on each side, so each bubble is just catching some golden brown. If you're planning on eating them within the next 20 minutes or so, keep them warm and moist by placing between the layers of a dish towel. Or, you can lightly butter and stack up in a tower.

9. If you're planning on drying them for later, don't add any fat. Allow air to get around them, and leave them somewhere draughty and away from critters. Alternatively, these freeze excellently.

Simit

Y

(Sweet Sesame Bread)

Simit – a sesame-encrusted, torsional ring of sweet, crusted delight. Sometimes maligned as a Turkish bagel, it's far from it; this is merely ring-based generalization. There's no boiling stage, for one, and the level of sesame of the typical Istanbul version I've written here is off the scale. The sesame, first mildly toasted, then toasted again during the bake in the oven, turns a deep golden brown, and with the subtle sweetness of the dough, is plenty as a meal or snack in itself.

Head to Istanbul and you'll find vendors – *simitci* – touting something akin to this recipe. But you could try regional variations: using poppy seeds as well as sesame, which is a nice one. Consider that not far away, the use of poppy seeds in several countries – such as the UAE and Saudi Arabia – is prohibited by law, and there have been reports of arrests for tiny, bagel or simit-related infractions. My garden is full of beautiful opium poppies and so in those countries I'd be in jail.

Elsewhere, there are variations on how it's served: a bare *simit* and yogurt to break the fast, dipped or rolled in za'atar, or with Western influence, increasingly used as a sandwich roll.

***Makes* 4 simits**

350g strong white flour, plus extra for dusting
1 tsp table salt
1 tsp instant yeast
250g tepid water
100g toasted sesame seeds
50g grape or pomegranate molasses
50g water

1. Start by weighing out your flour, salt and yeast in a large bowl. Add your tepid water on top, then use a wooden spoon to mix everything into a dough.

2. At this stage, you can get straight on with kneading if you're pushed for time. I'd recommend, though, giving it a 15-minute autolyse (rest) before you start, and you'll find it much easier to work at the next stage.

3. Knead for 5–10 minutes or until smooth and elastic. Alternatively, follow a no-knead method (page 45) or use an electric mixer (page 35).

4. Return your dough to your bowl and cover it with a dish towel, plastic bag or clingfilm (plastic wrap). Leave it at room temperature for about 90 minutes, or until puffy and risen. If your sesame seeds aren't pre-toasted, now's a good time to give them a light toast in a frying pan (skillet) over a medium heat until they're starting to catch a golden brown. Set aside.

5. Scrape your dough out onto a floured surface. Add a bit more flour on top, then use your dough scraper to cut it into quarters. Taking each in turn, roll a lump between your hands and the surface into a long sausage shape – as long as you can and at least 45cm (18in) – then fold this sausage in half, halving its length. Twist this round and round at least five times, then take your ends and join them to create a ring, slightly overlapping. Press down lightly to seal, and you can even roll your hand back and forth for extra closure.

6. Once your *simits* are shaped, line a baking tray with baking parchment, and find two bowls big enough to contain a *simit*. In one, mix your molasses and water. Into the other, put your sesame seeds. In turn, dip each simit in the watery mixture, then into the sesame seeds, completely coating the dough. Place them on your prepared baking tray for the final prove.

7. Give it another 30–60 minutes of proving so that the rings increase in size but they aren't too fragile. Make sure you preheat your oven to about 200°C (400°F) fan (220°C/425°F/gas7), about 15 minutes before you plan to bake.

8. Bake them for 25 minutes or so until you can see the dough has turned a deep golden brown, helped along by the molasses. Let them cool, but you won't want them to cool completely – these are so, so good hot.

NORTH AMERICA

NORTH AMERICA

Buttermilk Biscuits with Gravy

BP

To me, 'biscuit' means what Americans would call 'cookie' – short, sweet, flat, baked crumbling things. This recipe is a quick scone-like bread, layered with butter. Delicious comfort, if not a biscuit as I know it.

No, I still can't get over the name. It's derived from Latin: *biscoctus*, or twice-cooked (*bis* = twice, *coctus* = cooked). The evidence goes back to medieval England, where hard flatbreads were cooked, then sliced and cooked again. So, in my mind, I'm justified in feeling uncomfortable referring to anything soft as a biscuit.

But you can imagine the innumerable threads that led to the soft-centred, long-life, unleavened flatbreads that travelled well with settlers across the Atlantic being called biscuits. These stale breads, an evolution of hardtack, were revived with the soaking in 'gravy', and improved and lightened with the layering of fats, such as butter or shortening. When chemical raising agents were popularized in the 19th century, you can see the birth of the soft, flaky thing we know today.

Gluten is our enemy here. It helps to have a little to create the layers, but we want to limit its formation as much as possible. The best way I've found is to use frozen grated butter.

Makes 10–12 biscuits

For the biscuits

- **450g plain (all-purpose) flour, plus extra for dusting**
- **1 tsp table salt**
- **2 tsp baking powder**
- **½ tsp bicarbonate of soda (baking soda)**
- **200g unsalted butter, frozen for at least 12 hours beforehand**
- **250g buttermilk**
- **egg yolk or milk, for egg wash (optional)**

1. Into a large bowl, weigh your flour, then add your salt, baking powder and bicarbonate of soda. Stir these together roughly to combine. Then use a coarse grater to grate your frozen butter into the bowl. I tend to freeze a whole block, then grate all but a little, and stick any remaining back in the fridge.

2. Gently rub the butter into the flour, just to distribute it and so that all the flour is covered in butter. Then add the buttermilk and stir the whole thing with a wooden spoon until you've got something that barely comes together as a dough. Please, please don't spend too much effort here. You want to have loads of bare flour and lumps.

3. Generously flour a work surface, then turn your lumpy mix onto it. Form it into a rough, craggy lump, then use a rolling pin to roll it out at least 45cm (18in) long. Then we're going to fold this dough like folding a letter to fit in an envelope, in thirds. If you've ever made puff pastry, that's what we're trying to do: fold it one-third down, then close it over by folding again – except this will break and tear and crumble and that is fine, at this stage.

For the gravy
6 good pork sausages
60g plain (all-purpose) flour
1 litre whole milk
plenty of sea salt and freshly ground black pepper to taste – at least ½ tsp of each

4. Turn your dough around by 90 degrees, sprinkling with more flour, if needed, and repeat your rolling and folding step three more times until all the lumpy bits have gone and the dough looks like one smooth, cohesive lump.

5. Stick your dough on a tray and put it in the fridge (I use the baking tray I'm about to use, to avoid more washing up) to allow the now-formed gluten to rest, and to allow you to roll out the dough a little more easily. You can chill the dough for several hours at this point, if you wish, but the action of the bicarbonate of soda will lessen with time and your biscuits will be denser, the longer you leave it.

6. Preheat your oven to 200°C (400°F) fan (220°C/425°F/gas 7). Turn your dough back onto your floured surface, dust with more flour and roll it out until it's about 1.5cm (⅝in) thick; this is down to personal preference, as is whether you choose to use a scraper to cut your biscuits into squares, or whether you want to use a cookie cutter (read: biscuit cutter) to make rounds, and re-roll the less-than-perfect offcuts. Place the finished biscuits on a baking tray.

7. Optionally, brush your finished biscuits with a little egg wash or milk for a deeper golden hue but avoid dripping any down the sides, as this can affect the lamination (page 61). Bake for 20–25 minutes, while you make some gravy.

8. Into a frying pan (skillet), squeeze the filling out of your sausages. Place over a medium heat and, as it fries, use a spatula to roughly chop your sausagemeat up into little lumps no bigger than 1cm (½in). Shake the pan and move them about as they brown, so that they are golden and have released a good amount of fat. Add your flour and just 1–2 tablespoons of your milk, and stir so that everything clumps together into a gluey mess. Perfect.

9. Add about a quarter of the rest of your milk, heating and stirring all the time, and continue to stir until your gravy turns smooth, except for the lumps of sausage. Add another quarter of the milk and repeat. Keep going until all the milk is mixed in or you're happy with the thickness of your gravy. Add plenty of salt and pepper to taste. Serve with warm biscuits.

Sea Gull Inn

Modern Sourdough

S

(Cali County Loaf)

I'll keep this short. This is what I do – and if you like this recipe, I've written a whole book that goes deep into how to make this recipe and ones similar to it. But this is distilled into my basic guide on sourdough: follow this, and follow it well, and this will be very good bread indeed.

This is the one recipe that I make more than twice a week, at least, every week. And while it's called a country loaf, this isn't the French *pain de campagne* on which it's based; we're talking about the Californian country loaf. This loaf is engineered for lightness, for an open texture. It is refined and fiddled with for maximum aeration and maximum ear for a maximalist society. It may have French roots, but it's All American.

With a Scottish twist, in my case. While this takes the technique from the USA, to import ingredients from there would be unsustainable. If we want the super-strong wheat from America, trade deals actually give us Canadian red spring wheat in the UK: this excellent, unbelievably glutenous wheat is farmed on a massive scale and has excellent capacity to carry lightness in sourdough and resist the enzymes that are intent on disrupting the process.

But it lacks flavour, and using it involves shipping it halfway across the world, so let's not, and let's use local wheat, wherever you are. And if I want some of that American strength, I managed to find some hard spring red wheat of amazing strength at a farm called Kilduff, about 50 miles away from my house. You'd be amazed what's in your back yard.

Makes 1 large loaf but is easily scaled

400g strong white flour, plus extra for dusting
50g wholemeal rye flour
1½ tsp table salt
330g water
100g sourdough starter, fed with any flours (page 50)
semolina, for dusting

1. Start by ensuring your starter is happy, so if it hasn't been fed recently, feed it the night before you plan to bake. Feed it at a ratio of 1:2:2 and leave it for 5–8 hours at a warm room temperature before starting the recipe. I tend to leave this while I'm at work during the day, do the below steps in the evening, then prove overnight and bake first thing the next morning.

2. In a large bowl, weigh your flours. Add your salt and mix everything together. Run the warm tap and fill a jug with water so that it is just warmer than tepid, about 25°C (77°F), then add this too, followed by your active sourdough starter. Mix using a wooden spoon or a dough hook until you've got a lumpy, messy dough.

3. Let your dough autolyse (rest) for 20–30 minutes. If you like, you can cover the bowl, or you can just mix in any dry skin that forms.

4. Knead your dough for 5–10 minutes, or until the dough is starting to become smooth and supple. The slap and fold method tends to work well (page 36), as does using an electric mixer (page 35). If you choose the latter, give it a stretch and fold immediately after (page 47).

5. Cover your dough with clingfilm (plastic wrap) or a dish towel and leave your dough to rest for 4 hours or so at a warm room temperature. This can vary significantly depending on temperature. During this rest, conduct two to three stretches and folds (page 47), usually about an hour apart. The necessity of this will depend on how conscientiously you kneaded: I'd always do at least one.

6. If you've scaled this recipe, use a dough scraper to scrape your dough out onto a clean, unfloured surface. Pre-shape (page 62) by roughly tucking in two sides, then rolling it up. Leave your dough on the bench for another 15–20 minutes.

7. Flour a proving basket, or make one using a floured dish towel inside a mixing bowl. Then flour a work surface and scoop your dough onto it, smooth-side down. Shape so that it will fit nicely in your proving basket (page 60).

8. Place your proving basket in the fridge – I no longer tend to cover these: any dry skin that forms won't do any harm. Prove in there for 8–18 hours. Preheat your oven with a cast iron pan or Dutch oven inside for at least 15 minutes before you plan to bake. The temperature should be 220°C (425°F) fan (240°C/465°F/gas 9).

9. I tend to score after turning the loaf directly onto the lid of my cast iron pot or Dutch oven, but if you're baking within a high-sided pan, it helps to do this on baking parchment, then lower it in. Score lengthways down the loaf, or in a square pattern if it's a round loaf.

10. Enclose your loaf in your pan, and turn your oven down to 200°C (400°F) fan (220°C/425°F/gas 7). Bake for 20 minutes initially, then take the lid off and bake for another 15–20 minutes, or until a dark golden brown. Let it cool down before slicing. If slicing whole loaves for freezing, this is best done the next day.

Salt-risen Bread

This loaf and method has almost mythical status amongst bread bakers: it's different to any recipe in this book. It is a microbiological marvel. As new Appalachian settlers arrived in the USA, they adopted this technique. Little is known about its exact origin, but it may have been because sourdough could be difficult to maintain in the heat of the journey, and perhaps this bread, with a starter that could be started anew every night and left to grow in the heat, was just easier. If I've learned anything about innovation, studying food and medicine over the last 20 years, I'm confident it came about through a combination of necessity and luck, like everything else.

This recipe uses neither yeast, sourdough nor chemicals to rise the bread, but bacteria: specifically, the bacteria that often cause food poisoning, and much worse. As a doctor, I was hesitant to include this one, because I've seen the horror of this bacteria directly. But the risk to you is very, very tiny – wash your hands well after handling the dough, and then the bread is baked, so those bacteria are dead.

Clostridium perfringens is the name, and it smells cheesy. It creates spores, or the 'escape pods' of the bacterial world, that can survive extremely harsh conditions and from which the bacteria can thrive, given the right conditions. To create our starter, we're using just boiled milk, which eliminates lots of other bugs that could take over. This one survives. The salt-risen name refers to the fact that many recipes use salt to inhibit the growth of unwanted bacteria. We're using bicarbonate of soda here, as it works better, in my experience.

If this bread doesn't work, you've likely cultured the wrong bacteria, or you've not cultured any. Your environment should be warm but not hot: body temperature. If you cannot maintain this, for example using a modern oven, an oven with the light on or a proving drawer, it won't work out, sorry.

Makes 1 medium loaf

For the starter

25g coarse yellow cornmeal (polenta)
25g strong wholemeal flour
¼ tsp bicarbonate of soda (baking soda)
50g milk

For the dough

400g strong white flour, plus extra for dusting
1 tsp salt
300g warm water
50g salted or unsalted butter, very soft, plus extra for greasing

1. This takes a while. If you start the evening before, your bread will be ready some time mid-afternoon the following day. In a jar or Tupperware, weigh your cornmeal, flour and bicarbonate of soda.

2. Into a small saucepan, weigh your milk then bring this to a simmer over a low heat. Once bubbling, remove from the heat, pour into your jar and stir. Cover the jar loosely with clingfilm (plastic wrap), then place somewhere warm, between 36–38°C (97–100°F).

3. It will likely take about 10–12 hours to get properly going. It should have risen up, and be properly bubbly and smell of strong, horsey cheese. Lovely. Congratulations, you're a bootleg biologist.

4. Now, make the dough. Due to understandable trepidation about the spread of pathogenic bacteria over my kitchen, I've mixed this one in an electric mixer. Put your starter into a large bowl, then weigh in your flour and salt. Add your water – this should be really warm, above body temperature, so that it brings your whole dough up to 36–38°C (97–100°F) again. I use one-third boiling water plus two-thirds cold water from the tap to get the right temperature.

5. Mix, or knead, for 5 minutes until the dough has switched from being wet and shaggy to smooth and elastic. This will always be a wet dough. Then add your butter and mix until this is incorporated. The bowl now goes back in your warm place for 2–3 hours. Wash your hands with warm soapy water and clean any surfaces thoroughly.

6. Grease a 900g (2lb) loaf tin, preferably an oblong one. Your dough should have risen moderately. Turn it out onto a floured surface (it will be fragile) and shape for a batard (page 41). Place this in your greased tin, seam-side down. Again, wash your hands and wipe down after any contact.

7. Place the dough back in your warm place and leave for another 3–4 hours, or until risen but not to the extent that it looks overproved and fragile. If it's getting that way, don't score it, but bake it directly.

8. When it's getting there, preheat your oven to 180°C (350°F) fan (200°C/400°F/gas 6). Score your loaf, and bake in the presence of steam by putting a tray of ice or water in the bottom of the oven for about 40 minutes until it's got a good crust. I would bash out of the tin about 10 minutes before it's done and return it to the oven to ensure crusty sides.

Morning Muffins

Y

YS

S

Evidently, the fact that English muffins are called English muffins suggests that their place of reference is not England, where they are called muffins. You might question their position in this chapter, but then you'd be able to argue that the muffin, in turn, came from the German *muffen*, or French *moflet*. As with many cultural and geographical ties, the twine unravels and the historians can argue. We can get on and bake.

Makes 12 muffins

450g strong white flour
1½ tsp table salt
1 teaspoon instant yeast (optional)
300g warm water
100g sourdough starter, fed with white flour (page 50) (optional)
semolina, for dusting

1. Start the night before the morning you want your muffins – if making sourdough, you'll need to start at least a couple of hours before going to bed. For a yeasted loaf, weigh your flour into a large bowl with the salt and yeast and stir to distribute, then add the water. For extra flavour, add the sourdough starter with the water. For a full sourdough, leave out the yeast but include the sourdough starter at the same time as the water. Mix everything together using a wooden spoon until you've got a rough dough.

2. Leave this to autolyse (rest) for 20 minutes, then knead your dough until smooth – about 10 minutes. I like to use the stretch and roll, English knead (page 37) for this dough, or an electric mixer (page 35). This is one where it helps to give it a good working.

3. Return your dough to your bowl and cover it over with a dish towel, clingfilm (plastic wrap) or a plastic bag. If making a yeasted dough, stick your dough straight in the fridge. For sourdough, it's 2 hours at a warm room temperature, then a stretch and fold (page 47), then the fridge.

4. The next morning, sprinkle a work surface with semolina, then turn your muffin dough out onto it. Add more semolina on top, then gently use a rolling pin to roll your dough until it's 2.5cm (1in) thick: add more semolina if need be. Use a cookie cutter to cut into rounds, and transfer to a baking tray to rest. Rest for 45 minutes if yeasted, or about 90–120 minutes for sourdough.

5. Preheat a heavy pan (preferably cast iron) over a low–medium heat for about 5 minutes. Don't add any butter. Place a few muffins at a time in your pan and heat for 3–4 minutes. They will rise, probably unevenly. Once a deep golden, turn them over and cook for another 3–4 minutes on the other side, and any squintiness will even out. Repeat until you have used all the dough.

6. Leave to cool for at least 10 minutes before slicing. In an airtight container, they will keep for 2–3 days. They freeze particularly well: slice in half before freezing, and that way they can be toasted straight from the freezer.

Heather Honey Cornbread

BP

A quick bread, and a good one to have up your sleeve. Not just for when you run out of plain flour and only have a long-forgotten packet of polenta (possibly infested with weevils) at the back of the cupboard. Not just for when you're serving Southern barbecue or fried chicken. Serve, perhaps, with soups. Serve instead of rice with a chilli, or instead of potatoes with a stew. This is awesome; it is easy, it is fast and it is delicious.

At its heart, it is essentially a quick cake or muffin recipe, with the sugar scaled back and flour cut with cornmeal for an easy tear and a grainy, crumbly texture. The corn is the star.

Or it would be, until you start slathering it in butter and honey, and as is my own cultural allegiance, I'd avoid using generic runny honey if you want it to shine, without causing it to be too sweet. Go for something a bit fancy, and there ain't nothing fancier than Scottish heather honey. It's a punchy, floral and an intensely honey-y honey, and is perfect here.

Makes 1 medium loaf

170g coarse yellow cornmeal (polenta)
150g plain (all-purpose) flour
50g light soft brown sugar
1 tsp baking powder
1 tsp table salt
30g salted or unsalted butter (or better, lard), plus extra for finishing
2 large eggs
250g milk

For the honey butter
25g salted or unsalted butter, softened
1 tbsp heather honey, or other nice honey

1. Preheat your oven to 190°C (375°F) fan (210°C/410°F/gas 7). Place a small cast iron skillet, sealed (not loose-bottomed) cake tin or enamelled tin in the oven to preheat.

2. Into a large bowl, weigh all your dry ingredients. Crumble in your 30g butter or lard until it has mostly disappeared, and what you can see looks like breadcrumbs. Add your eggs and milk, then use a wooden spoon to mix the whole lot together until you've got a loose, lumpy batter.

3. Remove your skillet or tin from the oven and pop in a knob of butter. It should start sizzling and popping. Use oven gloves to give the skillet or tin a tilt to spread around the butter. Then pour in your batter. Bake for 20–25 minutes, or until it feels nice and bouncy when you press down on it.

4. There's no need to make your honey butter separately – just take your big knob of butter and stick it on top of your hot bread. Pour over your heather honey and use a brush to spread it around, or a spoon to baste the bread until it is absorbed. Serve hot.

Boston Brown Bread

BP

Bread in a can. Yes. This New England quirk seemed to emerge from a frugal, pragmatic but also comedic approach to baking: evidently, it wouldn't be thrifty enough to just recycle your tin can. You've got to re-use it. The plastic-lined (food safe) cans tend to be pretty non-stick, conduct heat well and the resulting bread is moist and hearty.

While it might have been conceived over an open fire, or more likely, in the dying ashes of a fire, I don't like to think what this intense heat does to the plastic lining of the can. So this recipe is steamed.

Makes 4 small loaves

100g coarse yellow cornmeal (polenta)
100g wholemeal rye flour
100g wholewheat flour
1 tsp bicarbonate of soda (baking soda)
½ tsp table salt
280g buttermilk
180g black treacle (molasses)
75g raisins (optional but recommended)
butter, for greasing

4 empty, thoroughly cleaned and de-labelled tin cans, lids removed completely

1. Start by greasing your cans well – watch the rim, as it's sharp. I like to then doubly stop sticking by coating the sides in baking parchment: this can stick out of the top by up to 1cm (½in).

2. In a large bowl, weigh together the cornmeal, flours, bicarbonate of soda and salt. Mix to distribute evenly. In another, bowl, weigh your buttermilk and treacle, and whisk these together so they are combined. If it's taking ages, heat for 30 seconds in the microwave.

3. Pour the wet ingredients into the dry ingredients and mix together until you've got a lumpy batter. Then add the raisins, if using, and keep stirring until it's pretty smooth. Pour this batter into your prepared cans, filling them no more than two-thirds full to allow space for the breads to rise. Then make a little cover for each using kitchen foil, tying with string to keep it in place.

4. Place the cans in a deep pot with enough water to come halfway up the sides of the cans. Cover the pot with a lid and bring the water to a simmer.

5. Steam the bread over a low heat for about 2 hours, or until a skewer inserted in the middle comes out clean. Don't check them for at least the first hour, unless you can smell burning. You might need to top up the boiling water in the pot from time to time.

6. Once done, remove the cans from the pot using tongs or thick waterproof oven gloves, and let them cool for at least 10 minutes. Then tilt each can and carefully tap out the bread: if you used paper, it should fall right out. If you try to slice it too quickly, it will just gum up, so let it cool before slicing. Serve untraditionally as part of a fried breakfast, or traditionally, toasted and covered in baked beans and cheese.

Banana Bread

BP

While many countries and cultures can claim to have made cakes and breads using bananas (based almost entirely on imported fruit), this version isn't quite like the ones you'll find in the average home. Its sweetness is dialled back, but still it's more a sweet cake than anything approaching a bread.

Like all banana breads, this one works best with really, really overripe bananas. Entirely black and leaking? Perfect. It's infinitely customizable, too – and in fact, I rarely make a plain old loaf. You can break it down into little loaves for baking in mini loaf tins or friand moulds, and you can add whatever you like: blueberries, raspberries and blackberries work really well, the acidity cutting through the cake. Otherwise, stirring in a handful of oats, sprinkling with oats before baking and adding a drizzle of honey can fool people into thinking this is somehow healthy.

Makes a 900g loaf, 2 × 20cm (8in) round loaves or 12 individual loaves

125g salted butter (or unsalted and a pinch of salt), plus extra for greasing
200g caster (superfine) sugar
3 large or 4 small overripe bananas
1 tsp vanilla extract
2 eggs
250g plain (all-purpose) flour
3 tsp baking powder
berries, chocolate chips, oats, nuts or any other filling of your choice
1 extra banana, for topping (optional)

1. Preheat your oven to 140°C (275°F) fan (160°C/325°F/gas 4) if making one large loaf. If making smaller loaves, heat to 160°C (325°F) fan (180°C/350°F/gas 4). Line your loaf tin(s) with baking parchment, or grease your little loaf tins.

2. Start by measuring your butter into a large bowl – mine usually comes from the fridge, so I weigh it and give it a buzz in the microwave until softened, or even just melted. Then add your sugar, bananas, vanilla and eggs, and use a whisk or an electric mixer to beat them all together.

3. Add your flour and baking powder on top, gently distributing the baking powder with your fingertips. Then gently mix everything together until you've got a very lumpy mixture but no bare flour is visible. At this point, add your fillings and stir gently to just distribute and no more.

4. Scrape your batter into your prepared tin(s). It can be nice to reserve some of your filling for scattering on top, or you can top it with another banana, sliced in half lengthways and laid cut-side up.

5. Then it's time to bake. For a large tin, it will take 50–60 minutes, and you can't rely on it being bouncy to know if it's done. Stick a skewer or sharp knife in – it needs to come out clean, except for fruit or chocolate residue. A loaf or cake that's half this size might take 30–40 minutes, and individual loaves will likely be done in 20–25 minutes.

American Pumpernickel

Y

YS

S

Unlike with most breads in this book, here we're after a bit of density. Yes, we still use yeast, and preferably sourdough, but the rise is secondary. Instead, it's for the fermentation: we want to break down those starches into sugars, soften the bran and create a bit of a tang. Once cooled, this bread slices very well, and freezes excellently for instant toast.

If sliced thickly, pumpernickel can be tough and dry; the key is to slice it thinly and top generously with toppings, so that its strong flavour can complement and not overwhelm what it's accompanying. Try topping with roasted figs, goats' cheese and honey, or smoked salmon, cream cheese, lemon and dill. Or butter: good butter, and thick, so you can see your teeth marks when you bite.

Makes 1 large loaf

250g wholemeal rye flour
200g strong white flour
100g 'cracked' rye (crushed rye berries) (optional, but recommended for a denser, more earthy texture, plus an extra 50g water, if using)
15g cocoa (unsweetened chocolate) powder
1½ tsp table salt
1 tsp instant yeast (optional)
60g black treacle (molasses)
400–450g tepid water
100g sourdough starter, fed with rye flour (page 50) (optional)
butter, for greasing
rye flour, for dusting

1. In a large bowl, weigh your rye and white flours, your 'cracked' rye, if using, cocoa and salt. For a yeasted loaf, add the yeast, treacle and tepid water, 400g if you have not included the cracked rye and 450g if you have. For extra flavour, include the sourdough starter – even an inactive, neglected starter will do here. For a full sourdough, leave out the yeast but include an active sourdough starter. Mix everything together until roughly combined. Don't try and work your dough too hard just now – it will seem very wet until the water is properly absorbed.

2. Leave it to autolyse (rest) for at least 30 minutes, then give your dough a knead for 5 minutes – this isn't essential, but I find it really helps with the texture of your final loaf. You'll find the gluten developing and the dough holding its shape far better.

3. Cover your bowl with a dish towel or clingfilm (plastic wrap) and leave somewhere at room temperature. Prove for 2 hours if using yeast, or 3–4 hours if going full sourdough. Whichever you choose, I recommend one stretch and fold (page 47); you might find it just breaks, but this can help redistribute moisture if this dough begins to split.

4. You might not notice much of a rise, but there should be something. Use a dough scraper to turn the dough onto a floured surface and form into a long lump: shaping in a traditional sense can be quite difficult with these loaves. Grease a 900g loaf tin, or your chosen tins, with plenty of butter, and stick your lump inside.

5. Cover your tin with clingfilm or place inside a plastic bag, and leave to rest for another hour if using yeast, or 2 hours if sourdough. This also works excellently in the fridge overnight, or for up to 24 hours. Preheat the oven to 180°C (350°F) fan (200°C/400°F/gas 6) about 15 minutes before you plan on baking.

6. There's no need to score, and you can even sprinkle with bare flour and watch as you get nice random cracks open up during the bake. Place your tin in the oven and add some steam by putting a tray of ice in the bottom of the oven.. Bake for a good hour, or until you've got a thick, caramelized crust. Cool completely before slicing.

Pueblos Bread

Y

(Native American Clay Oven Bread)

This bread caught my eye following my outreach to find underrepresented breads from around the world. It turns out you could write an entire book on the bread of the Pueblos – a diverse group of Native American tribes across the Southwestern US.

Until Spanish colonization, the tribes would have made flatbreads out of native beans or corn – but then with the introduction of wheat and the iconic beehive-shaped *horno* clay oven, these breads evolved. The doughs themselves are fairly simple things: they tend to be white and, crucially, moderately enriched with butter or lard. Depending on the interpretation, an egg might be added. Following testing, I've found the egg, in particular, allows these breads to rise well, despite the lack of steam and the very dry heat of the oven.

The oven is crucial here. It was my temptation to start this recipe with 'First, build a clay oven', but my editor won't let me. For those of us without one already rising from our New Mexico back yard, you can still create the necessary environment at home. A pizza oven, kamado grill or even a kettle barbecue will be perfect. The idea is to bake in the hot, dry heat as the oven cools, for an hour or more. These improvized modern ovens don't have the heat inertia of the grand clay structures of the Pueblos tribes, some of which can take 50 loaves or more – so we might have to add a bit more fuel during cooking to maintain the heat.

Makes 1 large loaf

400g strong white flour, plus extra for dusting
1 tsp table salt
1 tsp instant yeast
25g lard or salted or unsalted butter, plus extra for greasing
200g tepid water
1 large egg

1. In a large bowl, weigh your flour, salt and yeast together. Then add lard or butter, and rub these in so they are mostly combined. Then it's your water and egg, and mix everything together until roughly combined.

2. Leave to autolyse (rest) for 20 minutes, especially if choosing a no-knead method, then knead the dough. If possible, cut it in half and get a friend or a family member to knead half of it while you do the other half, and talk about something unrelated. You'd be amazed how a bit of kneading gets the conversation going. This is in the spirit of the Pueblos, who still congregate at big social gatherings to prepare this bread together. Or you could use an electric mixer and do something else entirely for 10 minutes.

3. Return your dough to your bowl, cover with clingfilm (plastic wrap) or a dish towel and leave it at room temperature for 60–90 minutes. Alternatively, stick it in a cold fridge for 8–10 hours.

4. Grease a large cake tin 20–23cm (8–9in) with plenty of butter or lard. Then lightly flour your surface and flip your dough onto it. Cut it into seven roughly equal pieces, then shape each into a ball (page 40). Place one ball in the middle of your tin, then space each of the rest around it, to create a flower pattern. Cover this by gently draping in clingfilm or with a dish towel. Leave to prove for another 60 minutes, or in a cold fridge for up to several hours.

5. Now you could just bake this in your standard oven, preheated to 180°C (350°F) fan (200°C/400°F/gas 6), but where's the fun in that? Get your barbecue, pizza oven or kamado grill going using ethical lumpwood charcoal. You want to get it properly hot, then allow your coals to burn down to an ashy smoulder. It's at this point you want to put your bread inside; if you bake with hot flames rising, it will just burn. Bake slowly for at least an hour: I use an infrared thermometer and monitor the temperature. If it's dropping, add a few more coals. This will create some hot spots, but it's better than raw bread.

AMERICA
CENTRAL
& SOUTH
AMERICA

Corn Tortillas & Flour Tortillas

U

In writing this recipe, I've had the agony of balancing accessibility of ingredients with the flavour of the final product; I'm thousands of miles from this bread's heritage. Ingredients are difficult to come by, and is it really sustainable to suggest using flour that's been shipped halfway across the world?

But I wonder if it's my job to insist; that by suggesting only traditional corn tortillas, I could play some small part in creating local supply chains. It wasn't long ago you couldn't get anything but basic 'brown' and 'white bread flour' in a big supermarket, but things are changing. We need to keep demanding that change.

Masa harina, the essential ingredient in making corn tortillas, isn't really produced anywhere else but in Central America. It's nixtamalized corn, meaning it's been boiled in a highly alkaline solution, usually lime, before hulling. This softens the corn and allows it to be easily ground: you'll notice the texture is far more akin to flour than traditional cornmeal or polenta.

This allows it to form into a dough, and there's not really a substitute for it elsewhere. Using fine cornmeal produces something grainy that you'll struggle to shape. You could, by all means, start with bare corn, and go through the process of boiling with lime, grinding into a paste and shaping, but it does lead to something quite crumbly, and it doesn't pass the midweek meal test.

I've therefore included two variations: traditional corn tortillas that you'll need your *masa* for, or a simple variation made from wholemeal flour: if you can use a local, finely milled version (or better yet, mill it yourself on your mill's finest setting), this makes the best tortillas. Alternatively, substitute chapatti-style, finely ground wholemeal flour, which works well too.

If you are planning to make these more than once, it might be worth investing in a tortilla press. Otherwise, you can use the bottom of a cast iron pan or a rolling pin.

Makes 12 tortillas

For corn tortillas
250g masa harina, plus extra for shaping
½ tsp salt
300g warm water

For flour torillas
250g wholemeal flour, plus extra for shaping
½ tsp salt
170g warm water
30g vegetable oil

To make corn tortillas

1. Weigh your *masa* and salt together in a bowl and roughly combine using your fingers. Add your water and mix together until it comes together into a dough. Keep mixing until all of the *masa* is incorporated and you've got a smooth dough.

2. Cover and rest your dough for at least 15 minutes to allow the corn to hydrate. At the end of this time, put a heavy-based pan or skillet on a medium heat while you shape.

3. Turn your dough out onto a bare surface and use a dough scraper to divide it into 12 individual lumps. Use your hands to form these into balls. One at a time, place a lump on a piece of baking parchment. Add another piece of baking parchment on top, and roll out until flat and round, about 1–2mm thin and at least 15cm (6in) in diameter. Alternatively, use a tortilla press.

4. Cook for about 90 seconds each side, or until blushing dark brown and speckled on both sides. Set aside to cool; I like to cover with a dish towel to keep them warm and soft. As one cooks, roll out another, continuing until all are done.

To make flour tortillas

1. Weigh your flour and salt together in a bowl and roughly combine using your fingers. Add the water and oil, then form into a dough. This is a dry dough and you might have difficulty bringing it together. Once formed, give it a knead for a couple of minutes to ensure the flour is well hydrated and distributed.

2. Cover your bowl and rest for at least 20 minutes – but longer is fine, and will make it easier to roll out. At the end of this time, put a heavy-based pan or skillet on a medium heat while you shape.

3. Turn your dough onto a lightly floured surface. Use a dough scraper to cut into 12 roughly equal portions and use two hands to form each into a ball shape. Using a little flour, roll them out one by one, until they're at least 15cm (6in) wide and 1–2mm thick.

4. Cook for about 90 seconds each side, or until blushing dark brown and speckled on both sides. Set aside to cool; I like to cover with a dish towel to keep them warm and soft. As one cooks, roll out another, continuing until all are done.

Pan de Yema

Y

Yolk Bread (& Thick Hot Chocolate)

This is a local *pan de muertos*, a Day of the Dead celebration bread, found in the southern Mexican city of Oaxaca. My own culture shies away from the taboo of death, so I'm glad these recipes are here to break down these barriers and we can bake bread to celebrate the passing of time. I think my own little society has a lot to learn: to accept what has been, to celebrate a life and to honour and remember those who are no longer here.

Pan de yema literally translates as 'yolk bread'. If you use really high-quality eggs with dark orange yolks, this bread turns a stunning hue, especially when torn. Mix in a touch of cinnamon (though anise is also traditional) and some orange zest, then you've got the base for a super-soft and enriched roll that's traditionally torn and dipped in hot chocolate.

The hot chocolate recipe is for a traditional Mexican-style hot chocolate, spiced with cinnamon and, if you like, a touch of cayenne.

***Makes 12* pan de yema**
and hot chocolate for 2

For the *pan de yema*
4 medium eggs plus 2 yolks, at room temperature
500g strong white flour
1 tsp table salt
2 tsp instant yeast
60g caster (superfine) sugar
120g warm water
100g unsalted butter, at room temperature
sesame seeds, for dusting

For hot chocolate for 2 people
500g whole milk
100g high-quality dark chocolate
20g caster (superfine) sugar
1 cinnamon stick
a pinch of cayenne (optional)

1. Start by cracking your eggs into a cup, one by one in case any broken shell makes its way in, then pour into a large bowl. Separate your two yolks, keeping back your whites for brushing later, and add them to the bowl. Weigh your flour, salt, yeast and sugar on top. Finally, add your water and combine to a dough. If your butter is in the fridge, it's worth getting it out now so it's softer in half an hour or so.

2. Leave your dough to autolyse (rest) for 10–20 minutes if you've got time, then start kneading. This is a sticky dough, but easily manageable. It can take a bit of working in order to come together. When it's becoming smooth, work in your butter, continuing until all the butter is completely combined. An electric mixer works well (page 35). If using the no-knead method (page 45), you can work in your butter after the first stretch and fold (page 47), which acts as a bit of a knead anyway.

3. Leave your dough to rest at room temperature for about 90 minutes or so. Alternatively, you can leave it overnight in the fridge – because of how much sugar we're using here, that inhibits the yeast.

4. Line a baking tray with a piece of baking parchment. Scrape your dough out onto a lightly floured surface, then ease it into a sausage shape, so that you can easily cut out 12 equal dough balls: cut the length in half, then half again, then each piece into three. Shape these as for rolls (page 40) and space out on your baking tray. If you're keen for them not to touch, you might want to use two trays.

5. Gently lay a piece of oiled clingfilm (plastic wrap) over the top of your rolls and let them prove for a final 45–60 minutes. About 15 minutes before it's ready, preheat your oven to 200°C (400°F) fan (220°C/425°F/gas 7).

6. Just before baking, use your reserved egg white to brush the top of the breads, then sprinkle on some sesame seeds. Slice each roll in a cross shape, and bake for 20–25 minutes until golden brown and baked but still soft.

7. As they cool, you can make the hot chocolate. In a saucepan, weigh the milk, then break in the chocolate. Add the sugar, cinnamon and pinch of cayenne. Place over a low–medium heat, stirring occasionally, until all the chocolate has melted. Don't let the milk boil. Once hot but not boiling, pour into a mug. Tear your still warm rolls and dip.

Conchas

Y

YS

(Mexican Sweet Bread Rolls)

These are one of the *pan dulce*, or sweet breads, of Mexico and feature with such ubiquity, I couldn't leave them out of this compendium. Here, the soft, enriched and brioche-like roll is encrusted with a sweet shell. It's a bit like a sweet tiger bread, which is brushed with a flour mixture that, as the dough underneath springs in the oven, cracks open. It's even more like *craquelin* that's draped over modern choux. Except with *conchas*, you don't tend to leave the topping to randomly crack, but score it into a shell pattern for that iconic effect.

Every Mexican bakery in the world will sell *conchas*, I'm sure, and there are infinite variations: even if you don't follow my recipe exactly, the nice thing is you can create a few different flavours from a single batch. Keep the dough consistent, and you can change the topping to the flavour (and the colour) of your preference.

You might notice many recipes use vegetable shortening for the biscuity crust, but I've switched out butter for flavour and to avoid the worst sort of rehydrogenated vegetable fats (trans fats). Yes, butter is the healthy option. Gotta draw the line somewhere.

***Makes 16* conchas**

For the conchas

500g strong white flour, plus extra for dusting
1½ tsp table salt
70g caster (superfine) sugar
2 tsp instant yeast (optional)
100g sourdough starter, fed with white flour (page 50) (optional)
200g milk
2 large eggs
1 teaspoon vanilla paste
100g butter

1. Start by weighing your flour, salt and sugar into a large bowl. For a yeasted loaf, mix in the yeast, reducing by half to 1 teaspoon if you plan on leaving your dough overnight at either point. For extra flavour, add some sourdough starter with the liquid portion. I wouldn't recommend this one for a full sourdough as it can struggle with the amount of sugar in the dough.

2. Weigh your milk in another bowl or jug, then warm it in the microwave or by placing it in a sink with some hot water. You want it tepid – neither hot nor cold. Add this to your flour, along with your eggs and vanilla paste, and combine to a dough.

3. Leave it to autolyse (rest) for 10–20 minutes if you've got the time, then knead. This is a sticky dough, so the slap and fold method will work well (page 36). As it's coming together and you think it's nearly done, add your butter: this should be soft, so use the microwave if it isn't. Instead of hand kneading, you can use an electric mixer (page 35), or you can use a no-knead method (page 45) if you prefer, so long as you use your second stretch and fold to incorporate your butter fully.

For the topping

100g butter, plus extra for brushing
100g icing (confectioners') sugar
100g plain flour (or cornflour/ cornstarch), or other gluten-free white flour
½ tsp ground cinnamon (for a cinnamon topping)
2 tsp cocoa (unsweetened chocolate) powder (for a chocolate topping)

4. Leave your dough to rest at room temperature for about 90 minutes or so. Alternatively, you can leave it overnight in the fridge – and you'll have reduced the yeast quantity.

5. Meanwhile, make the topping. In a bowl, soften your butter if it isn't so, using the microwave. Add your icing sugar and beat together to a paste. Finally, add your flour, and beat until it comes together to a dough. Divide this in half, and work in your cinnamon to one half, and your cocoa into the other. These can be covered or wrapped until needed.

6. Line a baking tray (or two to give them extra space) with plenty of baking parchment. Scrape your dough out onto a lightly floured surface, then gently ease into a long sausage shape. Use this to chop it into 16 pieces, and then shape as for rolls (page 40). Arrange these on your trays, and prepare your toppings. It helps to have some butter prepared, very soft or just-melted in the microwave, for brushing.

7. Divide each topping dough into eight pieces. Using the palm of your hand (or a rolling pin), squash each down into thin discs about 2mm thick. Brush your dough with a little melted butter, then lay the disc on top, pressing gently so it sticks. It will overlap the sides and that is fine. Once each dough is used up, use a blunt knife to cut a shell shape through the topping in each, using parallel wavy lines.

8. Once they're all topped, let them prove for a final 45–60 minutes at room temperature. About 15–20 minutes before they are proved, preheat your oven to 200°C (400°F) fan (220°C/425°F/gas 7).

9. Your doughs should be noticeably risen but not at the edge of stability: they need oven spring to give you the shell shape and cracking. Bake for 20 minutes or so, or until the dough is golden brown, but the topping remains white. Serve fresh, or that day, with coffee or hot chocolate (page 232).

Pan de Camote

Y

YS

S

(Sweet Potato Rolls)

This is a sweet roll from Peru that triumphs both in its colour and its softness; the incorporation of cooked sweet potato means the dough clings onto moisture to give a soft, tearable bun that's naturally sweet. Then, of course, we enrich it more – for that super orange colour, use the best eggs you can find.

Adding root vegetables, and sweet potato in particular, can be a problem: the first time I made this, the bread ended up an overly wet flop, with rolls that I couldn't shape and that spread over the sides of the trays. I then tried a version where instead of boiling the sweet potato, I baked it slowly for an hour. The flavour was so much more intense, the dough sweeter and the colour saturated. And most importantly, the dough didn't turn over into a gummy mess.

Still, this is an enriched dough, and so should be treated like a brioche roll for serving purposes. If you're after a savoury rather than sweet use, then try sprinkling some sea salt over the top after your egg wash. If it's for having as a sweet snack, icing sugar makes its saccharine nature clear. If you're that sort of person who likes mixing sweet and salty popcorn, why not both?

Makes 12 rolls

1 large sweet potato – at least 250g unbaked weight
500g strong white flour, plus extra for dusting
1½ tsp salt
50g caster (superfine) sugar
2 tsp instant yeast (optional)
100g sourdough starter, fed with white flour (page 50) (optional)
40g butter
3 eggs, plus 1 for brushing
100g tepid water
icing (confectioners') sugar or sea salt, depending on your sweet-savoury preference

1. Start at least an hour, but up to a day, before you bake. Set your oven to 180°C (350°F) fan (200°C/400°F/gas 6), then wrap a sweet potato in kitchen foil. Roast it in the oven for an hour. Using a dish towel or oven glove, give it a squeeze to ensure it is soft. Leave to cool as you start the dough, or store in the fridge for later.

2. Start by weighing your flour, salt and sugar into a large bowl. For a yeasted loaf, mix in the yeast. If you are planning to leave the dough overnight in the fridge, reduce the quantity of yeast to 1 teaspoon. For extra flavour, add some sourdough starter too, along with the liquid ingredients. For a full sourdough, leave out the yeast altogether, and you'll need an active, happy, recently fed starter that's at peak rise.

3. Once you've mixed together your dry ingredients, add your butter, then rub this in so that it's mostly combined. It doesn't need to be perfect. Add your eggs, water and scoop in your soft sweet potato – you're aiming for 200g cooked weight. If your potato is hot, use cold water. If it's cold from the fridge, use warm water. Simple.

4. Leave it to autolyse (rest) for 10–20 minutes if you've got time, then get started with kneading. This should be a sticky dough, but manageable. The slap and fold method will work well (page 36). You can also use an electric mixer (page 35), or use the no-knead method (page 45).

5. Leave your dough to rest at room temperature for about 90 minutes. Alternatively, you can leave it overnight in the fridge – in which case you'll have reduced the yeast quantity.

6. Line a large baking tray with baking parchment. Turn your dough out onto a lightly floured surface and, using floured hands, ease into a long sausage. Divide your dough into 12 roughly equal balls, then shape like rolls (page 40). Place these on the baking tray to rest, leaving as much space as possible between.

7. Leave the rolls to prove for another 45–60 minutes, uncovered. Overnight or all day in the fridge is fine as long as you've got a very cold fridge, but cover them with a piece of clingfilm (plastic wrap) rubbed with a little oil and draped over the top.

8. About 15 minutes before they're ready, preheat your oven to 220°C (425°F) fan (240°C/ 465°F/gas 9).

9. In a small bowl, beat your egg with a little salt. Brush the tops of your rolls with egg wash, and sprinkle with sea salt for a savoury finish. Bake for 25 minutes, or until golden brown and crisp looking. Allow to cool, but you can re-warm to serve by baking in a similarly hot oven for 5 minutes. Dust with icing sugar for a sweet finish.

Arepas

U

(Fried Polenta Cakes)

Arepas break my rules of bread making. I had a belief that every palatable bread is either risen in some way, or rolled super-thin so they don't end up gummy and tough. *Arepas* are neither. The key to their success is the corn: cooked corn, naturally sweet and without gluten – tasty even in dough form. They are, basically, fried polenta cakes.

If you read every recipe for *arepas* (and I must have read a hundred or more), they'll insist on a special flour, appropriately called *masarepa*. This is only available in specialist shops in the UK, it's shipped across the world (so is expensive) and many readers won't have access to it.

Masarepa is made by cooking corn, then drying it out and grinding it up: this means that when mixed with water, it forms an instant dough. Obviously, this can be hacked: just take regular cornmeal, and cook it. Boil it to create a paste, then cool this down, form it into dough and fry. Pedants, don't panic, I go into a little more detail – a little.

***Makes 6–8* arepas**

For instant *arepas*

200g masarepa, such as Harina PAN
1 tsp salt
400g water
vegetable oil, for frying

For cornmeal *arepas*

200g coarse yellow cornmeal (polenta)
1 tsp salt
350g water
vegetable oil, for frying

For instant *arepa* dough

1. In a large bowl, weigh your *masarepa* flour and add the salt. Gently mix to combine. Add your water and mix everything together into a soft dough – if it won't come together, you could add a tablespoon more water. If you think it seems a bit wet and sticky, leave it for 5 minutes and come back to it.

For cornmeal *arepa* dough

1. In a saucepan, weigh your cornmeal, salt and water, and place over a medium heat. Stir all the time until it comes to a thick, bubbling paste. Turn the heat down to low and simmer for 25 minutes, or until the cornmeal has fully hydrated and the mix is on the smooth side – this can vary depending on the grind of the polenta.

2. Optionally, place a stick blender in and give it a buzz for an extra smooth dough. Then cover your pan with clingfilm (plastic wrap) and leave it to cool and set. Once cooled to room temperature, you should have a mouldable dough.

To make the *arepas*

1. Preheat your oven to 200°C (400°F) fan (220°C/425°F/gas 7). Then stick a cast iron skillet (or other ovenproof pan) over a medium–high heat.

2. Take a handful of dough and roll it between your hands to create a ball. Squash this down between your hands until it is 1cm (½in) thick. Repeat with three other lumps, or as many as you can fit in the pan. Cover the rest of the dough.

3. Slosh some vegetable oil (about 2 tablespoons – be generous) into your pan, and fry your *arepas* for 3–4 minutes on each side until golden, (do NOT press down on the tops with your spatula). Stick in the oven and bake for 15 minutes, or until puffed up and set.

4. If you have leftover dough, you can repeat immediately if you have another skillet and space in the oven for crossover. Otherwise, wait until the first is done. Watch that handle – don't forget it's hot when it's back on the hob.

Marraqueta Integral

Y

YS

S

(Brown Crusty Rolls)

I've mentioned that my original idea for this book was a kind of *World Atlas of Bread*, where I would try to represent bread from every country around the globe. I sought help from people around the world using the power of social media, and received hundreds of impassioned suggestions. These were fiercely loyal to their local breads and keen for representation. I'm very sorry I couldn't adequately research, test and write about them all, for this would take up about 10 volumes and be a life's work.

Sometimes, as you'll see, I've had to pick a bread to make an important point, and that's why I've picked a *marraqueta*, a variation on the baguette and on the simple white roll. The trouble is, there are other breads from around South and Central America of almost identical construction: *pan felipe*, *pao cacetinho*, *pan marsellés*, *pan francés*, *pan blanco* and even the iconic *bolillo*. I didn't want to write recipes for the same bread over and over again, and I'm sure you don't want to read that. I want to get into the difficult discussion of their origins. There is a portrayal, I feel, that breads such as these spread due to the natural migration of French bakers seeking new horizons, and that popularity was driven by the passion of the people.

But the domination of certain breads is not natural. Bread has been adopted through colonialism, through poor industrial practice and through governmental policy. Bringing in the wheat has driven out many native species, resulted in huge deforestation and replaced more sustainable, local forms of agriculture for the purposes of placation, of evangelism and, above all, of profit.

This rant is unfair on the *marraqueta*, which is wonderful. As I write the recipe for this crusty roll, I'm thinking about its history, and what we should do about it, if anything. My suggestion is that you find a local flour mill, which gets locally grown wheat and uses the whole grain. You can look into the increasing practices of promoting biodiversity and soil health in arable agriculture. You can become interested in the origin of flour as we know it today, and what we can learn and enjoy of wheats of old.

So this isn't quite a traditional *marraqueta* recipe: it honours it. It's a full 50% wholemeal, and I'd suggest using wholemeal that you know was grown somewhere nearby in a sustainable way.

Makes 8 marraquetas

250g strong white flour
1½ tsp table salt
250g wholemeal flour, plus extra for dusting
1 tsp instant yeast (optional)
100g sourdough starter, fed with any flours (page 50) (optional)
330g tepid water
50g just-boiled water

1. Weigh your white flour and salt into a large bowl. Sieve your wholemeal flour on top (specified weight includes bran), and reserve the bran for later. For yeasted, mix in the yeast. For extra flavour, mix in sourdough starter next. For a full sourdough, leave out the yeast and add the sourdough starter.

2. Add your tepid water and mix everything to combine into a sticky dough. It will feel wet, so I highly recommend you leave it to autolyse (rest) for 20–30 minutes if you've got time, before you knead.

3. Meanwhile, place your bran in another bowl and pour over your boiling water. Mix until combined into a paste. Cover this bowl and set aside until cool.

4. Knead your main dough for 5–10 minutes, using your chosen method, or you can use an electric mixer (page 35). The no-knead method works well for this dough (page 45). Leave your dough to rest at room temperature for about 30 minutes for a yeasted dough, or for sourdough, at least an hour. Then turn your dough out onto a wet surface, and using wet hands, stretch it out, as for the lamination method (page 61). Spread over your bran paste, then fold and roll up your dough.

5. Prove for another 30–60 minutes, or stick it in the fridge overnight or all day. For sourdough, prove for 3 hours at a warm room temperature.

6. Set two baking trays aside. Flour a work surface, and turn your dough out onto it. You want to cut it into eight equal pieces: cut your dough in half, then each in half again, then each in half again. Shape each as for batons (page 42). Then, rather than shaping them for baguettes, place the side of one hand in the middle of your baton, and rock back and forth into the surface until the two halves come apart completely. Place these two sides right next to each other on the baking tray, just as they came apart. Repeat with the rest.

7. Prove for a final 30 minutes, or 90 minutes for sourdough. If you've gone full sourdough, feel free to stick these in a cold fridge for up to 12 hours. About 15 minutes before it's ready, preheat your oven to 200°C (400°F) fan (220°C/425°F/gas 7).

8. Score down the lengths of each dough, running from one hump into the next. Bake for 25–30 minutes or so, or until a deep golden brown and very crisp. Allow to cool at least slightly, then tear and eat.

Hojaldres

BP

(Deep-fried Doughnuts)

If you're a Spanish speaker with a repertoire of pastry-related language, you may know *hojaldres* as puff pastries, or kinds of viennoiserie.

In Panama and neighbouring Central American countries, *hojaldres* means something completely different compared with Europe: a puffy pastry of different origin that's far more similar to the well-known churro. This is a deep-fried, old-fashioned style doughnut, which can be made as quickly as it takes the oil to heat up (but is improved with a little rest). It is really, really easy, but must be eaten fresh: they stale quickly.

The dusting of icing sugar, while still hot, is crucial, as it crisps and caramelizes slightly on the crust. Be careful with frying – use a deep-fryer, or a digital thermometer to check the temperature of your oil exactly.

***Makes 16* hojaldres**

400g plain white flour, plus extra for dusting
20g caster (superfine) sugar
2 tsp baking powder
1 tsp table salt
1 egg
240g cold water
vegetable oil, for frying (at least 1 litre)
plenty of icing (confectioners') sugar, for dusting

1. Start by making the dough. In a large bowl, weigh your white flour, sugar, baking powder and salt. Add your egg and water, and stir into a dough. It might be a bit wet at this stage – just cover the bowl and leave the dough to rest for 30–60 minutes.

2. Set your deep-fryer, or put your oil into a large, high-sided pan over a low heat. Gradually heat the oil to 170°C (340°F) on a digital thermometer. This will take 10 minutes or so. Prepare a tray nearby, lined with kitchen paper.

3. Turn your rested dough out onto a lightly floured surface. Add some flour on top and, using a dough scraper, chop it into 16 small pieces – for example, chop it in half, then each piece in half again, then each of those in half again twice more.

4. Use your hands (no need for precision) to press down on a lump of dough and squash it into a disc, about 5mm (¼in) thick or so. Drop as many of these into your hot oil as you can fit in the pan. Fry for 2–3 minutes on each side, or until golden brown. Use a slotted spoon to scoop them out and place on your kitchen paper to soak up any excess oil. Transfer to a plate and dust with icing sugar.

5. Repeat with the rest, re-dusting with icing sugar whenever a new batch is ready. Eat fresh, or at least warm.

Fugazza & Fugazzeta

Y

YS

S

(Onion Flatbread and Stuffed Crust Onion Flatbread)

Fugazza. *Focaccia*. *Fougasse*. All have the same Latin derivation: 'focus', meaning the bread made in the intense heat of the fire. While *focaccia* and *fougasse* have evolved somewhat into more dumpy and wholesome expressions of the flatbread, I see *fugazza* as still true to the original principles, and so suggest you bake it as close to the heat of a freshly fuelled wood fire oven as you can get. If you've got a pizza oven or a kamado grill, use this, and you're aiming for it to be as hot as rated, up to about 450°C (840°F). In your own oven, you can aim to re-create this environment by pre-heating a stone, pizza steel or a cast iron skillet to as hot as it goes, or to use the skillet-broiler method (page 118).

This bread does share some similarities with pizza, but rather than just being topped, you have the option of stuffing it: *fugazzeta*. In this variation, you create two discs of dough. In between, a layer of cheese runs the full area of the disc, then you top the whole thing with even more cheese, and sliced onions. Because you're creating a thick layer here, you want to turn down the heat a tad.

The onions can be further customized: you've got the option to cook them down first, allowing them to caramelize during the final bake. Or you can do as I do: shred them fine, and put them on raw. They will still be crisp and tangy when the bread is fully baked, the spiked edges catching a little. This cuts through the heft of the cheese, in a bread that might be otherwise overwhelmingly rich (the tang of some olives can balance this).

The beauty of baking is knowing which rules you can break and which you can't, and once you know that, you can have a lot of fun. **Before starting, I'd recommend reading my pizza masterclass on page 108, as many of the principles apply here.**

Makes 4 **fugazza** *or 2* **fugazzeta**

400g strong white flour, plus extra for dusting
1 tsp table salt
2 tsp instant yeast (optional)
260g tepid water
80g sourdough starter, fed with white flour (page 50) (optional)
semolina, for shaping and baking

For the topping
1 large white onion
200g mozzarella, preferably pre-grated
100g provolone (Provoleto) or grated Parmesan (ideally aged 12 months)
salt and freshly ground black pepper
olive oil, for drizzling

1. Start by weighing your flour and salt into a large bowl. For a yeasted bread, mix in the yeast. If you are planning to leave the dough overnight in the fridge, reduce the quantity of yeast to 1 teaspoon. For extra flavour, you can add some sourdough starter with the wet ingredients. For a full sourdough, leave out the yeast and add the sourdough starter, although I wouldn't recommend this one for a full sourdough.

2. Add your water, and mix everything together into a dough. Leave it to autolyse for 10–20 minutes if you can, then get started with kneading. This dough isn't too wet and should come together with ease. If you've got an electric mixer, this is a good time to use it (page 35), but you could use any other kneading method (page 35).

3. Leave your dough to rest at room temperature for about 60 minutes, or 4 hours with two stretches and folds for sourdough (page 47). Alternatively, you can leave it overnight or all day in the fridge – and you'll have reduced the yeast quantity if using yeast, and left it for a couple of hours at room temperature first if sourdough to get it going.

4. Turn your dough out onto a floured surface. Chop it into four, and shape each of these into very loose boules (page 39). You just want them ball-shaped rather than tight. Add plenty of flour and semolina to a large tray or container, and place the dough balls in there with plenty of space between. Cover with more flour and semolina, then cover with kitchen foil or a lid. You can stick these in the fridge until needed, up to a day in advance, but at least another hour (regardless of sourdough or yeasted). Make sure you remove from the fridge 30 minutes before you plan on baking.

5. Get your toppings sorted – finely slice your onion into lengths, and if you've not got grated mozz, get it chopped thinly and finely and dried between a couple of sheets of kitchen paper. If you've got provolone, grate this coarsely.

For a *fugazza* – thin dough (*media masa*), unstuffed crust

1. Heat your pizza oven to 450°C (840°F) fan (full guide on page 113), or as close to this as possible. Otherwise, for the skillet-broiler method, set your pan on a medium–high heat and get your grill (broiler) turned to high. If neither of these suit, turn your oven with a pizza steel or pizza stone inside to as hot as it goes.

2. Scoop your portion of dough out onto a well-floured and semolina-dusted surface. Flip over so both sides are covered, and shape into a large flat disc. Cover your disc with a quarter of your cheese, and sprinkle over a quarter of your onion. Season with salt and pepper and drizzle some oil on top. Bake using your chosen method until the base is cooked, the onions are just blushing burnt (call it caramelized) and the crust is golden. This might take less than 2 minutes, so watch it closely. Repeat.

For a *fugazzeta* – stuffed and topped

1. Heat your pizza oven to 350°C (660°F) (full guide on page 113), or as close to this as possible. Otherwise, for the skillet-broiler method, set your pan on a medium heat and get your grill (broiler) turned to medium. If neither of these suits, turn your oven to 220°C (425°F) fan (240°C/465°F/gas 9) with a pizza steel or pizza stone inside.

2. Scoop your portion of dough out onto a well-floured and semolina-dusted surface. Flip over so both sides are covered, and shape into a large flat disc – you want the thickness to be as even as possible middle to edge. Then repeat and make an identical disc.

3. Spread a quarter of your cheese over your first disc, leaving a gap all the way around the edge. Then place your other disc on top, pressing all the way around to seal tightly. Sprinkle with more cheese and top with loads of onions, some oil, salt and pepper.

4. Bake using your chosen method for about 4 minutes, until the base is cooked, the onions are just blushing burnt (call it caramelized) and the crust is golden. Repeat with the rest.

Sopa Paraguaya

BP

(Paraguayan Cornbread)

This is a traditional bread that's unique in this compendium: I couldn't resist the traditional version that eschews the relatively modern (nearly two centuries old) invention of chemical raising agents. Rather, it uses only eggs to give this bread its lift.

It's often served at barbecues and makes a mean burger, or a dipper for soup or stew in the winter. It's got a reputation for being dense, but it's really needlessly so. This is a fairly straight down the line recipe, but I've simply divided some of the ingredients in non-traditional ways. Indeed, I've borrowed techniques from French and Italian pastry, where we separate the eggs, whisk both of them separately with added flour or sugar to stabilize, and then carefully fold everything together. It's easy stuff, so long as you don't mind dirtying three bowls.

Makes a 20cm (8in) square loaf

2 large onions
a large slosh (3 tbsp) vegetable oil, or rendered meat fat
1 red (bell) pepper (optional)
200g fresh corn (you can use frozen, defrosted)
250g cornmeal, preferably fine
150g cottage cheese (queso panela) or ricotta
200g milk
4 tsp caster (superfine) sugar
3 eggs
50g hard dry cheese, such as sardo (substitute pecorino or Parmigiano Reggiano)

1. Start by getting your onions on – finely slice them into thin strips, then stick them into a large skillet with your oil or rendered fat, over a very low heat, to soften while you finely slice your pepper and stick this in with the onions. Keep frying for 10–15 minutes until soft.

2. As those are frying slowly (keep half an eye on them to prevent burning), follow the steps below to make your batter. Before you do, preheat your oven to 180°C (350°F) fan (200°C/400°F/gas 6), and line a 20cm (8in) roasting or brownie tin with baking parchment.

3. For the batter, you'll need three bowls. In the first, weigh your corn. Use a stick blender to gently break this down into a very lumpy paste. Alternatively, pop this into a food processor and then tip it back into your bowl. Add in your cornmeal, cheese and milk and mix together into a thick batter.

4. Into your other two bowls, separate your eggs. If you're not used to doing this using the two halves of your cracked egg, just crack your whole egg into a cupped hand and let the white drip through your fingers. If the whites get any wee bits of yolk in them, fish these out.

5. Use a clean whisk, preferably an electric one on top speed, to whisk your egg whites until they form stiff white peaks: it's important you start with the whites to avoid contaminating them with the fat of the yolk. Then, add 2 teaspoons of caster sugar and keep whisking until this has disappeared and your whites are even more smooth and glossy.

6. Transfer your whisk to your yolks and beat these until they turn thick, pale and airy, and have at least doubled in size. Add the remaining sugar and keep beating: this will help them puff up.

7. Using a large metal spoon, mix in your fried peppers and onions – it doesn't matter if they are still hot. Then fold in your yolks, followed by your egg whites, as gently as possible to preserve as much of the air you've beaten in as you can.

8. Scoop your mix into your prepared tin, and grate your hard cheese on top. Bake until a deep golden brown, about 40 minutes, then allow to cool before slicing into squares to serve.

Galleta de Campana

Y

YS

(Uruguayan Flaky Rolls)

There are a few different ways to make these flaky Uruguayan breads, including an interesting 'reverse' puff by laminating bare flour into an enriched dough, but here I've kept it fairly traditional and simple. Make a bread dough. Roll it out, rub it with butter, fold it over and repeat. You don't want it as rich and flaky as croissants, but rather this could be seen as a more everyday pastry, as well as far faster and more accessible.

Makes 20 galletas

500g strong white flour, plus extra for dusting
30g caster (superfine) sugar
1½ tsp salt
2 tsp instant yeast (optional)
300g water
100g unsalted butter, very soft
30g vegetable oil
100g sourdough starter, fed with white flour (page 50) (optional)
icing (confectioners') sugar, for dusting

1. Start by weighing your flour, sugar and salt into a large bowl. For a yeasted loaf, mix in the yeast. If you are planning to leave the dough overnight in the fridge, reduce the quantity of yeast to 1 teaspoon. For extra flavour, mix in the sourdough starter.

2. Add your water, then mix everything together into a dough. Flour a work surface, and turn the dough out onto it. Use a rolling pin to roll your dough out into a big rectangle: at least 30×60cm (12×24in). It doesn't matter if it breaks. Add more flour if it starts to stick.

3. Soften your butter in the microwave, then mix it with your oil to create a paste. Use a brush (or just your fingers) to spread it across the entire surface of the dough. Then, you're going to fold the dough up like a letter (a letter fold in puff pastry): imagine the dough divided into thirds, and take one edge and fold it over the middle along one of the third lines, then complete the fold with the other edge.

4. Turn the dough a quarter turn (90 degrees) and roll it out again, adding more flour if need be. It might give you some resistance; if that's the case, leave it 5 minutes and try again. Do another letter fold, then repeat twice more, so there are four folds altogether. Your dough will be smooth and stretchy with all the rolling. Leave it to rest for at least 10 minutes before your final roll.

5. Roll your dough out until it's a 2cm (¾in) thick rectangle. Use a fork to prick all the way across this, right down through the layers. Use your scraper to cut it into squares, as large or small as you like; I like smaller ones, as it amplifies the height. Place on a baking tray and leave to prove for another 60 minutes or so.

6. About 15 minutes before it's ready, preheat your oven to 200°C (400°F) fan (220°C/425°F/gas 7).

7. Bake for 20 minutes, or until you have noticeably puffed up towers of golden brown goodness. I like to sprinkle with a bit of icing sugar and have with coffee, but the shape and height are perfect for tearing open and filling with just about anything, even if that's more butter.

Pao de Queijo

U

(Cheese Rolls)

Pao de queijo are Brazilian snacks that I first baked after my mindless scrolling landed on superstar baker Bryan Ford whipping up these cheesy little balls. It was the process that engaged me: it's not like any other bread, really. If I had to compare it to any European method, it's most like making choux pastry, but with tapioca flour (cassava flour or tapioca starch) instead of wheat.

It's traditionally made with *meia cura* cheese – a short-aged yellow cheese that is difficult to get outside of Brazil, so – like several of the recipes in this book – use what you can find locally. You want something that will melt and go a bit stretchy, and you want something with that salty bite. For me, I've gone for a mix of grated mozz and coarsely grated Parmesan for that extra bite.

***Makes about 12–16* pao de queijo**

270g whole milk
100g butter
1 tsp salt
500g tapioca flour
3 large eggs
150g pre-grated mozzarella
100g Parmigiano Reggiano, Grana Padano or similar hard cheese

1. Preheat your oven to 190°C (375°F) fan (210°C/420°F/gas 7). Line two baking trays with baking parchment: these rolls need plenty of space to puff up.

2. Into a saucepan, weigh your milk, butter and salt. Place over a medium heat and bring to a gentle simmer. As that's heating, weigh your tapioca flour into a bowl, preferably one for an electric mixer.

3. Once your butter has melted and your milk is just beginning to bubble, pour this onto your flour. Beat using an electric mixer or an electric whisk until a thick, smooth glossy dough. Keep stirring to allow it to cool; it might get a bit lumpy as this happens.

4. While still warm, but not so hot as to scramble the eggs, add your first egg (touch the side of the bowl, and if you can hold your hand there for more than 3 seconds, that's OK). Beat in this egg, then add your other, and then the last one. Beat until smooth.

5. Finally, stir in your cheese. Your dough may be cool enough to shape straight away, but if it seems a bit liquid, like it will just spread out when scooped onto the trays, set aside to rest for 10–15 minutes.

6. Use a spoon or ice cream scoop to make little piles of dough: 12–16 on a large tray, as they will spread out and puff up during baking. Bake for 15–18 minutes, or until still pretty pale but blushing golden brown. Enjoy fresh, and preferably warm, with a delicious beverage.

ASIA

Baozi

Y

(Steamed Buns)

Ovens are hot and dry, no matter how hard we try to add steam at the beginning, and that dries out dough: the longer a bread is in this environment, the drier and tougher it will be. Instead, steaming cooks the dough rapidly, but avoids significant loss of moisture: if you've not had a bun fresh from the steamer, you've not experienced how moist and light bread can be.

Having spent some months working in Hanoi, Vietnam, I'm more familiar with the *banh bao*, a Cantonese import to the country filled with pork, Chinese sausage, egg and noodles. I spent some time trying to get the dough right on returning, and in doing so developed an appreciation for the far simpler, original Chinese version, which I've shared here.

The trick, to avoid buns that are overly gluey, is to avoid high-gluten, strong flour, if possible. You can use the highly processed, ultra-bleached Chinese bun flour, which you can find in most East Asian supermarkets, to get that traditional white look. I don't here, instead using a local unbleached flour that gives a fantastic flavour and more rustic texture.

Makes 10 filled buns

300g bleached Chinese bun flour (or use strong white flour, as I've done here)
1 tsp instant yeast
1 tsp caster (superfine) sugar
280g tepid water

1. Start by weighing your flour, yeast and sugar into a large bowl. While I'm sure sourdough bao would be possible, because we're aiming for light fluffiness primarily, I'd suggest sticking with yeast. Add your water and mix together into a dry dough.

2. Leave it to autolyse (rest) for 10–20 minutes if you've got time, then get started with kneading. This is a dough that will take a bit of work to change it from dry and brittle, to soft and a little stretchy. I use an electric mixer (page 35) for most doughs this dry, but you could use the stretch and roll method (page 37). No-knead works (page 45), but can make shaping a little more sticky.

3. Leave your dough to rest at room temperature for about 90 minutes or so. Alternatively, you can leave it overnight in the fridge. While that's resting, make your filling if you want a filled bun.

4. Finely dice your onion. Then place a wok or large frying pan (skillet) over a high heat and add the oil until it starts to smoke lightly. Add your onion and ginger paste and quickly stir just until the onion turns translucent and the edges just start to catch. You've now got two options: turn the heat off, add all the other ingredients and form into

For the optional filling

1 small onion

1 tbsp vegetable oil

1 tbsp ginger paste (or 1cm/½in fresh ginger root, grated)

400g minced (ground) pork

1 tbsp shaoxing (or any rice wine)

1 tbsp oyster sauce

1 tbsp soy sauce

1 tsp caster (superfine) sugar

1 tsp sesame oil

2 spring onions (scallions)

1 sliced red chilli (optional)

a raw pork sausage, which must be well-cooked inside the buns. Or continue as below, without any risk. If the latter, add the pork and continue to stir, breaking up the mince. Stir-fry until all the mince is cooked (it doesn't necessarily have to be crisp and brown). Then stir in your rice wine, oyster sauce, soy sauce, sugar and sesame oil and stir to combine, and reduce for 1–2 minutes before turning off the heat. Finely slice your spring onions and fresh chilli, and stir these through. Set aside to cool.

5. Turn the dough onto a surface – it's dry enough that you shouldn't need much or any flour. Ease it into a sausage shape to make dividing easier, then use your dough scraper to cut it into 10 roughly equal pieces.

6. If making unfilled bao, they look rather nice just simply cut. Cut 10 little circles of baking parchment, place your buns on their own paper pedestal, and leave on your surface to prove, covered lightly with a dish towel. If making filled bao, then one by one, using a little flour if you have to, press or roll each piece into a flat disc about 15cm (6in) in diameter. Scoop a tablespoon of your filling into the centre, then bring the edges into the middle, making small overlaps as you work your way round to create a pleated pattern. Pinch the top hard to seal, using a little water if it won't stick well. Set these on individual pieces of baking parchment and cover as above.

7. Prove for a final 30 minutes or so at room temperature – by the end of this, they should have risen a little, but not be overly fragile. This is essential if you want to avoid them collapsing during the steam, as overproved buns inevitably will.

8. Bring a full pan of water to a boil over a high heat, turning it down to medium when you're at the boil. Arrange your buns in your steamer, bamboo or otherwise, on their little baking parchment rafts. Leave at least 2cm (¾in) between them as they can puff up a lot. By all means, use multiple levels. Steam for 15-20 minutes, or until the buns have puffed up and have a glossy sheen. If you've used any raw filling, check that it's over 75°C (167°F) on a probe thermometer before taking out.

Shaobing

Y

(Sesame Flatbread)

I wanted to include *shaobing*, a kind of Chinese breakfast sesame pancake-bread hybrid, because it showcases a few techniques that aren't really used anywhere else in this book. There's no reason why you couldn't use them elsewhere – and if you do, in breads from totally different parts of the world or your own, I'd be delighted to hear about it. Precedent has just meant I haven't.

The first is an informal variation on the Tangzhong method (page 278) that's far quicker and is used through a number of east Asian steamed or baked breads. Instead of creating a separate roux or hot water dough, you simply add a (measured) splash of just-boiled water into your main batch of flour, stir until lumpy, then add cold water to get somewhere the equivalent of tepid so as not to harm your yeast.

The second is a way of laminating that instead of using just oil or butter, uses a hot flour-oil paste. In a yeasted dough, it's easy to have the oil or butter used in lamination simply absorb into the dough and you lose the definition of your layers. I don't quite know why the flour stops this happening, but it appears to. This could be useful when making variations of viennoiserie, roti canai or paratha, but I've not yet tried.

This is a breakfast food, perfect for an omelette sandwich. To be sure it's fresh, make the dough the night before and prove in the fridge, and you'll find the rolling process much easier, with no getting up early.

***Makes 6* shaobing**

200g plain (all-purpose) flour
½ teaspoon sea salt
50g just-boiled water
80g cold water
½ tsp instant yeast
10g vegetable oil, plus more for greasing

For the oil paste
50g vegetable oil
50g plain (all-purpose) flour

To finish
100g toasted white sesame seeds

1. Start ideally the night before, by weighing your flour and salt into a large bowl. Add your just-boiled water and stir gently using a wooden spoon until you've got a lumpy, floury mix. Then add your cold water, yeast and oil, and stir everything together into a lumpy, slightly sticky dough. There's no real need to knead this one, though some recipes will ask you to. Just stick it in the fridge overnight, or let it prove for an hour at room temperature.

2. In the morning, take the dough out the fridge to warm up a little while you make the oil paste (this will make it easier to roll out). Heat your oil in a frying pan (skillet) over a medium heat until it's too hot to hold your hand above and has lost its viscosity. Add your flour, and stir until the flour starts to darken slightly. Use a spatula to quickly scrape out of your pan into a bowl before the flour starts to burn. Set aside to cool for 5 minutes, while you preheat your oven to 220°C (425°F) fan (240°C/465°F/gas 9).

3. Scrape your dough out onto a lightly floured surface, then grab the corners of the dough and stretch out into a rectangle – we're going to make a spiral, like in Chelsea buns (page 81). Flour the top of the dough and roll it out into a rectangle about 40×30cm (16×12in), then brush evenly with the floury oily paste, using nearly all of it. Roll your dough up like a roulade.

4. Cut your roulade into six equal pieces. Prepare a bowl of your sesame seeds. One by one, roll each piece out into an oval, at least 20cm (8in) long. Brush lightly with any remaining paste, and roll each one up again in a tight spiral. Press this firmly into your sesame seeds to coat.

5. Finally, adding a little more flour if you need to, roll each bun out a final time, squashing the seeds into the dough, until it's a flat oval shape about 5mm (¼in) thick and 15cm (6in) long. Place on a baking tray lined with a sheet of baking parchment, and bake for about 10–12 minutes or until blushing golden brown. Set aside to cool, make yourself a filling and enjoy. These freeze well, and you can toast them to defrost them.

Chole Bhature

BP

When asking for suggestions for this book, *chole bhature* came up several times, there is such a fierce love of it. I'm assured by Mehar in New Delhi that it's officially the most listed 'favourite food' in all of India, and even has a national holiday in its honour. In essence, it's a Punjabi marriage of chickpea curry (*chole*) with *bhature*, a fried, puffed flatbread.

The process of making the bread is very similar to making a *poori*, except *bhature* is made from a white, soft dough, with some rising agent and some natural yogurt: it's often left to ferment and bubble a bit for many hours prior to frying. Because they're bubbly, they're a bit more forgiving if you let them dry out or roll them too thick or too thin. The yogurt gives softness to the dough and they are rather addictive.

Makes 8 **bhature**

For the *bhature*

250g plain (all-purpose) flour
½ tsp salt
1 tsp baking powder
60g plain yogurt
100g water
enough vegetable oil to coat your pan about 1cm (½in) deep

For the *chole*

2 × 400g tins of chickpeas (garbanzos), not drained, (or 200g dried chickpeas)
1 white onion
2 tbsp vegetable oil or ghee
1 tbsp garlic-ginger paste (or 3 cloves garlic and 1cm/½in fresh ginger root, finely chopped)
1 or 2 green chillies
½ tsp Kashmiri chilli powder
1 tbsp chole masala powder
1 tsp ground coriander (or crushed whole seeds)
a pinch of turmeric
½ tsp table salt, or to taste
400g tin of chopped tomatoes

1. In a large bowl, weigh your plain flour, salt and baking powder. Stir these to combine them. Add your yogurt and water and combine to make a dough.

2. Knead your dough for a few minutes – not to the extent as for most yeasted breads but just to ensure you've got something that's stretchy and very smooth. Return the dough to your bowl and cover it, and leave this for at least a couple of hours at room temperature.

3. Start to make the curry. If you're using dried chickpeas, you'll need to cook these first. My favourite way is to use a pressure cooker, as there's no soaking needed. Simply cover with loads of water (at least 1 litre for 200g dried chickpeas) and cook at high pressure for 40 minutes, before allowing the pressure to drop slowly. If you are using tinned chickpeas, you can skip this step.

4. Meanwhile, you can finely dice your onion. Place in a pan with your oil, and stick onto a low–medium heat. Cook for 8–10 minutes, stirring regularly, until the onions are translucent.

5. Add the garlic-ginger paste and green chillies, and cook for another 2 minutes before adding your spices and salt. Stir to distribute. Then add the tomatoes and chickpeas and bring to a simmer. Cook for at least 20 minutes at a gentle simmer, so that the harshness of the tomatoes goes. I'd keep simmering, topping up with a little water if needed, until the *bhature* is ready.

To finish

more green chillies, sliced in half lengthways

a large knob of butter

fresh coriander

6. When your dough is rested, turn out onto a lightly oiled surface. Cut it into about eight equal portions. Using oiled hands, shape each lump into a round ball. At this point, they can be set aside on the work surface while you prepare a pan of oil – place this over a low–medium heat and gradually heat. You want it at 180°C (355°F).

7. As it heats, you can finish the *chole*. Place your sliced chillies and generous knob of butter in a separate pan over a high heat, and cook the chillies until they are soft and the skins are blistering and the butter is starting to go a nutty brown. Add this into your *chole*, and stir or leave on top as a garnish. Sprinkle with more coriander.

8. Roll out each ball of dough until you've got discs about 15cm (6in) in diameter and about 2mm thick. Fry for about 60 seconds on each side until they are golden brown. They should be crisp on the outside but not crisps; the middle should be soft. Serve immediately, with the *chole*.

Naan

Y

YS

S

Where I live, the naans are heroic. I live in Glasgow, Scotland, and I'm lucky to share it with a diverse population, especially from Pakistan, Iran, Afghanistan and India, who have given us (specifically, me) truly life-changingly good food.

If you're after an emulation of the best naans available, then the variations here can be used to create breads to equal curries of the highest order, or alongside some tandoori-style chicken, pickled cabbage, some raita and that spicy, tangy Indian kebab sauce, an astounding chicken kebab.

Even the most basic curry house in Glasgow has a tandoor, and the standard of naan (and often its size) is seen as a benchmark for the coming meal. If you want to make something of the same quality at home, you're going to have to get some serious heat on the go. I use my pizza oven, which can get up to the required very high temperatures to cook these naans within a minute or two (page 113) but you can use a barbecue with a pizza stone, a kamado grill, the skillet-broiler pizza method (page 118) or your own domestic oven as described here. If going down this route, I highly recommend a 'pizza steel' (Welsh baking stone) for maximum heat transfer, or a baking stone properly preheated as hot as the oven goes.

This is an ideal bread dough to make much earlier in the day, separate into balls and leave to prove slowly in the fridge until needed. And while you probably won't find a single restaurant doing sourdough naan in Glasgow today, it really does work well.

Makes 2 very large 40×30cm (16×12in) naan breads

400g strong white flour, plus extra for rolling
1 tsp table salt
2 tsp instant yeast (optional)
100g sourdough starter, fed with white flour (page 50) (optional)
250g tepid water
butter or ghee, for brushing

1. Start by weighing your flour and salt into a large bowl. For a yeasted loaf, mix in the yeast. If you are going to put it in the fridge overnight, reduce the yeast to 1 teaspoon. For extra flavour, add your sourdough starter. For a full sourdough, leave out the yeast and add the sourdough starter. Add your water and mix everything together into a dough.

2. Then I'd recommend leaving it to autolyse (rest) for about 10–20 minutes, to allow the dough to come together a lot easier.

3. Knead your dough for about 10 minutes or so until it's turned from a slightly sticky mess into something smooth that sticks to itself. You can use your hands, a mixer (page 35), or use a no-knead method (page 45) and add in an extra stretch and fold (page 47).

For garlic naan

3 garlic cloves, crushed or very finely chopped
40g salted butter, softened
fresh coriander (optional)

For peshwari naan

100g cashew nuts
1 tbsp honey, or a little more if the paste is too dry
a handful of sultanas (optional)

4. Leave your dough to rest at room temperature for about 90 minutes or so, or about 4 hours in a warm place if making sourdough, incorporating two to three stretches and folds during the first prove. Alternatively, you can leave it overnight in the fridge – and you'll have reduced the yeast quantity. If leaving a sourdough overnight, make sure to give it a couple of hours proving at room temperature first, before a stretch and fold.

5. As that's proving, decide whether you want plain naans, peshwari or garlic. For garlic naan, simply finely chop or crush your garlic and beat this into your softened butter. For peshwari naans, make the filling by combining your cashew nuts and honey in a food processor until it's a grainy paste. If it won't come together, add another tablespoon of honey. Mix this with some whole sultanas if you like.

6. When the dough is ready, get your pizza oven going: you want it properly hot, at least 400°C (750°F). Otherwise, you can use your oven with a pizza steel or baking stone inside, just preheat it as hot as possible, at least 15 minutes before baking.

7. Turn your dough out onto a lightly floured surface. Divide into two, add some more flour on top, and roll out into big flat sheets, at least 30cm (12in) in diameter. If making peshwari naan, divide your filling between your flat sheets, spreading across the surface but leaving a gap around the edge. Fold each over to completely envelop the filling. Roll out again until you've got big naans at least 30cm (12in) in diameter. For garlic naan, rub the garlic butter on the top of your naan just before baking.

8. For any naan, it's important to prick the top with a fork just before baking, otherwise you could end up with a huge puffball. Use a pizza peel or baking tray to get under the naan, and slide it into your pizza oven or onto your hot baking stone in the oven. If you don't have a stone, just bake on the tray itself. Your timings will vary depending on how hot your oven is: for a pizza oven, we're talking 90–120 seconds. For a very hot home oven, until you notice some dark speckling starting, about 5–6 minutes. Serve immediately, tearing some fresh coriander on top, if you like.

Chapatti

U

While you might be sceptical of this pale Scottish man who's about to tell you how to make *chapattis*, I do actually know how to make a decent chapatti. I'm not a professional, but I can hopefully convey what I've learned.

I got started after we did some filming in our local Gurdwara, or Sikh temple. As an outsider and someone who's never really got on that well with religion, I found it a powerful place. I received a warm and friendly welcome, then was quickly ushered into an entirely female kitchen and put to work: apron on, it was just like being back home in Shetland, being asked to butter the sandwiches in the village hall kitchen as I helped our local matriarchy prepare for the Sunday Teas. I felt right at home. Here, I was on chapatti duty.

By the third or fourth hundred chapatti, I think I got the hang of shaping to the extent that my supervisors simply nodded and gave an approving smirk, rather than the disdainful glares I got as I started out. Once the little circle of dough was formed by hand, we'd roll them out, quickly cook them on an array of pans and then stick them directly on the bare gas rings next to them, where they'd puff and gently char for a few seconds on each side. It was quick, hot work. The final step was to rub each chapatti with butter, held in block form, the folded-back foil becoming more and more encrusted in char. I'd stack them in ever growing towers, where their buttery mass kept them warm for the crowd outside.

Afterwards, sweaty and exhausted, I joined the rich and poor of Glasgow, Sikhs and not, those in desperate need and those with time and money to give, all together. We all sat on the floor, and we all ate with our hands using our chapattis as a tool, and smiled and spoke of nothing. And I found it humbling, and left puzzled about why the rest of the world wasn't like this.

Makes 6 chapattis

250g chapatti flour (atta, or finely ground wholemeal flour), plus more for shaping
220g just-boiled water
butter, for greasing

1. Start by weighing your flour into a large bowl. Then, keeping your bowl on the scales, pour in water from a just-boiled kettle until you hit 220g. If you go a bit over, that's no problem. Use a wooden spoon to mix the flour and water together until smooth: it will be a firm, gluey dough, and too hot to touch initially.

2. Cover your bowl with a dish towel and leave the dough for 5 minutes. Then knead – I suggest the stretch and roll, (page 37) – for 5 minutes, or until it's cooled down and is stretchy and malleable. Cover your bowl, and leave for another 20–30 minutes at room temperature.

3. Lightly flour a work surface, and make a small mound of flour next to it. Scrape your dough out onto your floured surface, and divide it into six equal lumps. In turn, dip each lump into your mound of flour to coat it, then using the index fingers and thumbs of both hands, work your way all the way around each lump to ease it into a disc shape. Place this disc on your floured surface and roll out until it's at least 15–20cm (6–8in) in diameter and only a couple of millimetres thick.

4. Repeat with your others, and it's usually fine to stack them up so long as they're well floured. As you do that, preheat a heavy-based frying pan (skillet), cast iron skillet, griddle pan or tawa on a medium–high heat.

5. Cook each chapatti for a couple of minutes on each side until they're going a speckled and dark golden brown. If you've got a gas ring, then I suggest lighting your wok ring and placing your just-cooked chapatti directly onto this, flipping it with a pair of metal tongs almost as soon as you've let go (be careful, the edges can catch fire easily).

6. As each one comes off, rub it with a little butter and place on a dish towel to keep warm. Stack them up so their collective mass retains the heat and moisture, and serve as soon as they're all cooked.

Roti Canai

U

(Malaysian Flaky Flatbreads)

These are a staple in our house – a shout-out to Julie, who runs our local Michelin-recommended Malaysian eatery, not for giving me this recipe (it's apparently traditional never to give out your recipe for *roti canai*, I found to my displeasure) but I have Julie to thank for getting me hooked. First it was one, then two, then three we'd have to order during our COVID Lockdown takeaways, giving some semblance of joy during an otherwise unpleasant time for all.

Soon, the focus turned onto making them myself. These are a kind of riff on the Indian *paratha* – unleavened, laminated dough that benefits from a heavy hand with the oil, or ghee if you want to go Indian style, where some versions even use yeast. Instead I've used milk, to give some sweetness to this unleavened dough, and if you object to the use of animal stuff then you can replace the milk and egg with 200g coconut water.

***Makes 8* roti**

600g plain (all-purpose) flour
1½ tsp table salt
150g water
150g milk
1 egg
200–300g vegetable oil for shaping and soaking

1. Start by weighing your flour into a large bowl, then add your salt and stir it to combine. Add the water, milk and egg, and stir this into a stiff dough.

2. Knead it for 10 minutes or so until it's smooth and stretchy. This one, I use an electric mixer for every time (page 35), but you could use the English stretch and roll knead (page 37).

3. Turn your dough out onto a work surface – you won't need any flour and this dough is easily and pleasurably handled using a dough scraper, but if you're struggling you can use some oil to stop it from sticking. Cut it into eight roughly equal lumps.

4. Shape it into rough balls – if you didn't use any oil, the roll shaping method works quite well (page 40), and they don't need to be perfect. Now, generously oil an oven dish or large Tupperware, and pour a drizzle of oil onto each lump of dough. As you pick them up, using oiled hands, make sure they're completely coated, and space them out in your dish. Add a drizzle more oil on top so they're sitting in a puddle of oil, and cover the dish with clingfilm (plastic wrap).

5. Leave the dough for at least a couple of hours, and preferably all day, at room temperature. If going longer than a day or overnight, stick the tray in the fridge, just remember to take it out again about 30 minutes before shaping, as cold dough is a nightmare to stretch.

6. Oil your work surface (a large area, at least 60cm/24in square) and place a lump of dough on top. Using oiled hands, gradually stretch your very stretchy dough out into a very large square, at least 50cm (20in), so you can see through it. Try to work on any thick areas as these can end up doughy. Don't worry about any small tears.

7. Then you need to fold the dough. There are loads of methods, but my preferred fold is a bit like the lamination method (page 61). Fold the left side of the dough into the middle, then the right, to create a central seam. Repeat this again at the left and right sides, and then do the same top and bottom, with just one fold. You should have a small rectangle, which you can twirl into a little spiral of a lump. Set aside, re-oil the worktop, and repeat with the rest.

8. Preheat a heavy-based pan over a medium–high heat. Use the heel of your hand to press down your *roti canai* and stretch it out until it's about 20cm (8in) in diameter (you can use a rolling pin if it's getting tough). Cook for 2–3 minutes on each side until a mixture of mottled golden brown and the shiny white of cooked dough. Stack and serve within 10 minutes.

Dosa & Idli

U

(Rice Flour Pancakes)

Along with salt-risen bread (page 214), this is one of those recipes that gets me excited and a little bit nervous, because its microbiology is not familiar to me like it is when working with sourdough and yeast.

Most of you will be familiar with *dosas*, I'm sure: the thin, crispy, bubbly pancakes filled with *aloo masala*, and a staple export of Southern India. You might not have had *idli*, which can be made using an identical batter: these are soft dipping breads shaped like little discs.

I'd made *idli* during research for *Super Sourdough*, after reading about that initial fermentation that comes as part of making a sourdough starter, which we ignore and stir through and wait for it to turn sour. This gas is produced by bacteria, and specifically species of *Leuconostoc*, which is going to provide the lift for making these doughs. It's important to think about where it's coming from, then: the rice and lentils that make up this bread are soaked for a lengthy time, allowing the dried bacteria to reactivate. If the rice or lentils are very old from harvests long past, they might struggle.

This recipe is as close to authentic as I could easily get in a city of a million people with relatively good access to Indian ingredients, but I get that it might be a bit much to ask you to buy a whole bag of specific idli rice for this purpose: use what you've got, and both basmati and jasmine rice have worked well for me. The urad dal is essential, and you're looking for the shelled 'white' version, rather than the black version used to make *dal makhani*.

The final thing to say is this recipe isn't possible in the cold, you'll need a reliably warm place, prover or an oven that can be turned all the way down to 25–30°C (77–86°F).

***Makes at least 24* idli *or 6–8* dosas**

75g urad dal (white or skinned)
½ teaspoon fenugreek seeds (methi seeds)
200g white rice (idli rice is traditional, but basmati or jasmine can be substituted)
½ teaspoon salt
180g water, plus more for soaking

1. Start with two bowls. To one, add your dal and fenugreek seeds and rinse under cold or tepid water (NOT hot, don't kill any bugs) until it runs clear. Cover with about twice the volume of water as lentils and set aside. With the other bowl, do exactly the same with the rice, but you'll likely need to rinse it many times. Leave both of these bowls for at least 5–6 hours or overnight, the night before you want dosa for dinner.

2. Drain your rice and urad dal mixtures and place them in a blender. Add your salt with 180g of fresh water and blend. It should be a smooth, frothy, gloopy mix, the thickness of double (heavy) cream. If it isn't able to be poured, add another 1–2 tablespoons of water.

3. Transfer to a bowl or large jar, cover loosely (don't seal or it will explode) and transfer somewhere warm – ideally about 30°C (86°F), but anything above 25°C (77°F) is fine. Leave the batter for about 8–12 hours and it should rise magnificently. To be honest, so long as you've got quite a few bubbles, the batter will work, but it won't be as sweet. If your *idli* taste sour, you're starting down the route of making a sourdough starter and have been fermenting too long.

4. For *dosas*, preheat a large heavy-based pan or flat griddle on a medium–high heat. Add a drop of oil and spread thinly using kitchen paper, or the traditional cut edge of a slice of onion. If you've ever made crêpes, you're aiming for a similar thickness to these. Ladle one scoop of *dosa* batter onto the pan, and use the bottom of your ladle to spread the batter thinly in a spiral. Cook for 1–2 minutes until the bottom is turning a deep golden brown and the edges are crisping and coming away from the pan. There's no need to cook the other side. Serve immediately.

5. For *idli*, these are traditionally steamed, and assuming you don't own an *idli* steamer, you can make an approximation of their shape using an egg poacher, if you have one: simply steam for 3–4 minutes until soft and spongy. If you don't, I've made them like Scotch pancakes by preheating a heavy-based pan on a low–medium heat and scooping the batter on top, but not spreading it like you would a *dosa*. You can fit three to four *idli* in a batch. Then stick a lid over the top and cook until they appear bubbly all the way through; you get a crisp edge on one side, but the rest are still just as light and soft.

Shokupan

Y

(Japanese Milk Bread)

No bread has gone viral like *shokupan* has gone viral, and I'm not sure how I feel about it. I kind of wish my seeded Scandinavian ryes went viral, or my complex ancient grain sourdoughs, rather than the super-white, super-soft, thick slices of refined wheat and milk. I'm torn between honouring my credentials as a doctor and as a proponent of organic and sustainable agriculture, but how I love white, oh so white, white bread.

This might trump the *pain de mie* or milk loaf (page 75) as the standard white bread favoured by my three-year-old daughter. This high hydration (very wet) dough is popular for its softness and stability, the freshness that lasts for days and days, and its ease of handling. This is all down to using a Yudane or Tangzhong method, both methods of pre-gelatinizing the starches to allow them to hold a lot more water for longer.

The Yudane is the Japanese style, and involves mixing about 20% of your total flour weight with boiling water and letting it sit overnight or all day. This may be fine in sourdough as this kind of corresponds with when you might feed your starter, but otherwise it's a faff requiring prior planning which – as you'll know by now – I'm not up for. I prefer the Tangzhong method, where you make a kind of roux, out of 5–7% of your total flour weight and plenty of water, to make a paste. Use much more flour, and I find you get something a bit gluey or rubbery, rather than the soft, fluffy tears of a proper milk bread.

The quantities here make a very large loaf, suitable for commercial-sized lidded Pullman tins. If you don't have one, reduce the recipe by half, or make two 290g loaf tins full (remember the long shelf life).

Makes 1 Pullman-style loaf or 2 large loaves

For the Tangzhong
40g strong white flour
120g water

1. Start with the Tangzhong. In a saucepan, weigh your flour and water. Place over a medium heat and, stirring all the time with a whisk or wooden spoon, beat until you get a cooked starchy paste. Set this aside to cool while you make the rest of the dough.

2. For your dough, weigh the flour, salt and yeast into a large bowl. If you are intending to rest the dough in the fridge overnight, reduce the yeast quantity to 1 teaspoon. Use your fingers to mix them together to distribute. Add your butter, then rub this in roughly so that it's mostly combined. Weigh your milk in a different bowl and warm it in the microwave until it's neither hot nor cold. Add this to your flour and combine to a dough, along with your egg.

For the dough

800g strong white flour, plus extra for dusting
2½ tsp table salt
2 tsp instant yeast
40g unsalted butter, plus extra for greasing
440g whole milk
1 egg

3. Leave it to rest for 10–20 minutes as your Tangzhong cools – this opportunity for an autolyse (rest) really helps this dough come together well and you can hit the lightness you want. Then it's time to mix the Tanghzong and the dough together – I use an electric mixer with a dough hook (page 35) but feel free to knead it in by hand. You could stop working when the dough is homogenous, but I'd give it a few minutes more until you've got something very smooth and glossy.

4. Leave your dough to rest at room temperature for about 90 minutes or so. Alternatively, you can leave it overnight in the fridge. If you're planning on doing this, I recommend reducing the quantity of yeast to 1 teaspoon.

5. Grease your Pullman tin (and lid) with plenty of butter – get it right into the corners. Scrape your dough out onto a lightly floured surface, then use your dough scraper to cut into four roughly equal lumps. To each lump, add a little flour on top then roll until it's about 5mm (¼in) thick – this is 'knocking back' the dough and also developing the gluten excellently. Fold over your edges to make your rectangle the same width as your tin, then roll it up into a tight spiral. Place this in your tin, then repeat with your other lumps until the base of the tin is covered evenly.

6. If your tin has a lid, stick this on. If it doesn't or you're using smaller tins, cover the top with a piece of kitchen foil. Prove for another hour at room temperature, or up to overnight in a very cold (2°C/35°F) fridge. About 15 minutes before it's ready, preheat your oven to 200°C (400°F) fan (220°C/425°F/gas 7).

7. Don't score this one. Bake with the foil or lid on for 20 minutes, then open the oven and open the lid to check it: if your dough has risen to make contact with the lid, close it again and bake for another 10–15 minutes until a golden brown colour. If it's not risen that far, that's OK, but remove the lid to allow the steamy top crust to brown, another 10–15 minutes. Leave to cool in the tin for at least 15 minutes before removing to a cooling rack, if you have to. I tend to let mine cool on the chopping board, knife at the ready. Don't forget to film yourself tearing this one open, for all the likes.

藤次郎
MADE IN JAPAN

AFRICA

AFRICA

AFRICA

AFRICA

Tapalapa

(Fulani Bread)

Y

YS

S

I've not written or talked about this before. I once did a bit of work in rural Ghana, helping bring medical care out into rural communities that had no access to it. Or, this is what I thought I was going to do, and indeed did do, but I only discovered after arriving that this was a guise by the far right American owners of the charity to convert people to evangelical Christianity. I went, I helped, I kept my head down, and left. I did not convert to evangelical Christianity, nor advocate this for anyone else.

One of the most difficult and rural trips we made was to a trading point with a still-nomadic Fulani tribe, who came both to trade cows and to get medical treatment – which we provided using a chain of interpreters. This bread, *tapalapa*, is widespread amongst Fulani people, after being taught by early French colonizers, in the 15th and 16th centuries. It has similarities to baguette, but with a portion of millet flour, and is traditionally baked in the dry heat of mud ovens.

Millet may be maligned in some circles, but this frugal grain from grasses gives a nutty flavour and slightly more crumbly-rather-than-chewy texture compared to a traditional baguette. Then, you can re-create the dry heat of a mud or clay oven using a pizza oven, kamado grill or a kettle barbecue with a baking stone, baking as the intense heat of the flames has started to die down. A home oven at max will do a similar job: you're wanting something dark and crusty.

***Makes* 4 tapalapa**

400g strong white flour, plus extra for dusting
100g millet flour
1 tsp salt
1 tsp instant yeast (optional)
100g sourdough starter, fed with any flours (page 50) (optional)
330g tepid water
a little semolina, for dusting

1. Start by weighing your flours and salt into a large bowl. For a yeasted loaf, mix in the yeast. For extra flavour, mix in the sourdough starter. For a full sourdough, leave out the yeast and add the sourdough starter.

2. Add the warm water and combine into a dough – we're using warm water to try and mimic a warm African fermentation. This will be fast and hot: aim for 30°C (86°F).

3. Let the dough autolyse (rest) for 15–20 minutes, then you can knead for 10 minutes by hand or machine, until it feels stretchy and smooth. Otherwise, by all means use a no-knead method (page 45).

4. Cover your bowl and stick it somewhere warm – ideally, you've got a warming drawer or an oven that allows you to set it as low as 30°C (86°F). Let the dough rise for about an hour if you used yeast, or 3 hours for sourdough, until it's doubled in size and light and fragile.

5. Prepare a couche (piece of linen or a thick dish towel) by adding plenty of flour, and placing this on a hard tray or baking tray. Scrape your dough out onto a lightly floured surface, and chop it into four pieces. Shape each as per baguettes (page 42) but don't worry about making them quite as tight and rounded: these are supposed to look a little flatter.

6. Transfer each to your couche, making a little fold in the material to stop them sticking together. I use a book or a bottle to support the ends. Cover loosely with a dish towel, and prove for just another half hour at room temperature, or an hour if you've used sourdough. If you overprove them, they won't open up at all.

7. When you're nearly at this stage, preheat your oven to 220°C (425°F) fan (240°C/465°F/gas 9), or you can spend this time creating a big fire in your pizza oven or kamado grill with a pizza stone inside, letting it die down to about 250°C (480°F) by the time you add the bread.

8. When ready, turn out your breads onto a peel or a baking tray dusted with semolina, leaving room between them to rise. Score, making long scores down their length. Then, bake on the tray, or slide them into your improvized clay oven. Bake for 40 minutes, or until the crusts are really quite dark; you'll probably need to turn them halfway through to stop them burning.

Cassava Bread

U

Cassava is native to South America, and was introduced to Africa by Portuguese traders in the 16th century. Despite its popularity and widespread use in West African cuisine, cassava is therefore relatively recent. This is relevant, as you can't consider Sierra Leonian cassava bread without thinking about *casabe*, an almost identically produced cassava pancake widespread in South America.

The process of making both is similar to a potato *rösti*, but with fine grating and a thinner bread. As far as I can find through quite thorough research, the co-origins of cassava bread and *casabe* breads haven't been studied in great depth academically, and while they could have developed separately, I would find this hard to believe. Common sense says that the people who brought the vegetables over might also have brought ways of preparing them.

I wouldn't have known about either bread if it wasn't for Mariama Jalloh from Sierra Leone, who contacted me and asked for it to be represented in this book. I had to include it because it is unlike any other recipe here, and contains just one ingredient, plus frying oil.

I'd then add a suggestion, or a signpost: that you check out some of the great content creators online, because I've found almost no other resource teaching outsiders like me how to make and shape these loaves, or make an accompanying stew or a fried *tilapia* dish. Please, keep more coming.

Makes 10–12 small flatbreads

2 medium cassava
oil, for frying

For a pepper dipping sauce
2 ripe tomatoes
5 habanero (or Scotch Bonnet) chillies
3 tbsp vegetable oil (any – palm is widely used)
2 garlic cloves
1 tsp bouillon powder
salt, as needed
fried fish or meat, to serve

1. Start by making your sauce. Put all your ingredients in a blender, except your salt for seasoning. Blend until smooth. Pour your smooth mix into a saucepan and place over a low–medium heat and bring to a simmer, cooking for 20 minutes or so until the harsh sulphury flavours of the raw ingredients have gone. Season generously with salt, tasting as you go.

2. As that cooks, peel your cassava, leaving only the hard white flesh in the centre. Use a box grater to finely grate it (don't use the coarser side of the grater or you'll end up with dry, crumbly bread).

3. In batches of about a quarter of the cassava at a time, use a muslin or cheesecloth to squeeze as much water out of the grated cassava as you can. Place your newly dried gratings on a plate ready for frying.

4. Place a heavy-based pan onto a medium heat and add a little oil. Heat for a minute or so, but not so long that the oil begins to smoke. Scoop 2 large heaped tablespoons of your dried cassava and place it on your pan, before spreading it out using the bottom of a plate (or the heel of your hand, if you're brave).

5. Cook for about 2–3 minutes or so before flipping and cooking the other side for the same time. In Sierra Leone, these tend to be a little thicker, paler and chewier than you'd expect if you're used to South American *casabe*, but this allows the flexibility needed for dipping. Serve with your sauce and fried fish or meat.

Injera

S

(Ethiopian Pancakes)

Ethiopia. Forever independent, where culture and biology seem to have uniquely evolved to provide a set of flavours that aren't found anywhere else in the world. I could merely be talking about Ethiopian coffee, another passion and addiction of mine, where wild varieties are still widely cultivated to give flavour found nowhere else.

The same is true in bread. *Injera* are unique pancakes, often made using teff, or the tiny seeds from an ancient domesticated grass that's unique to the horn of Africa. Teff is expensive, but you can order it to experience this bread fully. An approximation will work using wheat or rye flour only.

Injera is traditionally fermented as a batter, for up to four days, by which time it's plenty sour. It is then cooked on a *tawa* or pan to make a very bubbly, sour pancake. The process starts out a bit like *dosa* (page 275), but you go way beyond that initial fermentation, and so microbiological machinery found in sourdough starters takes over. Obviously, I checked to see if we could hack it a bit using a sourdough starter, and of course you can.

***Makes 6–8* injera**

150g teff flour
50g finely ground wholemeal flour (such as chapatti flour or home-milled)
100g sourdough starter, fed with wholemeal flour (page 50)
600g tepid water

1. Start by weighing your teff flour and wholemeal flour in a large bowl. Add your starter and 400g of the water and mix everything together into a loose batter.

2. Leave this at a warm room temperature, ideally up at about 25°C (77°F) for 24–48 hours, until a layer of hooch (dark liquid) has formed on top. If this forms early, don't worry, you can leave it until it's time to cook and it will develop a bit more of a sour flavour.

3. When about ready for your pancakes, weigh your remaining 200g of water into a saucepan and place on a high heat to boil. As that comes up to temperature, carefully drain off the hooch from your teff batter. Scoop a couple of heaped tablespoons of your thick under-batter into the boiling water, and whisk until it's thickened and gooey. Stir this new batter into the original fermented batter.

4. You should have something that's the consistency of crêpe batter, slightly thinner than dosa batter. If you have experience of neither of those, it should seem worryingly watery. Preheat a non-stick pan over a medium heat, and then scoop a ladle of the injera mix into the pan. Tilt the pan or spread with the ladle to coat the bottom.

5. Cook until the bubbles have risen and then burst, and the batter has turned from whiteish and bubbly to glossy all the way to middle – it can help to use a lidded pan, so you can stick on the lid for them to steam through if the middle is taking ages. Repeat with the rest. Serve with Ethiopian chicken or beef stew.

Banku

S

(Corn and Cassava Dough)

While a few recipes in this book stretch the definition of a bread, this one probably takes the biscuit. Or rather, the dough.

This is fermented corn and cassava dough, and a staple of many of the cultures and societies within Ghana since both non-native species were introduced during colonization over the last 500 years or so. I've been trawling the academic journals to look at what kind of fermentation *banku* undergoes, and there are only a couple of studies that have ever examined it. And? You guessed it: sourdough. This mix of *lactobacillus* and yeast kicks off usually within a couple of days, not surprising considering you're keeping it at African levels of warmth.

***Makes* 3–4 bankus**

200g coarse yellow cornmeal (polenta)
200g cassava 'dough' (cassava flour)
400g warm water, plus more for cooking

For a simple okra (ladies' fingers) stew
a big slosh (4 tbsp) vegetable oil
400g tough stewing beef or goat
4 garlic cloves, peeled
1cm (½in) piece of fresh ginger root, peeled
1 small onion, halved
1 red (bell) pepper, seeds and stalk removed
400g tin of tomatoes
5 habanero or Scotch Bonnet chillies, whole
100g extra water
¼ teaspoon salt, plus more to taste
175g okra (ladies' fingers)

1. Start by making your initial ferment. In a large bowl, mix your cornmeal and your cassava flour. Add your water and stir to combine. Place this somewhere warm, ideally 25–30°C (77–86°F) for about 48 hours until it is large and puffy and filled with air. If you don't have anywhere that warm, it will still work, but it might take 3–4 days.

2. At this stage, place the fermented *banku* in a saucepan with another 400g of water. Place it on a medium heat source and cook, stirring all the time. This is a bit like making a roux. As you stir, the mixture will cook and the water will gradually be absorbed. It should absorb all the water.

3. Gradually, add more water, a little at a time. It may absorb up to another 400g or so and take 20 minutes. Keep going until you've got a dough that's still thick but pliable and elastic – I think about the consistency of choux pastry, but if that's not relatable, a very soft bread dough. If in doubt, stop, because once you've gone too thin it's difficult to go back.

4. You can serve it hot straight away, but it tends to be bagged up in 3–4 individual plastic bags, depending on what size or how many you're making, or wrapped in clingfilm (plastic wrap). It can then be chilled for up to 2 days, then microwaved on full power for 3 minutes to re-heat, or immersed in boiling water for 5 minutes until piping hot all the way through.

5. This simple okra stew uses either a pressure cooker or a slow cooker (or a casserole pot in the oven set to 90°C (195°F) fan). Start by putting your oil in a pan, and the pan on a medium–high heat. In goes your meat, and gradually brown this all around.

6. As that's browning, you can make the sauce. Place all the other ingredients except the okra in a blender and blend together until no large lumps remain.

7. Once the meat is browned all the way around, stir in the sauce, then cook for 5–10 minutes on that medium–high heat until the harshness of the vegetal smell has gone.

8. Either transfer to your slow cooker and cook on low for 8–10 hours, or stick in a pressure cooker and cook at high pressure for 40 minutes, before turning it off and allowing it to come back down to pressure slowly.

9. Place the pressure cooker back on a medium heat and bring the stew to a simmer. Roughly chop your okra, and add this before cooking for 8–10 minutes. Season with salt to taste, then serve with your *banku*.

Roosterkoek

Y

(Grill Cakes)

Roosterkoeks are white rolls made directly on the grill. Think South African barbecue, or *braai*, and think relaxed gatherings round a roaring fire pit of crackling wood, slowly reduced to smouldering charcoals. As the flames die and the time for grilling approaches, an opportunity arises.

Cooked fast, these yeasted doughs puff into slightly scorched long rolls, and are best eaten hot, just off the fire, either with butter or a burger inside. So long as you've got an hour or so before your barbecue and some flour, you can make them. And contrary to popular belief, I find that having a slightly wet, sticky dough (within reason) leads to a lighter bread, but I do brush it with a little oil to stop it from sticking.

***Makes 12 individual* roosterkoek**

400g plain (all-purpose) flour, plus more for shaping (strong will work but they won't be as fluffy)
1 tsp table salt
1 tsp instant yeast
250g tepid water
oil, for greasing
a little semolina, for dusting

1. Start at least an hour, ideally 2, before your planned barbecue. Alternatively, you could start the morning or even the night before and fridge your dough until needed – if you do this, reduce your yeast by half.

2. Weigh your plain flour in a large bowl, then add your salt and yeast and stir to combine. Add your water and form into a rough dough.

3. Knead your dough until soft and smooth, about 5–10 minutes, using the stretch and roll method (page 37). If you've got one and have meat marinading or fire building to do, then use a mixer by all means.

4. Cover your dough and leave to rise for about an hour, or until noticeably risen and light, but not so fragile that it collapses with the slightest touch. Alternatively, stick in a very cold fridge and leave it in there until needed, up to 18 hours as long as your fridge is very cold (2°C/36°F).

5. When nearly ready to cook, turn your dough out onto a floured surface. Add some more flour on top and gently roll it back and forth into a long sausage shape. Use this to make it easier to cut into 12 pieces: I halve it, halve each new piece to make 4, and then cut each of those into 3 to finish with 12.

6. Add a little more flour to each, and roll them out until they're about 1cm (½in) thick. Space them out on a tray lined with some baking parchment, using flour or semolina to stop them sticking, avoid stacking them if you can.

7. Your fire should be hot but no bare flames should be visible. If you hold your hand just above, you should be able to hold it there for at least 3 seconds before having to take it away. I like to lightly brush each disc with some oil to stop sticking, but you might not need to. If you have a kettle barbecue, using a lid with the airflow fully open will accelerate the cooking process. Cook for 5 minutes on the first side, then flip over to crisp on the other, cooking for a further 3–4 minutes. Serve hot with butter, or let cool slightly, slice, and stick a burger inside.

Mahjouba

U

(Algerian Stuffed Flatbreads)

This is a typical Algerian street-food. The dough itself is unleavened, making it very simple and reliable, and the filling like a thick chilli *sofrito*. The filling is delicious, but it's the balance with the dough that works so well. It's made with semolina flour, which is certainly not the stuff the British call semolina. You're looking for finely ground durum wheat: it might be listed as durum flour, or as *semolina rimacinata*, meaning re-milled. It's often targeted at those looking to make pasta.

Semolina is so hard and dense it can be a bit tricky to work with. It absorbs water slowly, and can often feel dry and crumbly if not given time to rest. But go away and leave it for a while, and it comes together. You'll likely find it more stable than regular wheat.

This dough can be mixed well in advance – up to a day, if required.

***Makes 6* mahjouba**

300g semolina (durum wheat) flour
1 tsp salt
200g warm water
1 tbsp olive oil, plus more for greasing

For the filling
1 small onion
1 tsp cumin seeds
1 tbsp olive oil
1 carrot
2 whole green chillies
400g tin of tomatoes
1 tsp sugar
sea salt and freshly ground black pepper, to taste

1. Start by weighing your semolina into a large bowl. Add the salt and distribute, then add your water and oil, and use a wooden spoon to mix into a very grainy dough. Don't worry about this. Cover your bowl with some clingfilm (plastic wrap) and set it aside. This will need to rest for at least an hour at room temperature to properly hydrate, and you could leave it up to a day. Don't fridge it, or it will be impossible to stretch out.

2. Meanwhile, make the filling. Chop your onion as finely as you can be bothered. Grind your cumin seeds (or use ground), and place these in a pan over a medium heat. Lightly roast them until they are darker, aromatic, but not burned. Pour them out onto a plate to set aside. Stick your oil in the same pan, followed by the onions, and stir to coat. Turn the heat down a little to low–medium, and cook until translucent, about 3–4 minutes.

3. As that cooks, coarsely grate your carrot and finely chop your chillies, and then you can add these to the onion. Sweat this all down, sofrito style, until you're noticing bits starting to catch and turn a bit brown, another 5–10 minutes. At this point, stir in your tomatoes, add the sugar, season and whack the heat up to medium–high. As it is simmering, remove any brown from the pan by scraping the bottom of the pan with the acidic tomatoes. Simmer for about 15 minutes, or until reduced into a thicker, sticky paste. Season and taste.

4. The filling can be stored, covered, in the fridge until needed, so both parts can be made well ahead of time. When you're nearly ready to serve, oil a work surface with olive oil, and stick a heavy-based pan, griddle or *tawa* onto a medium heat.

5. Turn your dough out onto your oiled surface. Drizzle a little more oil on top and squash it with the heel of your hand. You can then roll these out, but it's traditional and probably easier just to stretch them. Imagine them as a square, and grabbing two corners at a time, stretch them out like you're shaking out a bedsheet. Little holes are fine. You want each piece about 20–30cm (8–12in) square and translucent.

6. Spread about a sixth of your filling, probably a couple of tablespoons, over the middle of the dough, in about a 10cm (4in) square. Fold your dough over this to envelop your filling, one fold from each of the four sides of the square: a bit like folding a crêpe over its filling, but stretching it so that the filling is completely covered.

7. Place your dough directly onto your pan (the residual oil should be enough) and cook for 3–4 minutes on each side until speckled and golden brown. As one cooks, you can shape the next one, adding a touch more oil to the surface each time, as needed. Serve warm, but watch you don't burn yourself: the filling can be very hot.

Khobz

Y

(Fluffy White Bread)

If you've ever spent any time in urban Morocco, you'll have been drawn to the early-morning queues, winding out of tiny archways and alleyways, being born from a tiny window, out of which stacks and stacks of golden, squat breads are passed.

Not quite a flatbread, *khobz* is a crisp, fluffy white bread that's thick enough to slice in two for sandwiches, and with the structural integrity that means it can be torn open and used as an implement to scoop sauces and salads.

It's essential that it's eaten fresh, on the day it was baked, but it really does suit part-baking and freezing well – both because you're guaranteed a crisp, crackling crust, and due to its shape, it stacks beautifully.

Most variations of this recipe you'll find have added sugar and oil, but there's absolutely no need. Give this bread a proper, prolonged fermentation and a good knead, and you'll find that you get a golden caramelized crust with light, fluffy insides. I recommend the fridge for your first prove, but if you're in a rush you can finish this bread in a few hours. And while the use of a sourdough might have been the traditional way of making this, the bread we've come to know and love is usually made using yeast.

***Makes 2 medium* khobz**

400g strong white flour
1 tsp table salt
2 tsp instant yeast
280g tepid water
semolina, for shaping and baking
sesame seeds (optional)

1. Into a large bowl, weigh your flour, salt and yeast. Add your water and mix together until you get a roughly consistent dough.

2. You can get straight to the kneading now, or you can autolyse (rest) it for 10–15 minutes and you'll find the kneading far easier and less messy (see page 37).

3. Knead using your chosen method for a good 5–10 minutes until you've got a dough that's elastic. Alternatively, feel free to use a mixer, or avoid kneading altogether, by giving it a further 20 minutes' rest and doing some stretches and folds (page 47) instead.

4. Once your dough is smooth and stretchy, pop it back in the bowl, cover with clingfilm (plastic wrap) or a plastic bag, and stick it in a cold fridge for 4–12 hours. Alternatively, rest for 90 minutes at room temperature.

5. Scrape your risen dough out onto a work surface dusted with semolina. Chop it in half, then very gently shape each piece into a

circle by grabbing an edge and turning it over into the middle, just like when shaping a boule (page 39) except rather than flipping it over and reinforcing this shape, we want to flip it over and squash it down to spread it out into a round disc. Each disc should be about 20cm (8in) in diameter. If you're using sesame seeds, this is the point to squish them into the top. Use plenty of semolina top and bottom while you are working.

6. Place each disc on a baking tray. You can line it with baking parchment, if you wish, but I've not had a problem with these sticking. Let them prove for another hour at room temperature so that they're overtly puffy and fragile-looking.

7. About 15 minutes before you're about to bake, preheat your oven to 210°C (410°F) fan (230°C/450°F/gas 8). Place a roasting tray on the floor of the oven for something to pour water into for steam.

8. There's not much point in scoring – they'll collapse and the scores won't open up. Simply place the trays in the oven, and add a splash of water onto the tray on the floor of the oven. Bake for 15–20 minutes, or until light golden and crispy. Cool and serve that day.

9. I mentioned part-baking – in this case, you want to cut the bake short by 5 minutes: your breads should be baked through but look 'too light' – a pale golden brown is good. Once cooled, these can be wrapped in clingfilm (plastic wrap) and stored at room temperature for up to a few days, or frozen. Bake for 10 minutes, straight from frozen if necessary, with a little more steam.

OCEANIA
OCEANIA
OCEANIA
OCEANIA
OCEANIA

Parāoa Rēwena

S

(Root Vegetable Sourdough)

Of all my favourite breads in this book, I get most excited about the indigenous breads that use processes, specifically microbiological processes, that don't appear anywhere else in the world. See Salt-risen Bread (page 214) or *idli* (page 275). When I first heard of *parāoa rēwena*, my excitement built: here was an entirely different way of creating a sourdough, rooted heavily in tradition, using root vegetables along with flour.

The most often cited method today involves cooking and mashing potatoes, which are a relatively modern import brought in by colonizing sailors. So go for sweet potato or kumara, which has been with indigenous New Zealanders for over 700 years, and gives a nice tinge of colour. Regardless, what you are making is a sourdough starter, though one that is adapted to a particularly high-starch, moisture-retaining environment.

It doesn't look like side by side experiments have been done to compare the 'bug', as it's known in New Zealand, with common French or American sourdough starters, so I'd be interested in that if anyone fancies this. Just now, you can assume that your own sourdough starter will happily munch through the sweet potatoes here, but if you do start one from scratch, as below, your flavour and the rapidity of your rise might be a good bit different.

Makes 1 large loaf

For the bug

20g sourdough starter, fed with any flours (page 50) (optional)
100g sweet potato, peeled weight (half a large sweet potato)
100g wholemeal flour

For the bread

450g strong white flour, plus extra for dusting
1 tsp salt
300g tepid water
all of your bug

1. It's important to make sure your starter is happy, so if it hasn't been fed recently, feed it the night before you plan to bake and ensure it rises to at least double it original size.

2. Then, it's time to make your bug. First, peel and roughly chop your sweet potato. Place this in a saucepan and cover with water. Boil on a high heat for at least 15 minutes, or until soft. Drain, then run under a little cold water to cool: it should be lukewarm, at most, before mixing.

3. When cooled, mix with your flour and starter into a dough. Leave this for about 5–6 hours, or until markedly swollen. Use this as your starter for the rest of the bread.

4. In a large bowl, weigh your white flour. Add your salt and mix everything together. Add your tepid water – which should feel neither warm nor cold to your fingertips – and finally add your bug. Mix everything together with a wooden spoon or a dough hook, until you've got a lumpy, messy dough.

5. Let your dough autolyse (rest) for about 20–30 minutes. If you like, you can cover the bowl, or you can just mix in any dry skin that forms during this time. It doesn't matter.

6. Knead your dough for 5–10 minutes, or until the dough is starting to become smooth and supple. The slap and fold method tends to work well (page 36), as does using an electric mixer (page 35). If you choose the latter, give it a stretch and fold (page 47) immediately after.

7. Leave your dough, covered, for 4 hours or so, at a warm room temperature. This can vary significantly depending on temperature. During this rest, conduct two to three stretches and folds, usually about an hour apart. The necessity of this will depend on how well you kneaded: I'd always do at least one stretch and fold during the first prove.

9. Flour a proving basket, or make one using a floured dish towel inside a mixing bowl. Then, flour a work surface and scoop your dough onto it, smooth-side down and shape the dough to the shape of your proving basket (page 60).

10. Place your proving basket in the fridge – I no longer recommend to cover these: any dry skin that forms won't do any harm. Prove in there for 8–18 hours.

11. Preheat your oven with a cast iron pan or Dutch oven inside for at least 15 minutes before you plan to bake. The temperature should be 220°C (425°F) fan (240°C/465°F/gas 9).

12. I tend to score after turning the loaf directly onto the lid of my cast iron pot or Dutch oven, but if you're baking within a high-sided pot, it helps to do this on baking parchment, then lower it in. Score lengthways down the loaf, or in a square pattern if it's a round loaf.

13. Enclose your loaf in your pot, and turn your oven down to 200°C (400°F) fan (220°F/425°F/gas 7). Bake for 20 minutes initially, then take the lid off. Bake for another 15–20 minutes or until a dark golden brown. Let it cool down before slicing. If slicing for freezing, this is best done the next day.

Bush Bread

BP

I have claimed that the birthplace of bread is the Middle East, and the oldest direct and preserved evidence of bread, about 14,400 years old, was found there. But the indigenous Australians may just have a claim because evidence of tools used to grind foraged seeds goes back 30,000 years. Thirty thousand years!

Whether these were cooked or raw isn't known, but the simple tools of a round stone and a flat plate exist. We know about the ancient grains and grasses that were prevalent then, and there's significant ongoing work in Australia exploring these ancient connections further: perhaps indigenous Australians were the first human farmers.

If you look up bush bread today, you'll find recipes for a damper, or a simple white wheat bannock cooked in a griddle over a fire, at its simplest completely unrisen, but I think better with added lift using baking powder. And I've done that elsewhere in the book.

I wanted to explore some ancient flavours, but taking into account worldwide availability. So I've gone for flax, which can be picked up milled from lots of health shops, and millet, an old native grass. Mix this with whatever you've got from a local, unrefined wheat, and whatever whole seeds are available where you are. Then we'll have something approaching bush breads of old: health-promoting and sustainable.

Makes 4 large bush breads

200g local wholewheat flour, preferably ancient grain such as emmer or spelt, plus extra for dusting
100g milled flax seed
100g millet grain
100g whole seeds, such as flax, poppy or sesame
½ tsp salt
1 tsp baking powder
280g water

1. This recipe can be done outdoors, using a griddle over a campfire, or indoors over the hob. If outdoors, you'll need to roughly shape using your hands. You could prepare the dry ingredients mix in advance, mixing with water before cooking.

2. Start by weighing the flour, milled flax, millet, seeds, salt and baking powder into a bowl. Use your fingertips to distribute the ingredients. Add the water, and mix until it forms a sticky, grainy dough.

3. Heat your pan over a low–medium heat, so that's ready to go with your first bread while you shape the next ones.

4. Generously flour a work surface, then scrape your dough out onto it. Add more flour on top, then pat it down slightly, then divide into four equal pieces. Using floured hands, ease each piece into a round shape, and squash it flat until about 1cm (½in) thick.

5. Cook each flatbread for 3–4 minutes on each side, one at a time, until golden. Let them cool a bit, preferably somewhere cosy like between the folds of a dish towel. Serve still warm, covered in butter.

Hipster Potato Sourdough

S

The thing that I tried to avoid mentioning around the time of *The Great British Bake Off*, which was an amateur TV baking show, was that I had worked in a bakery. Or rather, I had had a summer job washing dishes in a unit kitchen that included a bakery. While the producers of the show were quite happy that this didn't affect my status as an amateur, it did give me an opportunity that not everyone gets: watching the making of bread for 8 hours a day while I washed dishes.

David, the baker, lent me a few books that helped pique my interest in sourdough. The book I learned from, more than any other that summer, was *Bourke Street Bakery*, and about the bread and pastries baked out of their Sydney kitchen. One sourdough stood out: Mr Potato Bread. I tried it once at the time, but it didn't work out well. It wasn't like the potato sourdoughs you encounter now that incorporate mash into the dough for moisture. This had big lumps of potato, cooked beforehand, and I used the wrong sort and cooked them too long, meaning when I tried to shape, I was just smooshing big watery lumps into the dough and it stuck to everything.

The key in this adapted recipe is to roast the potatoes beforehand, and only partially cook them. Let them cool completely, and incorporate the nearly cooked lumps during a final stretch and fold. I've changed part of the flour makeup to spelt for nuttiness that works well with the roast, and incorporated some chopped fresh rosemary.

Makes 1 large round loaf

400g strong white flour, plus extra for dusting
50g wholemeal spelt flour
1 tsp table salt
100g sourdough starter, fed with any flours (page 50) (optional)
200g new potatoes (about 4 small potatoes)
olive oil, for roasting
3 sprigs of fresh rosemary

1. Because I'd recommend a full sourdough here, it's especially important to make sure your starter is happy (page 54). Feed it at a ratio of 1:2:2 and leave it for 5–8 hours at a warm room temperature before starting the recipe.

2. In a large bowl, weigh your flours. Add your salt and mix everything together, using a wooden spoon or a dough hook, until you've got a lumpy, messy dough.

3. Let your dough autolyse (rest) for about 20 minutes. Then knead your dough for 5–10 minutes, or until the dough is starting to become smooth and supple. Given how wet this dough is, the slap and fold method (page 36) tends to work well, or use an electric mixer (page 35).

4. Prove your dough, covered, for 4 hours or so, at a warm room temperature. Alternatively, if you've used yeast, this will only be about 90 minutes and I'd recommend getting straight onto the next step.

5. Heat your oven to 200°C (400°F) fan (220°C/425°F/gas 7). Chop your potatoes into large dice (1cm/½in cubes or so), and drizzle with your oil. Roast for about 15 minutes, or until firm but not hard. They will finish off cooking in the bread, don't worry. Leave these to cool down completely.

6. During your first prove, conduct two to three stretches and folds (page 47), usually about an hour apart. During the first one, add your potatoes and some chopped rosemary. Leave some lumps of potato to place on top of your loaf prior to baking.

7. If you've scaled this recipe, use a dough scraper to scrape your dough out onto a clean, slightly wetted surface. Divide and pre-shape (page 62) by roughly tucking in two sides of your dough, then rolling it up. Leave your doughs on the bench for another 15–20 minutes.

8. Flour a proving basket, or make one using a floured dish towel inside a mixing bowl. Then flour a work surface and scoop your dough onto it, smooth-side down. Shape to the shape of your proving basket (page 60).

9. Place your proving basket in the fridge uncovered. Prove in there for 8–18 hours.

10. Preheat your oven with a cast iron pot or Dutch oven inside for at least 15 minutes before you plan to bake. Set the oven to 220°C (425°F) fan (230°C/445°F/gas 9).

11. Turn your dough out onto a piece of baking parchment, or directly into your pot or Dutch oven. Score in a pattern of your choosing, I go for a cross using a rounded shape for this one. Stick your leftover pieces of potato into the sticky openings made by your scores.

12. Enclose your loaf in your pot, and turn your oven down to 200°C (400°F) fan (220°C/425°F/gas 7) and bake for 20 minutes initially, then take the lid off and bake for another 15–20 minutes, or until a dark golden brown. Let it cool down before slicing.

Super-soft Barbecue Buns

Y

YS

S

If there's one thing I envy in those who live Down Under, apart from the weather, the nature, the space, the coffee culture, the wine, the sourdough bakeries, the surfing and the fact that I could earn much more and work far less, it's the barbecue culture. I live in the west of Scotland, and during the summer of 2023, as I sit and write, it has rained every day. Every single day. I've forced outdoor meals to test recipes for this book and that's about it.

The barbecue is never certain, here. We've got that never-certainty around the weather, combined with a traditional British uncertainty by nature, with a tendency to err on the conservative: it might rain, so let's not take any chances. Hopefully, the more people emigrate from elsewhere, the more that changes.

These buns are designed to be the perfect accompaniment for a barbecue – super-fluffy brioche-ish buns, with or without sesame seeds. I use the Tangzhong method for extra stability and softness. Serve filled with a burger and alongside cold lager.

Makes 8 big burger buns

For the Tangzhong

15g strong white flour
100g whole milk

For the buns

380g strong white flour, plus extra for dusting
1 tsp salt
2 tsp instant yeast (optional)
75g sourdough starter, fed with white flour (page 50) (optional)
50g unsalted butter, plus extra for greasing
200g cold milk
1 egg, at room temperature, plus 1 egg, for brushing
oil, for greasing

1. Start with the Tangzhong. In a saucepan, weigh your white flour and your whole milk. Place these over a medium heat and stir gently. Keep stirring until they've formed a thick paste, then stir some more. Remove from the heat and set aside to cool slightly.

2. Weigh your flour and salt into a large bowl. For a yeasted loaf, mix in the yeast but if you are planning to leave the dough overnight in the fridge, reduce the quantity of yeast to 1 teaspoon. For extra flavour, add some sourdough starter with the liquid portion of the dough. For a full sourdough, leave out the yeast altogether and just include the sourdough starter.

3. Mix your chosen ingredients together to distribute. Add your butter, then rub this in roughly so that it's mostly combined. Add your cold milk, which is warmed by your Tanghzong that you add next. Then add your egg and combine everything into a dough.

4. Leave it to autolyse (rest) for 10–20 minutes, then get kneading – I would use the slap and fold method for this sticky dough (page 36). Alternatively, you can use a mixer (page 35), or use a no-knead method (page 45) and add an extra stretch and fold (page 47).

5. Leave your dough to rest at room temperature for about 90 minutes or so, or 4 hours if you've gone pure sourdough. Alternatively, you can leave it overnight in the fridge – and you'll have reduced the yeast quantity. If you choose to fridge the first prove of a sourdough fermentation, it's important to give it a couple of hours at room temperature first to allow it to get going.

6. Prepare a baking tray by lining it with a sheet of baking parchment. For that burger bun shape, if you own crumpet rings, grease these with butter and space them out on the tray. Scrape your dough out onto a lightly floured surface, then shape into rolls (page 40). Place these into your rings or space them on your tray.

7. Spread some oil over a piece of clingfilm (plastic wrap), drape this over your rolls, then prove for another 1 hour or so at room temperature, or in a very cold fridge all day or overnight. If going sourdough, it might be up to 2 hours at room temperature, or 8–18 hours in the fridge.

8. About 15 minutes before it's ready, preheat your oven to 200°C (400°F) fan (220°C/425°F/gas 7).

9. Whisk the remaining egg in a small bowl and brush this over your proven buns. Bake for 20–25 minutes, or until shiny and golden but not overly crispy. Leave to cool before slicing and filling: these store well for up to a few days, so long as you heat on your burger pan or barbecue before serving.

Finger Buns

Y

I bloody love an iced finger.

Served fresh, iced fingers, or finger buns as they're often called, are one of life's great joys. The bread must be soft and moist, with the icing just enough to give that balance of sweet top and comforting bread; no fancy flavouring, no pretence, just the joy of freshly baked white bread and the hit of sugar.

While they've certainly waned in popularity in the UK, they remain bolstered in both Australia and New Zealand. This is a fairly standard recipe for a slightly enriched dough, which must absolutely not be sourdough: softness is key. Don't bake them too long, or they'll dry out. Just cooked, that's enough.

Makes 12 buns

500g strong white flour, plus extra for dusting
1 tsp salt
2 tsp instant yeast
40g caster (superfine) sugar
50g butter, softened
220g milk
100g hot water
150g raisins or sultanas (optional)
1 egg, beaten
300g icing (confectioners') sugar
a few drops of pink food colouring (optional)
30g water, plus a little more if necessary
desiccated (shredded) coconut (optional)

1. Start by weighing your flour, salt, yeast and sugar into a large bowl. Add your butter, then rub this in roughly so that it's mostly combined.

2. Weigh your milk in another bowl, and then add your hot water to bring the temperature up to around tepid. Add this to your flour mixture and combine to a dough.

3. Leave it to autolyse (rest) for 10–20 minutes if you've got time, then do some kneading. I'd recommend the English stretch and roll for this (page 37), or you could use a mixer (page 35). If you go for a no-knead method (page 45), give it at least a vigorous stretch and fold or two (page 47), otherwise you might struggle to get the lift required. Towards the end of the knead or during your stretch and fold, add your raisins, if you like.

4. Leave your dough to rest at room temperature for about 60–90 minutes. You could fridge this prove, but I wouldn't leave it as long as overnight. Whatever you do, you don't want it to overprove and ruin your structure.

5. Line a baking tray or roasting tray with a piece of baking parchment. Scrape your dough out onto a lightly floured surface, then ease into a sausage shape to facilitate cutting into 12 roughly equal buns. One by one, sprinkle each with a little flour, then roll up like you're shaping for batons (page 42). Place in your tray, relatively close together. Repeat with the rest.

6. I use a roasting tray, so they can be easily covered in kitchen foil to stop them drying out and to lock in steam during the bake. Prove for another 50–60 minutes or so until they have noticeably puffed up and are pressing against each other (unless you placed them too far apart).

7. About 15 minutes before it's ready, preheat your oven to 200°C (400°F) fan (220°C/425°F/gas 7).

8. Remove the foil so you can your brush the finger rolls with an egg wash, then bake for 10 minutes, covered, and then another 15 minutes or so uncovered, until a pale golden brown. Remove from the oven and let cool while you make the icing.

9. In a bowl, weigh the icing sugar, food colouring and water. Use a dessert spoon or whisk to combine, adding just a little more water if necessary. Tear apart your cooled buns, and dip in the icing, top first. Sprinkle with coconut, if using, and set aside for the icing to dry. Store in an airtight container and eat within a day.

Cheesymite Scrolls

BP

I'm not here to judge. You read the 'mite' in this recipe to be Vegemite, as was originally intended by the conceivers of these scrolls, or Marmite, the British original that's better in every way.

This recipe takes the original concept of the cheesymite scroll and enhances it somewhat, incorporating some butter like in a biscuit dough (page 209) for extra flakiness. The butter is only partially incorporated when you're rolling this out, and so may stick to the rolling pin and may leach out during cooking. These are minor inconveniences.

What you really do want to leach is the cheese – use plenty, and be a bit reckless, so the Cheddar gently oozes from the scrolls during baking to form a bit of a buttery, cheesymitey crisp. So long as you use baking parchment, it should just lift right off after a few minutes of cooling.

Makes 12 scrolls

450g plain (all-purpose) flour, plus extra for dusting
½ tsp table salt
2 tsp baking powder
½ tsp bicarbonate of soda (baking soda)
125g unsalted butter, frozen for at least 12 hours beforehand
250g milk

For the filling
3–5 tablespoons Vegemite or Marmite
120g Cheddar, coarsely grated

1. Into a large bowl, weigh your flour, then add your salt, baking powder and bicarbonate of soda. Stir these together roughly to combine. Then use a coarse grater to grate your frozen butter into the bowl. You could freeze your whole block and grate directly into your bowl on the scales – that's what I do.

2. Gently rub the butter into the flour, only to distribute it and so that all the flour is covered in butter. Then add the milk, and stir the whole thing with a wooden spoon until you've got something that barely comes together. It won't be a proper dough.

3. Generously flour a work surface and turn your lumpy mix onto it. Form it into a generally cohesive lump, then use a rolling pin to roll it out at least 45cm (18in) long. We're going to fold this dough like folding a letter to fit in an envelope, in thirds. If you've ever made puff pastry, that's what we're trying to do: fold it one-third down, then close it over by folding again. Except this will break and tear and crumble and that is fine, at this stage.

4. Turn your dough around by 90 degrees, sprinkling with more flour, if needed, and repeat your rolling and folding step twice more, until all the lumpy bits have gone and the dough looks like one smooth, cohesive lump. If this hasn't happened, give it a final turn and roll.

5. Stick your dough on a tray and put it in the fridge (I use the baking tray I'm about to use, to avoid more washing up) to allow the now-formed gluten to rest, and to allow you to roll out the dough a little more easily. You can chill the dough for several hours at this point, if you wish, but the longer you leave it, the less puffy they'll be.

6. Preheat your oven to 180°C (350°F) fan (200°C/400°F/gas 6). Turn your dough back onto your floured surface, dust with more flour and roll it out to a large rectangle, at least 40×30cm (16×12in). Spread over your marmite or vegemite, and then add your grated Cheddar. Roll it up like a roulade, or for Chelsea buns (page 81).

7. Using a scraper, cut your roulade in half, then each half in half again. Cut each quarter into 3, and you've got 12 equal buns. Place these on your baking tray and bake immediately for 20–25 minutes, or until properly puffed and the cheese has melted. Serve on the same day, or freeze and reheat in the oven for 5 minutes each time.

Index

Acknowledgements

Many people have been involved in creating this book, and I'd first like to thank the contributors who engaged on social media or by email. Namely:

Jeroen Loopstra, Reilly O'Hara, Khusro Jaleel (@cosmoscooking), Volta Voloshin-Smith (@colorsnack), Mehar Saxena (@houseofmehar), Arsen Khachatryan, Raluca Vacaru (raluspantry.com, @raluspantry), Ignacio Díaz, Zuli PG (@zulipg), Tabitha Steemson, Pilar Hernandez (thechileankitchen.com), Georgina Adams, Jill Skelton, Anita Šumer (@sourdoughmania), Mariama Jalloh (@FulbeNomadicCuisine), Dominik Holters, Yusuf Patel (@spinoffbakingpage), Adam Frost, Alokya P. Perera, Sarah Pisanu, Christine Watts, Lesley Lupo, Wendy Fletcher, Mark Reeves, Daniel Ors (@starbakeriguess).

Also from Instagram: Roz MacAllan, @kissafishtas, @j9nah, Karen Barnes @editorkarenb, Helen Cross @grow_cook_inspire, Ken Noakes @kc_psm, @choitamara, Jonathan Bowers @sumba2014, Mare @mare_panadera, Michael James @michaeljamesbakes, Ruth King, @roo.f.king, Ben Taylor @bjm.taylor, Ceri Sidwell @cerisidwell, Rachel McPherson @dandyroll125, Leila @leiorla, Heather Short @short2420, Heidi Chapman @heidij.chapman, Mika @mikamooth.

Then, I've got to thank **Stacey Cleworth**, not just for being a wonderful editor and top human being, but also for her understanding, patience and the gentle nudges that have led to this book actually existing. Thank you Stace; this is for you and because of you.

Evidently, none of this would happen but for the great **Sarah Lavelle**, who demonstrates that you can indeed get to the very top of a competitive industry while maintaining compassion and empathy. If you're as talented and hardworking and plain brilliant as she is, that is.

Tim Hayward actually let us take over his entire home for two weeks to shoot most of this book. What a top bloke. He inspires, he challenges, he gives great enjoyment to others. Thank you Tim, and to Alison and Liberty Wright, for putting up with us.

Luke Bird might be listed as this beautiful book's designer, but he's far more. He filled a van full of props and furniture from his own kitchen and drove it to Glasgow for this book. He attended every shoot, he got stuck into baking, food styling and washing up. It has been such a joy.

And **Andy Sewell**? I mean, you just need to look at those photos. I know of no other food photographer who could have done what Andy did for this book. Next, try to save the world.

Wendy Hobson, your patience and diligence are unreal. Thank you for creating a book that people can actually use and understand, rather than the direct rants and ramblings of my brain.

Fenella, **Lily** and **Eve**, the three wonderful women of my life. I'm so grateful for the joy you bring, and for your understanding and encouragement and nurturing through this process. For the times I've been absent, I'm sorry: rest assured, they tore me apart too.

I've got to thank a couple of brands, too: **Ooni**, for supplying a fantastic pizza oven and associated supplies for the purposes of this book: while this may make me biased, rest assured, I used them for years before this, and indeed nothing else comes close. And thank you to **Le Creuset**, who supplied a couple of pots to add to the two I currently have, gifted to my parents for their wedding in 1983 and still in near-daily use today.

Write to us @quadrillebooks | @bakingjames

Managing Director Sarah Lavelle
Commissioning Editor Stacey Cleworth
Art Direction and Design Luke Bird
Photographer Andy Sewell
Food Styling James Morton
Prop Stylist Faye Wears
Head of Production Stephen Lang
Production Controller Martina Georgieva

First published in 2024 by Quadrille Publishing Limited

Quadrille
52–54 Southwark Street
London SE1 1UN
quadrille.com

Cataloguing in Publication Data: a catalogue record for this book is available from the British Library.

9781787138742

Printed in China

MIX
Paper | Supporting responsible forestry
FSC® C018179